Historic Homes of Minnesota

Historic Homes
of Minnesota

Roger G. Kennedy

MINNESOTA HISTORICAL SOCIETY PRESS

Frontispiece: *Sam Brown House, Brown's Valley,*
moved from Fort Wadsworth, South Dakota, 1866

www.mhspress.org

The Minnesota Historical Society Press is a member of the
Association of American University Presses.

Manufactured in Canada

10 9 8 7 6 5 4 3 2 1

∞ The paper used in this publication meets the minimum
requirements of the American National Standard for Information Sciences—Permanence for Printed Library Materials,
ANSI Z39.48-1984.

International Standard Book Number
0-87351-557-9 (paper)

Library of Congress
Cataloging-in-Publication Data
Kennedy, Roger G.
   [Minnesota houses]
   Historic Homes of Minnesota / Roger G. Kennedy.
      p.   cm.
Originally published: Minnesota houses, an architectural
and historical view. Minneapolis : Dillon Press, 1967.
Includes bibliographical references and index.

ISBN 0-87351-557-9 (pbk. : alk. paper)
   1. Architecture, Domestic—Minnesota.
   2. Historic buildings—Minnesota.
   I. Title.
NA7235.M6K46 2006
728′.3709776—dc22   2005025344

The photographs on pages ii, 7, 17, 31, 38, 40, 46, 50, 57, 58,
60, 61, 67, 69, 70, 85, 90, 92, 94, 107, 110, 113, 128, 130, 132,
133, 137, 158, 160, 171, 175, 181 are © by Doug Ohman. The
photograph on page 184 is © by Joe Michl and is used by per-
mission. All other photographs are from the Minnesota Historical Society Collections.

To John and Lee

Contents

List of Illustrations

Preface

SOME OF THE GREATEST OF MINNESOTA HOUSES have been relatively small. That was true during the Greek revival and Gothic revival periods, which lasted in Minnesota until about 1870. It was also remarkably true of some still surviving in the stick and shingle styles, despite the gallimaufry of the 1880s and 1890s, and especially true of the best buildings of the Progressive Era, between 1900 and 1917. William Gray Purcell, the most eloquent among the Progressive architects, Frank Lloyd Wright the most celebrated, and the others worked hard to make good architecture available to middle-class people. I think especially of the $2,700 studio house Purcell and George Elmslie created for a woodworker friend, and a later small residence, near what is now the Southdale Mall, for their dentist. Purcell's own house on Lake Place, in Minneapolis, now treated as it should be, as a precious artifact, by the Minneapolis Institute of Arts, is among the nation's best manifestations of how elegance can be achieved in small space and with small means.

The distilled taste of these masters was also expressed in mansions, such as Wright's for Francis Little, and Purcell and Elmslie's for Edward Decker, both at Minnetonka, and in George Maher's works near Winona, but their sheer size—and a subsequent decline in taste—led to their seeming surplusage and being broken apart for wholesaling to museums. Perhaps it is just as well that the Metropolitan Museum of Art in New York has a little piece of Minnesota, but the view from the windows is not nearly so beautiful as it was from the windows of either the Little or Decker Houses.

Looking backward, beyond the Progressive Era, to me the most endearing epoch in the social and architectural life of the state so far, this book presents examples of previous occasions in which Minnesota builders and architects availed themselves of opportunities to make great houses, large and small. After the passing of the frontier, respectability presented itself in the middle of the nineteenth century in the solemn mansard era. After the nation recovered from the Civil War, it celebrated with an outbreak of structural candor in the stick style, architecture by X-ray. Then came the shingles and turrets and vertiginous projections of the Carpenter's Frenzy of the 1880s. In the 1890s increasing social unrest and the rise of the plutocracy brought fortress-like Romanesque mansions now thoroughly defensible in stone, with slit windows and boulderous foundations.

After 1905, resistance to plutocracy worked its way into aversion to pretentiousness in architecture. Some of the best of the Romanesque designers, such as Harvey Ellis, moved from its forbidding grandeur toward a more folkish medievalism, through the Arts and Crafts Movement, breaking the way for the Progressives. Ellis worked with Henry Hobson Richardson at the onset of his career, and (according to Purcell) with the Progressives, Elmslie, and Louis Sullivan, and, finally, for Gustave Stickley, developing the Craftsman style.

The grandest medievalesque mansions are gone from the Twin Cities and Duluth, though there remain along the otherwise genteel streets of Crocus Hill several dozen examples of Carpenter's Frenzy, which is also well represented in these pages with examples from communities outside the Twin Cities. This was still the time of St. Paul's hegemony, which from the 1850s onward was sometimes content to stake its pride in elegant cottages. I remember one of these, in a racially mixed neighborhood near the Cathedral, later obliterated by "urban renewal." I recall especially an evening in which its owner, my parents' friend Mary Downie, a schoolteacher and a deeply cultivated lady, played for us on a piano that filled nearly all her living room.

A few blocks away, there were still in the 1930s stone and brick mansions along Summit Avenue too monstrous to survive even in institutional hands. Norman Kittson's was one. As they went down, one after another, the great elms that sheltered them went also. Other, older stone mansions had been in the way of "railroad renewal" in what became the warehouse district of St. Paul. The Hardenburg and Blood fortresses were bulldozed to make way for the vast artificial prairie below the Capitol.

Until the 1920s, building costs were low for houses large or small.

Cass Gilbert produced a grand neoclassical house on Heather Place in St. Paul for $5,200 in 1891; the construction contract is gone for his own Arts and Crafts house across the street, but it probably cost less than that. Forests went into cheap housing and the work was done with labor unprotected by unions, safety requirements, insurance, or retirement benefits. Bungalows were sold from the Sears catalog for less than $2,000.

Prices rose after the First World War, and it is fair to say that for a long time taste declined. In the 1920s, bland opulence took over, presaging that of the 1990s. Wright and Purcell went on living, but there was little work of genius done in the Twin Cities in the intrawar period. There was, however, high competence. The Arts and Crafts tradition was sustained by two gentlemen known as "Mr. Lundie and Mr. Jemne." Edwin Lundie and Magnus Jemne found clients willing to permit architecture free of derivative tags in summer camps such as Beaver Bay, Encampment Forest, and Madeline Island, but seldom around Minnetonka or White Bear Lake. Lundie was still working wonders on the North Shore of Lake Superior as late as 1949.

Minnesota got its confidence back architecturally about then. The small house came back into its own, and so did the big house for the techno-rich, the rebel bankers, the retailers of civil dispersion, and the skillful purveyors of packaged foods. Unlike the torpid though prosperous 1920s and 1990s, the 1950s, '60s, and '70s were decades of architectural vigor. Michael McGuire's Bancroft house, near St. Paul, remains one of the masterpieces of that period. In the Minneapolis suburbs, the leaders of the Minneapolis Renaissance either built or bought great houses. Edward Larabee Barnes provided John and Sage Cowles with a splendid house for grand-scale entertaining, which they turned over to the Spring Hill Conference Center when they moved in town. The Michael Wintons bought Philip Johnson's Curtis glass house of 1954 and added a Frank Gehry guest house. Ralph Rapson executed some elegant houses as well as the first Guthrie Theater, on which the Cowleses and Wintons were two of the chief Medicis, along with the Zelles, Von Blons, Walkers, and Daytons—always, it seems, in good things in Minneapolis, the Daytons—who also had good eyes for architecture. (I had the pleasure of serving as the theater's first chairman while living in a little house designed by McGuire.)

The most exciting developments in recent years have come from the increasing possibility that there can now be greater houses of smaller size. The exuberant 1880s and 1890s are gone, but so have the Boring Twenties. Talented designers such as David Salmela, Charles Lazor, Tim Alt, and those producing Weehouses are once again showing that great houses can be small. The Progressives of the Prairie School learned that from Harvey Ellis, who could do it big or do it small. I look up from my computer at some of his stained glass for a fortress-house in St. Paul, long gone, and in the next room are other glass panels of his, rescued from the basement of a Craftsman bungalow in Rochester, New York—all these are bound for the Minneapolis Institute of Arts when mortality intervenes. I believe that Ellis and Purcell—who told me about Ellis forty years ago—would be pleased to see great-in-small carried forward by a new generation making clever use of computer-driven systems, demonstrating that the lessons Philip Johnson learned from Mies van der Rohe could be made available to the kind of clients that once employed Purcell.

From the architects of the new millennium we have learned that glass can be a friendly material, capable of being transparent to nature as well as reflecting back the proud visage of the client and the architect. That's progress—the Progressives might say.

ROGER G. KENNEDY
September 2005

Historic Homes of Minnesota

1

The Sources of Pioneer Architecture

The French

IN 1804 THOMAS JEFFERSON sent out a series of expeditions to find out in detail what he had bought from Napoleon. Lewis and Clark set forth from St. Louis up the Missouri River toward the Pacific through the midst of the Louisiana Purchase. Zebulon Pike went northward up the Mississippi to explore its headwaters. Along the great river Pike found a series of French settlements, some already a century old, extending as far north as Prairie du Chien, Wisconsin.

Even beyond these villages, beyond what was then thought to be civilized territory, he found French traders placidly smoking their clay pipes in encampments to which they often returned to meet their Indian suppliers in the fur trade. About three miles below the present town of St. Peter, on the Minnesota River, he "passed the encampment of Mr. Ferrebault, who had broken his peroque," presumably by running afoul of the rapids which were the bane of traders whose fragile boats traveled downstream heavily laden with furs. American explorers were often startled to find that they were not bringing light to an empty continent, but were trespassing upon hunting and trading grounds long occupied by the French.

How long they had been there is not easy to certify. In Minnesota they established no settlements which have survived, and their forts and fur-trading posts have long since disappeared. Throughout the seventeenth century, while Frenchmen were prowling the woods and pushing through the swamps of the Great Lakes region, the light of history glinted upon them infrequently. Great, chronicled expeditions were rare; there were, instead, many wide-ranging forays by men contemptuous of records. We know, for example, that when Etienne Brulé reached Sault Ste. Marie in 1622 (or was it 1615? The records are vague) the Indians there were already calling the rapids the "Sault de Gaston" after the brother of Louis XIII. Among the certainties are these: Quebec had been founded in 1608, twelve years before the English set foot upon New England's stern and marshy shore. By 1634 Frenchmen were already exploring the fringes of Wisconsin. That was the year in which the General Court of Massachusetts ventured to authorize the construction of a frontier post called Concord, fourteen miles west of Boston.

Most of the French settlements along the central Mississippi owed their origins to soldiers and missionaries rather than to farmers or bourgeois (though they had become trading centers surrounded by small farms by the time Zebulon Pike passed them on his way northward). Soldiers in the service of Louis XIV built a chain of military posts along the central Mississippi late in the seventeenth century. A group of missions came a few years later followed by civilian settlements. Cahokia, across the Mississippi from modern St. Louis, was established as a mission in 1699 atop the remnants of a great Indian town of the twelfth century. Kaskaskia, established the next year fifty miles to the south, grew to have a population five times larger than French Cahokia, though only a twentieth of that probably in the ancient city there. Ste. Geneviéve, across the river from Kaskaskia and about equal in size, was thriving before 1750. St. Louis, which grew to be the metropolis of the middle Mississippi under the leadership of the great French fur-trading families, was established in 1764 before Daniel Boone broke over the Appalachians into Kentucky. The northernmost of the French towns, Prairie du Chien, located on the edge of the wilderness stretching north to the Arctic and west to the Rockies, had a population of between five and six hundred in 1806.

In these settlements the French developed a distinctive domestic architecture, in its most primitive form a stockade under a roof. Stakes were driven into the earth as close to each other as possible, chinked with mud or homemade mortar, and roofed with split rails. This was known as "poteaux en terre" construction and was the French alternative to the cabin of horizontal logs which is more familiar to Americans.

Their second and more sophisticated mode of construction was called "poteaux sur sole." A stone foundation was built. Then, across it was laid a sill, an adze-squared timber. Onto the sill were placed the evenly cut vertical timbers, 8 to 12 inches apart, and across their top was placed a heavy timber rafter. This technique descended from the ancient timber-framed construction of hardwood areas of Northern Europe, with adjustments to North American climate. The radical changes of temperature encountered in the New World forced the posts closer together to avoid disastrous cracking of the mud, mortar, chopped-straw, or plaster which filled the space between. The Francois Roi cottage built during the American Revolution in Green Bay, Wisconsin, shows this sort of a wall underneath later clapboarding, and several other examples can be found in the old French towns of Missouri and Illinois. The noblest of these is the Louis Bolduc house in Ste. Geneviéve.

There is abundant evidence that the French who settled the mid-Mississippi region aspired to still more ambitious architectural achievements. Those who came from Canada seem to have been largely Bretons and Normans in origin, and for them the traditional house was of stone. The Quebec census of 1660 already showed masons and stonecutters in residence and some stone houses had replaced those of "poteaux" in Kaskaskia by 1723. Two- and three-story stone residences were sold there by 1763 and in the metropolis of St. Louis, Lewis, Clark, and Pike were impressed by the stone mansions of the great fur-trading families.

It was characteristic of all these French houses that after 1725 or so they were surrounded by porches or galleries. The origin of the porch, along the Mississippi, is subject to considerable scholarly dispute with one school favoring the West Indies or Brazil and another, more persuasive, suggesting independent development. It seems reasonable to presume that the rain-lashed mud or mortar between the posts of the "poteaux" houses required some protection and that the roofs were extended to provide it. When these extensions reached a sagging point, posts were provided. Thus the midwestern front porch came into being. At any rate, travelers through the mid-Mississippi villages noted galleries facing the river, and sometimes completely surrounding the houses. What had been shelter for walls was soon found to provide shelter and shade for people as well. From New Orleans to St. Paul the homes of Frenchmen were distinguished by steep-sloping roofs, some of which broke straight toward the horizontal to cover the galleries, and some curved outward to form a "bell cast."

While there are early references to such structures in St. Paul, the only remaining example in Minnesota was built not by a Frenchman, but by an observant and adaptable Kentuckian, General Israel Garrard. He was the son of a governor of Kentucky and came from a family which had successfully speculated in real estate in Cincinnati. He explored the prairie around the head of Lake Pepin while on a hunting trip, finding the land broad, fertile, and protected by bluffs from the northwest wind. His sharp eye saw its potential value as a town site. The same eye saw the virtues of French colonial architecture as each year he traveled down the Ohio River into the Mississippi and up the great river past town after town where old French houses presented to the river their broad, shaded, breezy galleries. In 1856, when he built his lodge, which he called St. Hubert's after the patron of hunters, he incorporated double galleries into its design.

At first Garrard built only two sets of small rooms at each side of the entrance hall which led back from the center of the lower gallerie. Bedrooms opened onto the upper tier. About 1860 he added a large living room with a bay window looking southward over the park, and various service rooms to the rear. In the years just before the Civil War, Garrard's hospitality attracted many friends making the "grand tour" of the Upper Mississippi and the town of Frontenac, growing up about St. Hubert's, became Minnesota's first summer resort. Architects Grant La Farge and Christopher L. Hiens there discovered the Frontenac limestone they later used in the sanctuary of the Church of St. John the Divine in New York City; Joseph Jefferson was the first actor to arrive and Marie Dressler came back so many times that even in the General's old age a romance was rumored. John LaFarge, painter and artist of stained glass, and Henry Ward Beecher were also among the General's guests. When his service in the Civil War was finished, Garrard began building more houses along the terraces above the river to accommodate his family. His dining room became too small to seat the growing tribe, so the barn was moved against the house and a great hall made of it. The old board-and-batten house was extended in the back toward the General's racecourse. Still there was not enough room for friends, so in 1867 Garrard converted one of his granaries into a hotel with wide verandahs like those of his own house. Here congregated southern families each summer, retreating northward before the humid Delta summer, bringing their servants with them. In the fall they would mi-

grate home again, many of them back to raised cottages in the old French fashion, much like St. Hubert's itself.

In the early 1870s General Garrard confronted a crisis: the Chicago, Milwaukee and St. Paul Railroad had crossed the Mississippi and was laying track up the west shore toward Frontenac. He could capitalize upon his real estate holdings and convert his terraced, bluff-protected town site into the bonanza his father had made of Cincinnati. The price would be the desecration of the shoreline by the railroad. Frontenac was a thriving port for the shipment of grain; Garrard had sawmills and gristmills. Garrard and the community could have used profitably the transportation which the railroads would have offered. But Garrard chose, instead, to donate to the railroad a right-of-way four miles to the west along which the tracks and the highway run today, passing by the old town. There St. Hubert's Lodge remains today. Beside it is a row of houses along the terrace but the racetrack and the mills and the grana-

General Israel Garrard House, St. Hubert's Lodge, Frontenac, 1856

ries are gone. Rows of tall elms mark where streets once passed and in the winter when the summer residents have gone the place is very quiet.

St. Hubert's Lodge remains the only example of the French-American galleried style in Minnesota. There once were more. An old map of St. Paul with sketches of houses standing in 1857 shows the residence of Charles H. Oakes which had much in common with the Choteau house in St. Louis. Galleries, which surrounded three sides of the main structure, were reached on both levels by tall windows—French doors. The house, which was on Eighth Street in Lowertown, was described in the *Minnesota Pioneer* of December 25, 1851, as "a large new elegant mansion . . . well warmed and illuminated up to the observatory." Oakes was the son of a judge in St. Clair County, Michigan, who had come to Michigan territory from New England. He had early forsaken settled places for the wilderness and entered the service of the American Fur Company. In 1822 he was trading along the Yellow River in Wisconsin, and "signed on" with the fur company's chief northwest partner, Hercules Dousman, in 1834. With his brother-in-law, Charles W. Borup, he founded the first banking house in St. Paul. Where he acquired his architectural taste is unknown, but he married Miss Julia Beaulieu of an old French family of Sault Ste. Marie and, like most leaders in the early fur trade, he probably made frequent visits to St. Louis. His house modifies what he might have found either at Sault Ste. Marie or in the old French Mississippi towns: it bore a captain's walk on the roof. The captain's walk and the galleries must have satisfied both the New Englander (Oakes was born in Rockingham, Vermont) and his French-American wife.

Oakes and Garrard fully accepted the French galleried style. Other Anglo-Americans such as William H. C. Folsom modified the severity of a New England facade by annexing galleries. Folsom worked for a time in the area of the French settlements of the mid-Mississippi and in 1837–38 made a voyage to New Orleans. There is a family tradition that when he returned and built his mansion in 1856 on the escarpment above the Dalles of the St. Croix in Taylors Falls, he wanted to duplicate the double galleries he had seen to the south. Long, two-tiered porches were placed along the riverside of the house, which is now a historic site.

The Folsom and Garrard houses are tributes to the French, showing the influence of their architecture upon the Anglo-Americans who suc-

ceeded to power in the region. During the 1830s and 1840s the French
were joined by increasing numbers of men from the states who came
to join the ranks of the Indian traders. Garrisons were established at
strategic locations by a government anxious to pacify what Lewis,
Clark, Pike, and others had surveyed and what the War of 1812 had
substantially secured. Agents were sent out to keep an eye on the still-
resistant Indians, and a few missionaries and teachers took up residence. The houses built by some of these newcomers survive and they
illustrate several of the architectural traditions brought to Minnesota
to mingle with those of the French.

*William H. C. Folsom
House, Taylors Falls,
1856*

The Middle Colonies and Galena

Two main streams of western migration flowed together in Minnesota.
One, which will be examined shortly, came from New England through
the states bordering the Great Lakes. The other brought pioneers on a

long, indirect route from Virginia and the Middle Colonies, from the Atlantic littoral bounded by the Hudson River and the Great Dismal Swamp. It was primarily from these men of the mid-Atlantic states that Minnesota gained its most primitive forms of dwelling, the log cabin and the sod house; from them also came another masonry tradition to fuse with that of the French.

The log cabin has long been a staple property of American folklore. It was not a New England contribution. Fiske Kimball, Henry C. Mercer, and Harold R. Shurtleff have persuaded students of this problem that the pilgrims lived first in huts of sod or saplings and knew nothing of log cabins. So evaporates the image of a hundred Thanksgiving pageants. The facts seem to be these. The Swedish settlers of the Delaware Bay region introduced the log cabin to our shores as early as 1638 and it was little known outside their settlements for seventy or eighty years. Later, Germans in Pennsylvania, the Pennsylvania Dutch, developed their own log houses. They may have acquired the technique from the Swedes or they may have introduced it afresh from those areas of Switzerland and parts of Germany where it was known.

But it was the Scotch-Irish who made the log cabin the symbol of the American frontier. They, too, entered by way of the Delaware Valley and they spread widely north and south through the mountain valleys of the Appalachians, building log cabins there before they moved westward, taking their acquired technique with them. They had no log-building tradition in their homeland; they had probably learned of it from the Swedes or Germans.

The modern popular name of log cabin would have seemed most inaccurate to the pioneers of Tennessee and Kentucky. To them a cabin was a temporary building of unhewn logs, caulked with moss or straw, daubed with mud, and roofed by thin staves about four feet long and five inches wide held down by heavy poles being laid upon them. As one of the pioneers said, "If the logs be *hewed*, if the interstices be stopped with stone, and neatly plastered, and the roof composed of shingles nicely laid on, it is called a *log house*. A log house has glass windows and a chimney; a cabin has commonly no window at all, and only a hole at the top for the smoke to escape. After saw-mills are erected, and board can be procured, the settlers provide themselves more decent houses, with neat floors and ceiling."

In Minnesota, the earliest cabins were roofed with sod, with thick bark, or with handmade shingles. According to the late Paul M. Klammer of New Ulm, Minnesota's primary authority on the subject, many settlers continued to build of logs even after inexpensive lumber became available. The milled product appeared on the exteriors only on the gables and roof; it was also used for interior planking.

Nearly all the early settlers in wooded areas built log cabins. The French apparently ceased using the "poteaux en terre" method in the 1780s and adopted, instead, the horizontal-log technique employed by the newcomers pressing in from the states recently independent of Great Britain. The Yankees learned to build log structures as they crossed the Appalachian region toward the Northwest Territory. By the time of the presidential campaign of 1840 the log cabin was no longer merely the habitation of the Appalachian mountaineers. This should have been known by the Democratic orator who proclaimed that the White House was too good for William Henry Harrison who, he said, should have been content with a "log cabin and a jug of cider." That bit of architectural snobbery may have swung the election for the Whigs; it gained a place in history for the Log Cabin Tradition. The architectural historian Hugh Morrison says that when the Whigs countered that Harrison was "the kind of American who would be *proud* to live in a log cabin; the log cabin became a symbol of courage, simplicity, honesty, ruggedness and plain democratic homey Americanism."

All log houses were not alike. The craftsmanship of their builders could be judged by the type of corners they employed, by their precision in pegging their logs next to the window frames, and by their care in squaring their timbers. The most common way of bringing logs together at a corner is by a "saddle notch," which requires some chopping away of a resting place for one log upon another to diminish the space left between. The dovetail corner, better illustrated than described, calls for the most skill. It requires the mutual adjustment of square-hewn logs to provide for a nice joining along their length. The square-hewn corner requires wooden pegs to lock two logs together, and the blockhouse technique means cutting away half the end portion of each log to accommodate the other. The saddle notch, while most common, is not necessarily crude. When the upper surface of the log is pointed into a gable, a very neat and solid fit can be made.

Log houses are everywhere in Minnesota, some now reappearing from under clapboards which have rotted and fallen away. During the

1937 Centennial Celebration in Marine-on-St. Croix, two believed to have been built in the 1830s were brought in from the hinterland. One, next to the Shell gasoline station, served as a carpenter's shop and the other stands next to the old stone jail and Town Hall.

Paul Klammer concluded after a study of log construction in Minnesota that the immigrants who came into the state from Europe built in distinctive national styles. "The Scandinavians . . . seem always to have used the dovetail type of corner notching. They selected large logs, which they carefully sawed or hewed, and they erected neat and substantial buildings. The Germans and Austrians, on the other hand, employed several types of corner notching, featuring the gable type of saddle notch, and their workmanship varied greatly in quality. The Irish, who regularly used dovetail corners, usually did poor construction work."

The variance in skill shown by these groups is easy to understand, for the Scandinavians and many Germans came from pine-growing country. They were not baffled when they encountered pine again. The Irish, whose island had been stripped of most of its trees, were not likely to be good carpenters in pine. And they were never lovers of the exposed, unsociable countryside when, near at hand, there were cities to organize into caucuses.

The frontier was not a place but a period. It was an ocean frontier to western Europeans in the fifteenth century, a mountain frontier three hundred years later to those moving westward from beachheads on the Atlantic littoral of North America, and in the nineteenth century it was, for a time, a prairie frontier. We are apt to forget that until the 1870s many farmers feared to penetrate prairie regions. The woods had provided fences, fuel, and building material for houses. Where trees would not grow, they thought crops would not grow either.

It is possible that the sod house came to the prairie as the tribal style which the Indo-European migrants had brought from the treeless steppes of central Asia. It has been used for millennia in those regions which still today constitute a sort of permanent frontier in the inhospitable extremities of Europe. There remain stretches of barren countryside in Great Britain, France, and Scandinavia where human habitation has not taken root. Shaggy hills and windswept moors are inhabited by shepherds, charcoal burners, peat diggers, and, until the last fifty years or so, brigands and hermits. These people live as their prehistoric fathers lived, in pits dug in the ground roofed over by poles and bark, sometimes extended above ground by walls of sod.

It was in such shelters that many Dutch and English settlers of the sandy Eastern Seaboard of America spent their first years. The relief ships which arrived at Jamestown, Virginia, in January 1608, found the survivors "utterly destitute of houses . . . so that they lodged in cabbins and holes within the grounde. . . ." Cornelius Van Tienhoven, secretary of New Netherland, described how his charges would "dig a square pit in the ground, cellar fashion, six or seven feet deep . . . case the earth all round the wall with timber . . . floor this cellar with plank . . . raise a roof of spars clear up, and cover the spars with bark or green sods. . . ."

From the seaside sand barrens the frontier moved westward until it encountered, two centuries later, an area where the woods first straggled out into savannahs and then expired utterly in the great upswelling prairie, where lonely, parched cottonwoods, along the streambeds, gave the only shade. In Merrill E. Jarchow's book, *The Earth Brought Forth*, he reports: "In the 1860's, 1870's, and even later, western Minnesota was dotted with sod houses of various types and sizes. When Ole Hedman arrived in Cottonwood County in 1870, he dug a hole four feet deep and roofed it over with bark, slough grass, and sod; and most of his neighbors did likewise on the prairies. . . . Near Sleepy Eye a Danish family built a sod house large enough to accommodate not only themselves, but their cows and oxen as well."

However little leisure they may have had for the enhancement of the necessary with the beautiful, frontiersmen were impatient with mere shelter. They wanted more. They wanted the comfort of a home, in a familiar shape and material. And for the people who came to America by the middle route, out through the Appalachian passes into the Old Northwest Territory and thence to Minnesota, this generally meant houses of brick and, occasionally, of stone.

This had been true in the area of Europe from which most of them had come, that portion lying north of a line drawn due east and west, passing through Berlin, and extending from Russia to Holland, and including most of Britain except that southeastern corner (where timber for homebuilding was more common and from which, as we shall see, most of the settlers of New England came). From masonry country came the majority of the settlers of the Middle Colonies; from wood country, came the Yankees.

As early as 1611, brick was made in America at Henrico, Virginia. In 1628, the Dutch were manufacturing bricks on Manhattan, despite a lush supply of wood, and their compatriots in the Delaware Valley also built of bricks. The English colonists in New Jersey and Pennsylvania used both brick and stone, apparently tending toward brick as far west as Philadelphia and joining the Pennsylvania Dutch in their preference for stone further west.

The Pennsylvania Dutch were, of course, natives of Germany who were first solicited as settlers by William Penn in a tour of the Rhenish Palatinate in 1677. Into the southeastern counties of Pennsylvania they came, building first square-hewn log cabins, then half-timbered houses of hardwood (as the old German traditions of pine-growing and oak-growing areas fused in the new land) and finally, that solid, secure masonry which is today one of the chief attractions Bucks County offers to frazzled refugees from Manhattan. The masonry skills that the Pennsylvania Dutch carried westward on the emigrant trail contributed mightily to Minnesota's architectural history.

While the westering migration of men from the Middle Colonies carried along a richer and more diverse group of national traditions than the parallel movement of New Englanders to the north, these traditions tended to fuse by the time they reached Minnesota. An amalgam was formed, and its core was the metropolis of the Upper Mississippi—Galena, Illinois.

Galena was larger by far than Chicago or Milwaukee, vying with St. Louis. It had more than 10,000 people in 1830. While other settlements were building log cabins, Galena was erecting mansions of stone and brick. Galena radiated Middle Colonial influence throughout the Upper Mississippi region. It is a city of stone and warm, red brick houses; there are many streets which look much like Georgetown in the District of Columbia; or Alexandria, Virginia; or Baltimore, Maryland. Galena was founded in 1826 when its lead deposits were discovered. From southern Illinois and Kentucky, "southerners moved in, leaving their impress with the introduction of slaves, southern manners, and southern architectural traits that are still traceable in residential structures."[1] Around Galena, in southwestern Wisconsin and southeastern Iowa, there sprang up small towns which also were built of red brick. Even today this rolling, eroded land could be mistaken for piedmont sections of Virginia or Maryland.

Architectural influence is not susceptible to pedantic proof, but it seems logical to presume that Galena and its brick and stone houses were influential in Minnesota not only because it was the chief seat of civilization in the Upper Mississippi until the Civil War, but also because it was the great port of embarkation for points upriver. Oliver Kellogg's wagon trail first reached the Mississippi there in 1825, and the Illinois Central brought to Galena railroad communication with the East Coast by way of Chicago on November 8, 1854. Until the advent of rail communication all the way to the Twin Cities nearly twenty years later, it is probable that more people reached Minnesota by traveling overland to Galena and from there by steamer up the Mississippi than by any other route. Frontiersmen far up the river remembered this last center of civilized life and, when they could, built houses like Galena's. These lonely, uprooted people were very conscious of their perceived role as the exemplars of enlightenment. They got their supplies, their books, and their occasional opportunities to renew acquaintance with society in such cities on the edge of the wilderness. The greatest of these places of replenishment and reassurance was not settled by wood-building Yankees, but by southerners and men of the middle border, for whom brick and stone were traditional building materials.

The Yankees

It is ironic that the inveterate foe of Yankees, Jefferson Davis, was the first to invite their invasion of Wisconsin and Minnesota by demonstrating that a rich crop of pine was available in the area. In 1829, the future president of the Confederacy, then a lieutenant stationed at Prairie du Chien, took a squad of men up the Chippewa River valley to cut timbers and shingles, and his report of endless forests of tall timber did not go unheeded. The western migration of New Englanders had already begun through the North American pine belt, which commences on the seacoast and expires in Minnesota, and Minnesota and western Wisconsin became the final destination of many who hoped to make their fortune in pine.

In the decade of the 1820s, the population of New York State doubled; three-fifths of the increase apparently originated in New England. From the Hudson Valley westward, the way was made easier by two great events: the development of steam-powered navigation and the opening of the Erie Canal. The *Walk-on-the-Water*, the first steamer on the Great Lakes, went into service in 1818, and traffic vastly increased seven years later when the canal was opened, quickening movement from New York to Buffalo from twenty days to six, and cutting the cost of freight on that passage from $100 to $5 a ton. By 1834, as many as eighty thousand emigrants a year passed westward through Buffalo alone. Farmers, tired of plowing their ancestral rocks, and townspeople, seeking a new start, went west in a stream which spurted as new treaties opened new lands.

First, Ohio felt the wave of newcomers. New England veterans of the War of Independence and the War of 1812 claimed their bonuses in land in the Western Reserve in the northeastern part of the state. The great influx of New England settlement in Indiana and Illinois was from 1830 to 1837. In the same period Silas Farmer of Detroit tells us that "it seemed as if all New England were coming" to that old French town, where a Franco-Yankee synthesis was reached a decade earlier than in Minnesota. Passing through southern Michigan, Indiana, and northern Illinois, the surge of emigration reached Wisconsin. In 1837, the population of that state, settled almost entirely in the lead-mining area in the southwestern corner near Galena, was 11,683. A decade later it was 155,277; two years after that 210,546.

The settlers pushed on to lumber towns and camps along the St. Croix and the Chippewa rivers and their tributaries. By a series of treaties, the Indians had turned over the Chippewa Valley to the lumbermen in 1833 and, during the summer of 1837, Governor Dodge of Wisconsin territory secured the St. Croix Valley. Where smaller streams rushed down the bluffs or the rivers themselves passed over falls, Yankees followed their familiar pattern of creating mill towns. Such places as Taylors Falls and Marine-on-St. Croix came into being in this way, as New England colonies. They still show their lineage since they have been less corrupted by remodelings than other towns in the area. Most of their houses face the St. Croix or press close against the mill ponds which were once raucous with tearing saws.

Another unspoiled group of Yankee houses clusters near the site of the old Bolles Mill in the lost hamlet of Valley Creek, northwest of Afton. There, in 1856, Erastus Bolles, a silversmith who had followed his Uncle Lemuel into the valley and adopted the more profitable frontier pro-

fession of miller, built a simple white house like those of his native Oxford, Massachusetts. Around it grew a little village with conservative tastes. When Silas Geer bought some land across from Bolles and built his house in 1874, he avoided the use of any decoration, although the picturesque revivals were well under way elsewhere. These two houses are much like a house built before 1850 by Cornelius Lyman of Vermont, just north of Stillwater on the Arcola Road. It, too, is free of any picturesque detail and bears the imprint of firm puritan taste.

A few miles up the river, between Marine and Stillwater, the brothers John E. and Martin Mower had built in 1847 the first large house on the St. Croix, at the center of their barony of Arcola. The Mowers were from Maine and became leaders in the politics of Minnesota territory and later of the state. Additions made in the 1870s have cluttered the lines of the house somewhat, but the severe, powerful character

John E. and Martin Mower House, Arcola, 1847

given to it by the Mowers is still present. On the floor of the room which was their study, are still hobnail marks left by loggers' boots and below, along the river, remain the foundations of a half-dozen homes, a schoolhouse, a carpenter's shop, a smithy, and a general store—all part of the Mowers's domain.

It is probably deceptive to refer to the residences of Folsom or of the Mower brothers as houses. The domiciles of prosperous New Englanders both at home and in the West were composed of not one, but many buildings: the smoke house, the milk house, the barns, the wood shed, the privy, the chicken house, and the dormitory for the "help." The

Daniel S. Piper House, Medford, 1877

Mowers's ménage was really a small village. Early photographs of the Folsom house showed it surrounded by outbuildings, all architecturally related. And it was not only in the St. Croix Valley in the period before the Civil War that these New England compounds appeared. In Medford, a village north of Owatonna, settled by emigrants from the mountainous back country of New England, Daniel S. Piper of Sanbornton, New Hampshire, arrived in 1877 with his wife, Lavonia Whitney Piper, and their four-year-old daughter. Because he felt only Yankee carpenters could build a proper house, he brought four master carpenters from New Hampshire that summer. They remained six months to complete the buildings. Piper had been in a lumber trade in New Hampshire and personally selected his materials.

The foundation was limestone, and under the kitchen floor there was a brick cistern into which ran all the downspouts. The kitchen could thus be supplied with good soft water. The main floor had a front parlor, sitting room, downstairs bedroom, pantry, and a large "keeping room" or kitchen. There were no fireplaces; stoves were used for heating. A Franklin stove in the parlor was used only on special occasions. Many visitors came during the construction to see the marvelous windows that lifted by means of a rope concealed in the sash and to admire Mr. Piper's "elevator cupboard," forerunner of a refrigerator: a wood cabinet, lined with tin, which could be closed, locked shut, and the whole structure, approximately five feet high, three feet wide, and three feet deep, lowered through the floor into the cool basement. Yankee ingenuity also devised an umbrella-like drying rack which on cold winter days could be opened and raised to the ceiling of the kitchen, loaded with clothes.

The Piper and Bolles houses represent the dominant New England style: what might be described as the "pastoral puritan" style. It began as a simple rectangle under a gable roof, like a shoebox under a pup tent. When more space was needed, more shoeboxes were added. Nearly always these houses were made of wood, sheathed in horizontal siding and painted white. Wood was the traditional building material of New England. The first Englishmen who settled there were, of course, Puritans and Separatists, most of whom came from the east coast of England (the ancient Danelaw) where timber construction was common. In New England this wood-building habit coincided with convenience. Wood was plentiful; bricks and lime for mortar were not. Even in the eighteenth century when the Georgian and Federal styles were generally executed in brick, as they always were in England, many Yankees refused to abandon their preference for wood.

What the New Englanders meant by frame construction until the middle of the nineteenth century was similar to the heavy timber technique which we have described earlier as prevailing among the French. The use of siding in New England developed for the same reason as "poteaux sur sole" in New France: in response to the quick alternations of temperature of a violent climate. While the French were bringing vertical timbers closer together to make walls more solidly wooden, the English colonists were covering the outside of their houses with horizontal boards, overlapping downward to keep the rain from penetrating the cracks. Thus, the tradition of clapboard siding began.

In the 1830s the balloon frame was developed in Chicago and became almost universal in the West. The conception of this new technology has been the object of much scholarly study. The traditional method of framing a building with heavy timbers, pegged together, was replaced by a basket or grid of light strips of sawn lumber, standardized as "two-by-fours" and "two-by-sixes," nailed together. Such a frame could be put together on the ground and hoisted easily into place. It was probably called a balloon frame because of its lightness and in its early years because of what traditionalists thought to be its flimsiness. It worked a revolution in home building and created a vast market for Minnesota white pine. As John W. Root, one of the greatest of Chicago architects, described it: "No expert carpenter was needed, no mortise nor tenon nor other mysteries of carpentry interfered with the swiftness of its growth. A keg of nails, some two by four inch studs, a few cedar posts for foundations and a lot of clapboards, with two [sic!] strong arms to wield the hammer and saw—these only were needed and these were always to be had."

There are still houses remaining in Minnesota which show how Yankees built with timbers before cheap, milled lumber for balloon frames became available. One of the most interesting of these is the Ames-Florida-Stork house in Rockford on the Crow River, which shows what craftsmen could do with a few simple tools. Rockford was a Yankee colony, clustering about a sawmill and gristmill built by George F. Ames, Joel Florida, and G. D. George in 1856. The interior, which has been restored with great care, is paneled in fruitwood cut on the property. The doors, floors, and of course, the structural materials were entirely produced on the place. Much of the furniture, shaped there by hand tools, remains on display in this historic museum-house.

The simple gabled houses presented so far show one dominant strain in New England residential architecture as it moved westward, but there was another which had appeared early in the mill towns: the hip-roofed cube. The architectural historian, John Coolidge, suggests that the new rich of those places, in the middle years of the eighteenth century, preferred a "symmetrical, regular house, with few angles, but with order and method and distinctness stamped upon its unbroken lines of cornice and regular rows of windows." An unbroken cornice line meant an aversion to a gable roof, an attitude which might explain the preference in New England and among some New Englanders in the west for the hip-roofed cube. Mr. Coolidge asserts that it was the "snobbish symbolism of the square house that made it such a success. . . . In the eighteenth century, with the growth of the seaports and the rise of a commercial class, there had come to be a distinction between the pseudo-English architecture of the merchants [which later became the bracketed style] and the simpler buildings of rural New England. The seaboard style . . . culminated in the . . . great foursquare merchants' houses of Newburyport, Salem and Beacon Hill. Once and for all these established the pattern which the mansion of a conventional New England Gentleman was expected to follow. . . . As the square house increased in popularity, so the gable-roofed house declined."

It was noted earlier that New Englanders avoided the use of any material other than wood, but they often rusticated their siding to present the appearance of cut stone. This they did more often in building cubical houses, which partook of the formality of the Georgian mode, than in the simple, gabled houses of the countryside. In Stillwater, a growing lumber town, Mortimer Webster of Massachusetts built many humble houses, but he followed the pattern suggested for grander mansions when, between 1865 and 1870, he built his own cubical house high on a bluff at 435 South Broadway. His handiwork can be seen for miles up the river. Like earlier Georgian houses in New England and Mt. Vernon in Virginia, it has rusticated siding which can still be observed after a century of wear. It is a beautiful structure with distinctive moldings around the windows and a proud, small cupola on the roof.

Dean Theodore Blegen has emphasized the conscious harkening back to New England origins which led to the establishment in 1856 of the New England Society of the Northwest, the dubbing of St. Paul as the "Boston of the West," and a nostalgia for "New England industry, New England enterprise, and New England thrift." The New Englan-

Mortimer Webster House, Stillwater, c. 1870

der who made it all the way to the northwest frontier, that adaptable and resourceful Yankee who had weathered many storms and learned much was, in many ways, a "new man" but he was unwilling to abandon the familiar patterns which had defined home to him and to his family before him.

2

The Homes of the Fathers

THE HOMES BUILT BY MINNESOTA'S FOUNDERS are not characterized by purity of style, and it is perilous to explain their shapes and materials by attributing to their builders either a deference to contemporary fashion or a pious adherence to tradition. But, on the other hand,
speculation is one of the quiet pleasures of history, and there is no harm
in attempting to find out what might have molded the shapes and influenced the selection of the materials of these buildings. Not all can
be certain, some must be conjecture, but along the path of inquiry
something can be learned about these men and their times.

In the 1840s Minnesota was still a wilderness, insecurely gar-
risoned. Its two chief crops, furs and lumber, were the fruits of wild-
ness and once reaped, could never be replenished on a grand scale. The
majority of its population, the Dakota and the Ojibwe, were unenthu-
siastic about civilization.

In 1851, said a contemporary chronicler, "a vast region of country
large enough for a kingdom was released from barbarism and opened
to settlement and civilization." This was the Suland, all the southern
and central portions of Minnesota except for the lumberman's triangle
along the St. Croix and the enclave around Mendota and Fort Snelling,
which had been occupied earlier. A strip of land was reserved to the Indians along the Minnesota River into which they were thrust to brood
upon their injustices, to hunger, and to grow ever more impatient until they burst out in the desperate Dakota War of 1862. Their condition
concerned few of those who made the treaties by which this territory
was acquired. To them "the hand of civilization was reached forth to re-
claim it [the land] from the red savage and wild beasts. . . ." But many
of the old Indian traders knew better.

The most famous of these traders was Henry Hastings Sibley, whose stone mansion is the oldest house still standing in the state. It is as massive as a fort and could have served so had Sibley's always volatile Indian neighbors turned against him. In 1835, when Sibley began its construction, the symbol of American occupation was Fort Snelling on the opposing bluff of the Minnesota River. Sibley was the representative in the region of John Jacob Astor's American Fur Company. As such, he was as important as the commander of the fort's garrison, who lived somewhat less opulently in his quarters behind walls of limestone taken from Pike Island. The same quarry provided material for Sibley's house. The exterior walls were two and a half feet thick, and the window sills, flooring beams, and posts were of adze-hewn timber, pegged in place.

Sibley is such a familiar figure to readers of Minnesota history and his impeccable New England lineage has been emphasized so often that it may seem somewhat startling that his house has no Yankee features and is, instead, fairly representative of the houses built along the Upper Mississippi by French trappers and traders. It is true that Sibley was the scion of a distinguished New England family: his father had removed to Michigan and reached eminence in that new state. But it is also true that he deliberately broke away from that tradition and set out westward as (in William James's phrase) "an unencumbered man." He explained his motives in his memoirs:

> It may seem strange that men of education and culture could be induced to endure the hardships, perils, and exposure, incident to the life of an Indian trader, nevertheless many such could be found among that class. The love of money was not the incentive, for rarely did a trader accumulate, or become wealthy. . . . What constituted that fascination, it would be difficult to describe, except upon the theory that the tendency of civilized men, when under no restraint, is towards savagery as the normal condition of the human race. There was a charm in the fact that in the wild region, inhabited only by savage beasts, and still more savage men, one was liberated from all trammels of society, independent, and free to act according to his own pleasure. . . .

When Sibley built, at Mendota, a home which was also an office and a dormitory for friendly Indian clients, he adopted the architectural habits of the frontier, then largely French, as he had adopted many of its mores.

Though men like Sibley went to the frontier with the intention of adopting its free, untrammeled ways, they did not, when they prospered, live in primitive circumstances. The sheer mass of Sibley's house at Mendota was exceptional, but it must be stressed that many of his peers among the Indian traders were merchants, men of substance, not merely trappers as were the later "mountain men." The Minnesota traders often lived in fixed residences of considerable opulence, receiving the furs the Indians brought them at these regular trading stations. Joseph Renville, for example, lived "like an African King" at Lac qui Parle, surrounded by a bodyguard of Indian warriors and a large

Henry H. Sibley House, Mendota, 1835

corps of servants. He maintained schools for his pensionaries and presided as suzerain over the territory for miles about. At Prairie du Chien, Hercules L. Dousman, the chief agent of Astor for the Upper Mississippi region, presided over his satrapy in a mansion on an estate of 4,500 acres.

The trade in its peak years during the 1830s provided great return on little capital. In his first year as Dousman's partner, the twenty-three-year-old Sibley accumulated 389,388 muskrats, 1,027 otters, 1,139 buffalo robes, 3,243 deerskins, 2,330 mink, 609 fishers, and hundreds of coons, martens, bears, foxes, and beavers. But the company was badly hit by the panic of 1837, four years after the prescient John Jacob Astor had withdrawn to speculate in Manhattan real estate. Ladies everywhere, and the British army, suddenly agreed upon a preference for silk over beaver hats, and two great consumer groups thereby disappeared. Independent traders set up posts within the company's preserve, and the supply of furs in the area diminished as the number of trappers increased. In 1834, Sibley had traveled to his post at Mendota three hundred miles up the Mississippi after conferring with his partners at Prairie du Chien and reported seeing only one cabin along the way.

Ten years later, he encountered a dozen or more trading centers on the route. The wilderness was passing and with it, the fur trade. Sibley wrote in 1846 that "larger animals are fast disappearing and will soon be exterminated. Upon the plains where the elk and buffalo were to be found by the thousands, the hunter may now roam for days without encountering a single herd."

Sibley was Minnesota's most intriguing character of the frontier period. He had a Churchillian gift for romantic journalism about his own exploits, writing for national magazines under such names as "Walker-in-the-Pines" and "Hal-A-Dacotah." He was handsome, lithe, quick, and tough; he alone of the early territorial leaders could stand up to James "Bully" Wells of Frontenac in a fair fight. He had a flair for making and reporting expeditions to exotic places, for hair-raising escapes, and for big-game hunting quite beyond the call of the trade. On one long safari with the Dakota he and his companions shot "more than two thousand deer, fifty to sixty elk, many bears, some buffaloes, and even a few panthers." He wrote a biography of the old trapper Jack Frazer, known as "Iron Face," but his literary tastes were not limited to folk heroes or to frontier Americans. His library contained the works of Hallam, Prescott, Froissart, Thiers, and Sparks, and they were thoroughly read. The chivalric rhythms of Froissart and of Sir Walter Scott can be heard in Sibley's own prose.

For a time Sibley was the sole representative of the law west of the Mississippi and north of Iowa, "the only magistrate in this region and the county seat . . . three hundred miles distant." He became the first territorial delegate to Congress, the first governor of the state, donated his middle name to his real estate speculation which became the town of Hastings, and led the forces which put down the Dakota War of 1862. He had long sought to prevent that tragedy by advocating a more enlightened policy toward the Dakota. In Congress he had said, "Your pioneers are encircling the last home of the red man as with a wall of fire. . . . You must approach these with terms of conciliation and of real friendship or you must suffer the consequences of a bloody and remorseless Indian war. . . . The time is not far distant, when pent in on all sides and suffering from want, a Philip or Tecumseh will arise to band them together for a last and desperate onset upon their white foes." A decade later, Little Crow reluctantly assumed the mantle of Tecumseh, and the frontier fell back a hundred miles before a concerted and skillful Indian attack. After Sibley's forces extinguished that uprising, he negotiated the treaties of peace with the Dakota.

Though he served a term in the state legislature in 1871, Sibley ceased to be a dominant political figure in Minnesota in 1860. He was a Douglas Democrat and the long Republican hegemony had begun. One of his biographers, Wilson Shortridge, suggests that he was not really comfortable in the hurly-burly of public life. It seems likely, too, that a man who had sought freedom and dignity on the frontier may have been restless amid the haggling and huckstering of the late Victorian political life. Though without major office, Sibley was active and interested in all the large concerns of the state until his death in 1891. We know little of his feelings in these decades, for though he wrote a great deal, he had a strong sense of personal privacy. The last years of his life, spent as a regent of the University of Minnesota, as a corporate officer, as a Grand Old Man, saw the world of his gay, boisterous life as "Young Hall" pass away.

Sibley's old friend and neighbor, Jean Baptiste Faribault, did not live to see Minnesota become a commercial and industrial state. He died in 1862 at the end of a life which began during the American Revolution, bridging the days of the French regime in America to the era of the American empire. His father, a lawyer, had come to Canada as military secretary of Montcalm's army and had remained after the defeat and death of his general and the triumph of British arms. Jean Baptiste was born in Berthier, near Quebec, in 1774, and came to the northwest in 1798 to take charge of a trading post near the present site of Chicago. He was trading in central Iowa at the turn of the century and came to Minnesota in 1803. lt was on September 21, 1805, that Lt. Zebulon M. Pike, found "Mr. Ferrebault" encamped to repair his "peroque." Faribault later returned to civilization at Prairie du Chien where his trade goods, according to one report, were destroyed by hostile Indians while he was held captive by the British during the War of 1812. But his loyalty to the American cause, "his intelligence and knowledge of the Dakota language and customs" were rewarded when, seven years thereafter, Colonel Henry Leavenworth set forth up the Mississippi to establish American control of the region. In 1820 as Leavenworth was building Fort Snelling to be the Gibraltar of the northwest frontier, he suggested that Faribault move there and carry on his fur trading operations at Pike Island under the shelter of the fort.

After two spring floods, Faribault retired to higher ground at Mendota. First he built a log structure there and, finally, in 1839–40, a dignified stone house beside the home of Henry Sibley, and considerably more formal. It may have been modeled on a similar residence created a generation earlier for his colleague, Michel Brisbois, at the fur traders' headquarters, Prairie du Chien. But to Brisbois's simple pattern the old man added a square classic doorway and the hooked gable of the Greek Revival style which was coming into fashion in downriver settlements. Faribault's house presents a proud symmetrical facade balanced by end chimneys. Thus a formal facade fronted the dwelling of an old trader of no formal education, while the urbane Sibley inhabited the casual dwelling of a frontiersman. The Faribault house has been restored through the exertions of the WPA, the DAR, and the Minnesota Highway Department.

Joseph R. Brown was another of the early fur traders who made an uneasy adaptation into the role of a leader of a civilized territory. He came to Minnesota from Maryland in 1819, joining the first garrison of Fort Snelling as a musician, playing the fife and drum. He soon tired of

Jean B. Faribault House, Mendota, 1840

military life and began trading along the Minnesota River and at Grey Cloud Island below St. Paul. Aside from his musical skills, he was a gifted prose stylist who edited newspapers in St. Paul and Henderson, an intrepid soldier and explorer and, in the territorial legislature, the dominant parliamentarian.

Says William Watts Folwell, "the veritable Joe Brown . . . [was] . . . most skillful of all in the usages of conventions and legislatures." For a Fort Snelling drummer boy who had no formal education beyond the age of thirteen, that was no small accomplishment. He was competing with Henry Sibley, lawyers like Moses Sherburne and Lafayette Emmett, and such crafty statesmen as William R. Marshall and Alexander Ramsey. Brown was known as "Joseph the Juggler" for his legislative skill; this was no term of derision for he was extraordinarily popular with all factions. He had played host, in his tamarack log house near Stillwater, to the organizers of Minnesota Territory, had served in the Wisconsin legislature, and had laid out a town around his trading post. He was credited with being Minnesota's first (European) farmer, having broken prairie sod and raised a crop near Minnehaha Falls. When others sought to stake the first claim to the town site of Taylors Falls, with its ample waterpower, they found Brown there before them. Later, he sent the first log raft down the St. Croix and "this gave him the place of pioneer lumberman of Minnesota," according to the admiring Folwell.

Brown was, however, a drifter, for reasons which await the probing of a skilled biographer. He left each place he founded, each profession, each scene of triumph and adulation and removed westward, always forsaking the settlements he had led, always seeking a clear sky and unbroken horizons. From St. Paul, he went up the Minnesota River again, found a fit place for habitation and named it Henderson, possibly after a favorite aunt. He named the county thereabouts Sibley, after his lifelong friend and political ally. From Henderson there soon radiated no less than nine public roads, thanks to a compliant and generous legislature. On some of those roads there soon traveled Brown's marvelous invention, a steam wagon. It looked something like an early tractor and carried the mails for short distances. Brown, late in life, sought to displace Wells Fargo with a steamer mail service from the Mississippi to the West Coast. He remained in Henderson only for his customary sojourn of a few years and then repaired still farther westward up the Minnesota Valley where he built a nineteen-room limestone house overlooking the reservation lands left to the Dakota by the 1851 treaties. Three and a half stories high, it was dubbed "Farther and Gay" castle by a punning English visitor. Brown was in New York negotiating for support for his steam car when the inevitable backlash of the treaties struck; the Dakota rose up and massacred nearly five hundred settlers. Among them would have been Brown's wife, twelve children, and his retainers had she not been a Sisseton and kin to their chiefs, as she informed a group of warriors who intercepted them on the way to shelter at Fort Ridgely. She was a formidable woman and the Dakota treated her with respect, but they destroyed the castle.

Joseph R. Brown died in 1870 while at work on another steam wagon project, and is buried in Henderson. His town is a fit memorial to him; it is as distinctively of brick as Marine-on-St. Croix or Taylors

Joseph R. Brown House,
Henderson,
c. 1855

Falls are distinctively of frame. Brick stores line Main Street. There is a brick jail, a brick town hall, and at the top of the long slope from the riverbank, there is a group of cubical, hip-roofed brick houses like those of Galena or of the old seaboard cities of Maryland or New Jersey. The influence of Galena upon the frontier may well have been reinforced by the dominant role in Henderson of a son of Maryland.

Brown was impatient to get brick factories in operation; "a prodigy rarely met with . . . he was the organizer and leader in everything." Brown insisted that the new factories put color in the brick. The local clay was yellowish, but Brown wanted the same rosy hue as the brick of the Eastern Seaboard and of Galena.

What has now been fairly well established as Brown's brick house has now been painted yellow to protect the old sun-dried brick from further decomposition, and its interior has been altered, but Brown's innovative touches can still be seen. The structure has double thicknesses of basswood lath and plaster, basswood siding over maple two-by-fours, heavy oak sills and beams, and six-foot windows looking out on the park which he gave to his town. Under the eaves is a slight suggestion of Gothic revival tracery, enough to classify this house of a pioneer editor (to select one of his professions from many) with those of the literati who, in Minnesota, favored that style. (See chapter 5.) The land records indicate that Brown never troubled to record a deed to the property, but gave Henry Poehler the right to sell it for him, under a power of attorney, after he departed for "Farther and Gay" Castle. Poehler finally sold the house in 1864.

Even if Galena's masonry influence had not been so strong, brick would have appealed to men who had to deal with Indians. On the inflammable frontier, it was reassuring to know that brick walls, laid back-to-back, and heavy masonry provided good protection. Though log houses, of course, had acted as forts during the most primitive period, missionaries and Indian agents gradually found it possible to acquire brick and there seems to have been a general preference on their part to build of masonry.

The most imposing of the Indian agency houses in Minnesota was occupied by a great man who deserves wider recognition, Jonathan E. Fletcher. Fletcher practiced on the Winnebago reservation the Indian policy articulated in Congress by Henry Sibley and implemented among the Dakota by his colleague, Joseph R. Brown. Much has been written of the callousness of traders and agents like Andrew J. Myrick, who was said to have precipitated the Dakota War by telling the hungry Indians to eat grass (and who was found scalped, his mouth stuffed with grass). But during the same uprising, Fletcher's Winnebagos remained tranquil, probably a tribute to the agent and friend who had accompanied them through their tribulations, and had pursued an Indian policy which might have prevented the war had he and his colleagues not been replaced by political hacks like Myrick.

Fletcher's Winnebago agency house, built in 1855, was considered to be the finest residence in town; its red, sun-dried brick had a solemn eighteenth-century facade with twin chimneys at each end of

Jonathan Fletcher House (Winnebago Agency House), St. Clair, 1855

the gable roof, a symmetrical five-bay front and a cornice with handsome dentils.

Fletcher was born in Thetford, Vermont, and settled near Muscatine, Iowa, in 1838 where he served as a member of the Iowa Constitutional Convention. A Democrat, he was appointed agent to the Winnebagos when that tribe still reigned over most of southern Wisconsin. Folwell says they were then "a virile and prosperous tribe." In a succession of treaties, they gave up their Wisconsin lands and were herded across the Mississippi toward Ft. Atkinson, Iowa. There, despite Fletcher's best efforts, they were easy prey for whiskey sellers. Soon the neighboring whites were again conscious of the unworthiness of such "besotted idlers" to occupy good farmland, and the traders became anxious for more "lost credits." In 1846, a new treaty presented the traders with $190,000, "to settle their affairs," and one of them, Henry M. Rice, was selected to collect the tribe and transport it to the area of Long Prairie, Minnesota, where it was to be placed as a buffer between the Dakota and Ojibwe. Neither of these ancient enemies welcomed the newcomers to land they both claimed, and Sibley protested that Rice would clear $100,000 from his "infamous contract." Fletcher refused to accept Rice's accounting, and it was not until 1861 that Rice's assignees collected the last $23,327.46. But the Winnebagos were settled at Long Prairie. Soon again neighbors began to view the 890,000 acres allotted to them with interest. In 1854, a new treaty passed the Senate, replacing the Long Prairie reservation with 200,000 acres around St. Clair and providing $70,000 to assist the Indians "to meet their obligations" to the traders. This time Fletcher himself moved "a large majority of the vagrants to the Blue Earth River at very small expense."

There, "hunting and fishing was impossible, and the annuities . . . were insufficient for the support of the tribe. Fletcher applied himself vigorously . . . to lead it toward a civilized life. He induced many of the Indians to plant crops, to build houses, and to wear white men's clothes; he persuaded some to enroll their children in school. . . . They improved their farmland, gambled less, and many of them abandoned whiskey. They framed and adopted a code of laws. . . . There is reason to believe that, could they have been allowed to remain on this reserve, within a lifetime they would have become nearly, if not quite, as civilized as the Indians of New York and New England." But there arose a "storm of wild rage . . . among the whites after the Sioux Outbreak of 1862," though the Winnebagos had refused to join their kinsmen on the warpath. Vigilante groups called Knights of the Forest were formed, pledged to eradicate the Indians, and the Winnebagos were moved once again, beyond the Missouri River, and so, in Folwell's words, "they pass beyond our horizon."

Jonathan E. Fletcher had acknowledged defeat earlier. He was apparently relieved by a new appointee of the Lincoln administration. We do know that he returned to Muscatine after his Indian service and died there in 1872.

At the Upper Sioux Agency residence in Yellow Medicine County, now near State Highway 67, eight miles southeast of Granite Falls, is a brick structure with twin end-chimneys and a high-peaked gable roof pierced by three dormers. It was once two-storied, probably much like Jonathan Fletcher's house, and was built for the agency doctor soon after Agent Robert G. Murphy selected the site in July 1854. Around it were homes for a carpenter, a farm superintendent, blacksmiths, and other agency employees, a brick warehouse, school, stables, a brick kiln, a jail, four traders' houses, and a hundred or more brick houses for farmer Indians. Several of these who had been converted to Christianity refused to join the uprising in 1862, sheltered the agency residents, and led them to safety. But the agency itself was sacked and burned. After the war, it was abandoned until a farmer, George E. Olds, reoccupied the site in 1866 and rebuilt the shell of the doctor's house from the two-story, end-chimney style into the present single-story, end-chimney, dormered style.

Another form of house common on the Eastern Seaboard has already been noted, the hip-roofed cube. Its facade often was perforated by three windows above, and two and a door below. Its walls, like those of the gable-roofed rectangles discussed above, were often made of brick in the Middle Colonies, rather than of white-painted siding as they were, generally, in New England. Henry Sibley's French-American secretary, or assistant, Hypolite du Puis, built such a house at Mendota in 1854, of buff brick brought, the story goes, from Milwaukee. The house is very simple, with no decoration of any kind. It was placed behind the mansion of his employer, farther up the hillside and away from the river, and after 1930 was used as a summer-season restaurant. Today it is the visitors' office for the Sibley House.

A more imposing brick cube was erected in 1856 by Gideon H. Pond, overlooking the Minnesota Valley where for twenty years he had labored as a teacher and minister to the Indians. He and his brother Samuel had been charged with religious zeal at a revival meeting in their home state of Connecticut and came west by way of Illinois, reaching Minnesota in 1834, the same year as Sibley. They had no backing from any religious body, but they knew farming and carpentry. Gideon had taught school and, as a contemporary said of them, "they seemed the children of a king." Over six feet tall they were, and "stalwart and sinewy, alert and genial." On occasion they were assigned to do menial labor by ecclesiastical superiors who thought too little of their limited education and their lack of formal ordination, but together their influence not only upon the Indians but upon the entire region increased every year. They devised the Pond Alphabet of the Dakota language, worked at Indian villages at Kaposia (South St. Paul) and Lake Calhoun, developed a Dakota dictionary of three thousand words, and then divided. Samuel went East for formal education and ordination, returned, and finally settled in the neighborhood of Shakopee. Gideon went to Lac qui Parle where, with others, he worked on a translation of several books of the Bible into the Dakota language. Later he published a *Dakota Reading Book*; Samuel followed with a *Second Dakota Reading Book*, Gideon developed a monthly publication, the "Dakotah Friend," and later a study of Indian religion called *Dakotah Superstition*. (I wonder what he would title it today?) The two brothers learned Hebrew, Greek, Latin and French, and Samuel added German. In 1843, Gideon moved to a log structure in Bloomington township which he later replaced with the brick house. The house, now surrounded by suburban development, is at 401 East 104th Street.

The traveler who explores first that stronghold of the New England tradition, the St. Croix Valley, and then proceeds to Mendota and beyond, can be easily convinced of the importance of the influence of the masonry traditions of the Middle Colonies, of Galena, and, perhaps, of Prairie du Chien upon the Indian traders and teachers in the Minnesota River valley, for in that valley the oldest houses are not of white frame but of log, brick, or stone construction. When the transition from primitive shelters to more ambitious residences was made by Sibley, Faribault, the Ponds, Jonathan Fletcher, Joseph R. Brown, and their colleagues, it appears likely that they either fell back upon the French tradition of stone construction or followed the lead of the inhabitants of the closest centers of civilization and used brick. The Ponds had remained in the area of Galena for a period before proceeding to Minnesota, and Fletcher had first settled just across the Mississippi, in Muscatine, Iowa.

The chief negotiator of the Treaties of 1851 was Alexander Ramsey, first territorial governor of Minnesota, and preeminent representative of the Pennsylvania Dutch virtues in the Midwest. Ramsey was a hearty, heavy, hardfisted, practical politician and land speculator who "wasted no time on fanciful projects." The years after the Indian treaties, when Minnesota was growing into a strong, settled, mechanized, and urbanized society, were congenial to Ramsey. He was a leader of firm purposes, strong intelligence, and little patience for trifles or sentiment.

His father died when he was ten. He earned his education as a carpenter and clerk, was admitted to the bar and the councils of the Whig party and was elected to the United States Congress in a German-speaking district, "and he often attributed his election . . . largely to the fact that he canvassed the district thoroughly and addressed his audiences in their own vernacular, the Pennsylvania Dutch dialect." Though he bore his father's Scotch name, he made much of the fact that his mother, a Miss Kelker, was of German descent. During his second term in Congress, he applied himself to organizing pivotal Pennsylvania for Zachary Taylor's successful campaign for the presidency. In 1849, Taylor remembered and rewarded by making him governor of the newly created Minnesota Territory which then stretched from the Mississippi to the Missouri. Such posts brought honor and considerable pecuniary potentialities.

Ramsey arrived at Mendota on May 27, 1849. He was made welcome by Henry Sibley, with whom he stayed for a month while a house was made ready in St. Paul. The capital city was "just emerging from a collection of Indian whiskey shops and birch-roofed cabins of half-breed voyageurs" and had a population of three hundred. From the time that Ramsey and his wife were ferried there in June in a birchbark canoe until his death in 1903, he and Sibley were its leading citizens. After Ramsey arrived in St. Paul, he lived in a log house covered with plank siding, then in a more ambitious wooden structure as he accumulated the means to build what he called a "Mansion House." By this

term he meant the kind of large, impressive stone structure which he finally constructed in the years between 1868 and 1872 at 265 South Exchange Street. The architect, which in that period in Minnesota meant little more than contractor, was Monroe Sheire, who was of Dutch ancestry and came from the stone-building region of the Catskill Mountains in New York. Ramsey's house has a mansard roof, but one scarcely notices the roof above its broad-shouldered bulk. It has the brackets, hood molds, and bay window characteristic of the Italianate style, but they, too, flatten into relative insignificance against the sheer solidity of the structure. It sits upon its haunches behind a broad front porch, older in spirit, stronger, unmoved by the styles of its time which play about its surfaces, a Mansion House marking the full accomplishment of a Pennsylvania Dutch burgher. It dominates the neighborhood which Alexander Ramsey purchased for speculation when it was oak scrub and swamp and watched grow into the town's most prosperous and fashionable section.

In 1964, the Ramsey House passed into the hands of the Minnesota Historical Society under the terms of the wills of Anita E. Ramsey Furness and Laura Furness, who maintained the house much as it was when their grandfather completed it in 1872. The cavernous front porch was Ramsey's favorite retreat on summer evenings for conversation and reading. After passing through a marble-floored vestibule with niches for trays to receive calling cards, the visitor enters the front hall, and then the parlor to the left: forty feet long, fourteen feet high, twenty feet broad, lit by two crystal chandeliers which take a week to clean, drop by drop. Across the hall are a smaller parlor, library, dining room, and service areas. Upstairs are five bedrooms and Ramsey's office; above that, the nursery and servants' rooms on the third floor. There are broad grounds, and about them, a wrought-iron fence with wide gates carrying the wrought-iron letters "A R."

Through that gate every May 27 came Henry Sibley to call on his old friend on the anniversary of their first meeting. Unlike Sibley, Ramsey was seldom out of public office. He was always a leader of the Republican Party during its long hegemony, though he had been characteristically slow to abandon the moribund Whig Party; it was said that he "sat up with the corpse." He was twice United States senator, served as secretary of war under President Hayes, and after that served on two presidential commissions. President Hayes visited him in the Mansion

House during one of those processions through the province, delightful to an age much given to ceremony.

Near Alexander Ramsey's mansion there is a small stone house at 252 West 7th Street, thought to have been the home of his luckless brother, Justus. Justus C. Ramsey, who had also arrived in St. Paul in

Justus C. Ramsey House, St. Paul, c. 1850

1849, engaged in a modest real estate business and in his declining years grew less and less capable of comprehending reality. He died, alone, in a drab hotel room while his brother walked with presidents. The little house, which he is believed to have built, is now hidden away behind a small yard between two business buildings. The interior was pegged butternut, the walls local limestone, two feet thick, like those of Alexander Ramsey's Mansion House.

Justus Ramsey's may have been the first stone house in St. Paul; the abstracts indicate that it was built about 1850, and in the previous year E. S. Seymour reported that "there was not a brick or stone building in the place." This was despite the fact that limestone lay so close to the surface that an ordinance a few years later forbade householders to leave pits in roadways after quarrying stone for their houses. In the years of the great land rush, 1851 to 1860, when the population of Minnesota grew from 6,000 to 172,000, many more stone houses were built in St. Paul. A few were the product of the old Germans, the Pennsylvania Dutch, but most were built by German immigrants arriving fresh from Europe.

These newcomers were the agents of a change in Minnesota's architectural landscape, a change so profound as to deserve a chapter of its own. But in this broad survey of the early houses of Minnesota it seems worthwhile to note that the ancient masonry tradition of northern Europe was not inhibited by man-made frontiers. The French and the Germans built stone cottages very much alike, and their descendants continued to build them in Minnesota well into the last half of the nineteenth century. The French-Canadian strain, in particular, remained strong.

Francois Tetrault came from Quebec and settled in Faribault where his handiwork can be seen in his own house, built against the bank of the Straight River in 1870, at 224 NE 2nd Street. But the finest expression of that tradition, aside from the Faribault house, is the craftsmanship of Andrew and James Doig. Their story deserves to be related in some detail.

Stone buildings do not rot, neither do the rains wash them rapidly away. They outlast the men who build them, and stand as memorials to forgotten hopes, long after frame houses, built quickly to meet the need for shelter, have crumbled, and wild roses have overwhelmed their wooden fences. There is a group of empty stone buildings at Wasioja in Dodge County west of Mantorville, where Andrew Doig and his brother, John, settled after emigrating from French Canada in the 1850s to join a community headed by Colonel James George. They constructed fine buildings during that decade, built of stone quarried near the town: a bank, a two-room school, and, proudest of all, the seminary,

the largest educational institution in the state, erected when the population of the town reached one thousand in 1860.

When in 1861 President Lincoln called for volunteers, the seminary's president, Clinton A. Cilley, formed his student body into a company and, at its head, marched down the hill to Colonel George's still standing law office, which had become a recruiting station. Most of the students enlisted to form Company C of the Second Minnesota Regiment and both George and Cilley accepted commissions. Colonel George led them through many battles and, finally, at Chickamauga he rose from a stretcher to steady their lines under the pounding of the Confederate charges. When the day was over, a third of his command were casualties.

After the war the survivors returned to Wasioja. There they met the ghosts of friends and brothers as they sat in the hollow evening with those who had no sons left, and then, after a while, they boarded up the windows, piled the furniture in wagons, and moved on to start again somewhere else. Andrew Doig sold his house, with its meticulously cut lintels and sills, its squared stone laid in level courses, and followed Colonel George to Rochester. George became a successful lawyer there, and Doig established a monument business. A decade later, the seminary burned down, and no one had the heart to rebuild it. Wasioja is today almost deserted, but the house of Andrew Doig has been carefully restored. The seminary is a charred ruin, mourned by giant trees.

Finally, a house which appears to be simple, but represents a tangle of influences. The Heman Gibbs homestead at 2097 Larpenteur Avenue in St. Paul is made up of a central mass built in 1867 around a tamarack log cabin laid up in 1849. That central mass has a gable roof and is covered with the white clapboards typical of Gibbs's native Vermont, but it also has a broad gallerie which would have been unusual there at so early a date. The explanation for the porch may well be that Gibbs spent a considerable period in northwestern Illinois with his sister and was there exposed to the pleasures of the French south-facing porches. It could even be argued that the influence of Galena, itself, can be seen playing upon that Gibbs house for, instead of the central chimney which prudent Yankees placed where it could provide heat to the entire house, Heman Gibbs placed a chimney at each end of the gable roof. End chimneys were more common in Galena, in Virginia, and in Maryland than in New England. Of course, Gibbs may simply have liked the end-chimney shape, and his frame farmhouse is far too modest to claim the right to represent all the major influences upon Minnesota architecture in the pioneer period.

3

The Houses the Germans Built

THE FIRST GERMANS TO COME TO MINNESOTA were merely one group of emigrants joining the general westward movement. Most of them had already accepted many American customs, having spent years in the great German-American centers such as Pittsburgh, Milwaukee, and Cincinnati. In their first architectural essays in Minnesota they sustained their ancestral building habits only to the extent that local materials made it possible for them to do so easily. There was nothing self-conscious about this; they did what came easiest. Later, however, a spectacularly German architecture appeared in a burst of national pride. It is that phenomenon, which can be called, for reasons shortly to appear, "cahenslyite," that will occupy the central part of the argument of this chapter. First, let the early, easy tale be told.[1]

German immigrants exerted a powerful force upon the history of Minnesota. In 1860, only 30 percent of Minnesota's population were European immigrants, but the German-born nearly equaled the New England–born (18,400 against 18,222). In 1870, there were 41,000 Germans and 28,500 Yankees living in Minnesota. These Germans were largely concentrated in three areas: the Minnesota Valley around New Ulm, in St. Paul, and on the Upper Mississippi in the prairie about St. Cloud. They had begun to arrive early in the 1850s drawn by the advice of Father Francis Pierz, who wrote "glowing descriptions of the advantages and beauties of the region, and especially of the Sauk Valley," from his mission at Crow Wing. In 1856, a group of Benedictine monks traveled from Germany to Pennsylvania, then to St. Paul, and on to the new German settlements, established missions in St. Cloud and across the Mississippi at Sauk Rapids. In 1866, they built a large stone building to serve as the center of what became St. John's Abbey at Collegeville. Around that structure grew up a community of German farmers who built of granite (unlike their cousins to the south who employed limestone).

Granite fieldstones and outcrops had been used for the construction of houses in the mountainous areas of southern Germany for thousands of years, and when their plows rasped against the same recalcitrant rock in Stearns County, the Germans knew how to use it. Glanville Smith, of Cold Spring, Minnesota, the laureate of the granite industry, wrote of the use of seam-faced granite in a letter to the author in 1963:

> Granite outcroppings which occur in these regions where glacial action or water erosion had laid them bare—generally they are in river valleys— are often not of too sound quality in their exposed parts, that is, they are traversed by fissures and seams. Into these seams moisture has carried vegetable dyes from the plant life at the top, which means that the seams, if granite is split away from them, have non-granite colorings, and very color-fast, too-rusty tones, red tones, sometimes subtle greens, and so on. Since this top rock, full of seams and cracks, was easily broken loose, it was a cheap building material in pioneer times and ready-to-hand to the old country immigrants who had some knowledge of stonecutting and masonry work. (Granite itself is never yellow or rust colored.)

Throughout the Sauk River valley old farmhouses and barns disclose foundations of such seam-faced granite. Two houses (whose dates cannot be precisely fixed but probably belong to the 1860s or early 1870s) are to be found in the neighborhood of the old stone building at St. John's Abbey and are built entirely of this material. One is situated just across the highway from the new entrance road to the abbey. The other is on the grounds of the abbey itself, across the lake from the school and monastery.

Fieldstone houses, quite common in Wisconsin, are not so in Minnesota. One of the few was built by Reuben Freeman on the Old Pine Bend Road between St. Paul and Hastings. Freeman was a farmer of modest means but mighty energy, who spent many of the coldest evenings of the winter of 1875 reading *The House of Seven Gables,* and pledged to go Nathaniel Hawthorne one better: for two summers, he and his sons labored to lay up a house of eight gables, using stones they dug out of their fields and homemade cement. At one point Freeman grew bored with granite and laid a course of old bottles into the wall.

Reuben Freeman House, Inver Grove Heights, 1875

The roof is of a flapping butterfly design, defying more conventional description.

Freeman settled amid a band of German settlements which comprised rich farmsteads stretching across the promontory bounded by the Mississippi and Minnesota rivers, with its Teutonic concentration increasing as it moved westward. A few miles to the north in St. Paul, there was a strong German colony, which sustained its affection for masonry construction and added to the frame and log houses of St. Paul's French and Yankee founders many fine stone structures, "the materials for the walls and mortar being found in excavating the foundation." Several of these still remain. Doris Apitz, a widowed seamstress, built her small two-story home at 320 Smith Avenue in 1860. Two years before, George D. Luckert erected a dignified, two-story farmhouse in the middle of an orchard at 480 Iglehart, with precisely laid courses of limestone in front and random ashlar on the sides.

The Spangenberg brothers were led to the St. Paul area by Frederick, probably the eldest, who became a prosperous dairy farmer and milk distributor. He made it a practice to bring his brothers over from Germany, one by one, to assist in his growing enterprises. Between 1864 and 1867 he erected a large limestone farmhouse in the prairie overlooking the Mississippi River, west of St. Paul and south of St. Anthony. The stone was brought by heavy sled or stone-boat from the riverbank during the winter. The house, now surrounded by St. Paul's Highland Park district, has gained a street address (375 Mount Curve Avenue). A decade later his brother Charles followed the same process in acquiring stone for a home in the Cottage Grove area of Washington County. It was built into the hillside for protection from the northwest wind. Only two stories are exposed to the windward, but to the leeward, looking out over a valley and over crops and herds, it has three stories and a two-tiered porch. At the ends of the gable, there are scroll-sawed bargeboards (boards cut into patterns in the Gothic manner, running along the eaves as if a vine had grown there) above the windows of a fourth story. The Spangenbergs had done well with their cattle and their milk routes.

Other German settlers were not so fortunate. A group of them, several families of Ellringers, Marnachs, Kieffers, and Majerus, participated in the tragedy of the Whitewater Valley, northwest of Winona. This area was settled early in 1856 by men who tore up the prairie turf and plowed up and down the hillsides and cut away the trees whose roots had held the soil in place and soaked up the rain. When the topsoil began to follow the spring freshets downhill into the valley floor, the farmers were delighted. It was like the Nile Valley—fresh soil every spring. But soon it was sand, filling the riverbeds and forcing the water up over the fields. Twenty-eight times in one year the Whitewater River flooded; when the river receded and the sun came, the wind drove the dust into the air to cover everything. More sand flowed down the hillsides past the stumps and the abandoned cornfields—sand, and then mud. It is said in the area that one roadway built six feet above flood level was six feet below the level of the sand-covered fields a decade later. The Ira Card farm lay under sixteen feet of sand and mud. Hylon Appleby finally abandoned his house when the mud seeped over the windowsills. Today, the limestone Kieffer-Hemmelberg farmhouse remains, four miles west of Altura, in the midst of the Whitewater Recreation Area, eighteen thousand acres owned by the state of Minnesota, purchased in the 1930s and 1940s from farmers who could no longer survive in the devastated valley. The Nicholas Marnach "fort," a large, three-bay, two-story limestone house, had slots under the eaves for firing rifles in case of an Indian attack, which never came. It surrendered instead to the mud and has fallen into ruin, abandoned long ago.

Most of these first houses built by German immigrants to Minnesota were little more than shelters against a fierce and capricious climate. In a new scene, the newcomers re-created the humblest dwellings which had served them in the old country, warm places to cook, eat, and rest. They made them of traditional materials and, generally, in simple traditional forms.

Soon, however, the Germans were able to do more, and in increasingly sophisticated and self-conscious architecture they created a series of monuments to their changing attitudes toward American life. First to come to Minnesota were the "Forty-Eighters": individualistic, imbued with the idealism of the French Revolution, suspicious of established churches, opposed to restrictions on trade, and especially opposed to feudal impediments to the ambitions of persons. The Forty-Eighters made up an articulate and potent element in Minnesota's foreign-born population. Most of them were eager to adopt American ways.

After 1865, especially in the 1870s, a new group began to arrive, refugees from Bismarck's effort to clamp upon the diverse multitude of German states and customs, a Prussian mold which was, itself, anticlerical, industrial, centralized, and hostile to the remnants of feudalism. He drove out many who revered the old Germany of tiny states and autonomous villages and of inefficient but independent craftsmen. Many were attached to their parishes, their priests and pastors, and hostile to the heavy, mechanical autarchy of the Prussian system. When these post–Civil War refugees came to the New World, they resisted the ineluctable centralizing and industrializing of the American economy. They had little desire to be homogenized into a mass society like the one they had escaped. After 1865 these conservatives began building a self-consciously old-German architecture which persisted until they finally found a comfortable place in the American consensus after 1920. For both the Forty-Eighters and the conservatives, religious faith, language, politics, and architecture moved together. Each of these elements was braided into the others, and all four aspects of their culture changed sharply after the balance shifted from the liberals toward the conservatives after 1865.

This tangled tale can be pursued most easily, perhaps, by proceeding from the history and ideology of the Forty-Eighters to their architecture, and then advancing into the thicket of ideas which is associated with the great Cahenslyite controversy in the American Catholic Church, which was the most conspicuous symptom of the conservative reaction.

The Forty-Eighters were so called because of the year in which they participated in a revolt against the petty despotisms and the feudal economy which had persisted in Germany despite the challenge of the ideals of the French Revolution. They had sought to establish constitutional monarchies in the major German states, to open up ancient barriers to the physical movement of goods and the social movement of men, and to achieve a unity of the German states in a new confederation, inspired by the example of the United States. They failed. At Frankfurt they built cloud-constitutions while the Junkers and the Austrian oligarchs rallied, and soon Prince Schwarzenberg from the south and Prince Von Bismarck from the north clanged the gates of despotism together again. For the Forty-Eighters, America was an example and a promise. It became, in an ideological sense, their true homeland. America had succeeded in the first modern revolution to articulate its principles in liberal doctrines. It had chosen for its leaders intellectuals who wrote in much the same way as intellectuals among the Forty-Eighters. And it was a constitutional democracy, such as the Forty-Eighters had tried to achieve in Germany.[2]

With the exuberance of synthetic philosophy, German intellectuals mixed together Rousseau's noble savage, Goethe's Faust, and the American frontiersman, and produced an image of an American which would have been the wonder of the world. When people already given to a political philosophy of which enthusiasm was the principle component, and imbued with an idealized concept of American democracy and of the American as a type, reached these shores to find architecture in the grip of the Greek revival, they must have felt a new rush of intoxication. For, in Germany, most educated men revered classical Greece and Rome.[3]

For a brief time their identification with American society found expression in their houses. This was especially true in the most important settlement of the Forty-Eighters in Minnesota: New Ulm in Brown County. The town was burned by the Indians after it had been evacuated by its defenders during the Dakota War, but it was photographed, showing houses painted white. None were of stone or brick except two which had barely been started when the Dakota arrived. One of the town's founders built a small Greek revival house, typical of many, which survives at 220½ North Minnesota Street hidden behind a row of business buildings. Two houses built just after the Dakota War by Forty-Eighters show how earnestly they adopted American building patterns: 212 South German Street is the finest home left from this early period, built by Adolph Seiter in 1865. Its lineage, architecturally,

Adolph Seiter House, New Ulm, 1865

is impeccably American. Its builder was a tailor from Baden. That he chose such a form, as his colleagues chose other Yankee styles, tells us a great deal about these first settlers of New Ulm.

Seiter was born in Baden in 1826. He came to the United States on

May 1, 1847. After remaining in New York for two years, he migrated to Cincinnati, the center of the German-American turnvereins, secret societies which in Germany had provided cadres which fought nobly in 1848 and in America continued as centers of liberal activity. In 1856, Seiter and a group of turnvereiners headed by Colonel Pfaender departed for New Ulm to join a similar group from Chicago. With Pfaender he selected the site of the town and opened one of its first general stores. Just before the Dakota War, he erected a hotel called the Dakotah House, which was used as a hospital during the uprising. When peace returned Seiter erected a new house and chose as his model a familiar American pattern-book form. It had descended from Palladio through British reductions and simplifications into a thoroughly Americanized version in the hands of native craftsmen like Jonathan Goldsmith of Ohio and was popularized by Minard LeFever's *The Modern Builder's Guide.*

The roofs of two balancing wings, cut away in the front, rise in the rear in a continuous line to the sides of the hip-roofed central pavilion. A verandah across the front is a contribution of Seiter to LeFever's design, consistent with the predilection for the front porch already established in Minnesota.

At 15 South Valley Street is another thoroughly American pattern-book house, apparently built about 1865 by German-born Henry Hammer, a cabinet maker who came to New Ulm from Cincinnati about 1859. It is in the Villa style with a tower rising to a cap. There is a typical midwestern verandah in front and a bay window to the south. So it appears that the earliest German immigrants felt no need to display any distinctively German architectural style. The American amalgam effectively accepted even those who came directly from the Old Country, as rapid Americanizing took place. A good example is the home of Martin Schmidt, built about 1872 a mile south of Victoria, in Carver County. Schmidt emigrated from Munich in the 1860s, paused in the staging area of St. Louis, which had become almost as much a German city as it had been French, and came to Minnesota in 1871. His farmhouse was carefully restored by former State Senator Henry McKnight and his wife. It is a five-bay, end-chimney structure of yellow Chaska brick.

Between 1870 and 1895, the German colonies in Minnesota underwent a profound change. Many who had come to America full of hope for an idyllic life in a model democracy were disappointed. Their recoil from American society was encouraged by a new wave of immigrants who had left Germany for a new set of reasons and had no desire to embrace American ways. These parallel developments—disillusionment, and the introduction of a new immigrant group already hostile to the evolution of American society—reinforced each other and had dramatic effect upon the domestic architecture of those areas settled largely by Germans, particularly the area about New Ulm. Both the parallel causes and their effects are worthy of detailed examination.

From the moment they stepped ashore in America, the Forty-Eighters faced native American suspicion of all foreigners, which had been directed initially at the Irish but which was readily transferred to the Germans. Know-Nothingism was a strong force in America before they arrived. Smoldering among the ignorant, it was inflamed by the arrival of men who were quick to learn, to compete, and who often were better educated than the native Americans about them. The nineteenth-century Germans experienced much the same resistance as our twenty-first-century Asians.

This was particularly true when the new competitors were hostile to established forms of religious observance, and the German Forty-Eighters included many anticlericals. In Germany, the liberal revolt had been directed against the tyranny of petty princelings who often shored up their precarious power by reliance upon the parish clergy, both Roman Catholic and Lutheran. Therefore, both the State and the Church had seemed hostile, and radical French doctrines gave real grievances a theoretical framework. When the Forty-Eighters came to America, many of them sustained their antagonism to the Church, though many others, Roman Catholics and Lutherans, never coupled anticlericalism with their opposition to feudalism. Religious folk in New Ulm, for example, lived harmoniously with freethinkers, but the evidence indicates that for a time, at least, the freethinkers made up a large and sometimes oppressive majority. The original town charter of New Ulm called it a "home for every German laborer, popish priests and lawyers excepted." Father Alexander Berghold, the first Catholic priest to be resident in New Ulm, reported that in those early days "so called Church people were handled rather roughly. Many a zealous free-thinker exerted himself too much . . . Imbued with their socialistic views, they entertained the false idea that religious congregations in a free city were detrimental to the public welfare, and a prolific source of dissensions among the people."[4]

Such a disposition quickly caught the eye of Puritan neighbors like the redoubtable Harriet Baker McConkey, who had charged in her book *Dakota War Whoop* (1864) that New Ulm had been settled by a "class of infidel Germans . . . who had stipulated that no church edifice should ever 'disgrace their soil' . . . with no religious restraints, they became strong in wickedness . . . and resolved that no minister should be allowed to live among them: One they drove from the place and another was annoyed in every possible way." Her concern was not only with their anticlericalism but also with certain German folkways: the pleasures of a dance hall and the drinking of beer on the Sabbath. As a matter of fact, the drinking of beer on any day was thought by many Yankees to be a serious offense, and the Germans soon detected that their fairly liquid diet differed sharply from that prevailing in temperance communities about them like Ottawa or Carimona. Theodore Blegen has pointed out that it was not only the suspected Know-Nothingism of the fledgling Republican Party of the 1850s and 1860s, but its known tendency toward "desiccation" which led most Minnesota Germans to vote for the Democrats. Later, Carl Schurz led many Germans into the Republican ranks, which abandoned Know-Nothingism to open the party for them. But the differences between teetotaling, clergy-respecting people on one hand and the Forty-Eighters on the other was not healed in time to prevent an estrangement that lasted a generation.

A host of new immigrants in the years after 1870 brought with them a desire to perpetuate old German ways and a hostility to what they thought to be American secularism. These new arrivals caught many of the Forty-Eighters rebounding and carried the entire German community toward a strenuous sense of Germanism. Many of them had departed their homeland for precisely the opposite set of political and religious reasons from those sending the Forty-Eighters into exile; whereas most of the liberal generation of 1848 had sought a German national state, had opposed the Church and the division of Germany into a multitude of feudal divisions, and aspired to a modern commercial and industrial order, most of the next wave of refugees were fleeing Bismarck's effort to create, in an iron mold, just such a State (but without, of course, a liberal political system). His *Kulturkampf,* expressed most fiercely in the May Laws, was an effort to impose a uniform secular state upon the diverse and religious establishments which had been deposited by the wars of the sixteenth century.

The new immigrants to America, who might be called May Law Refugees, were encouraged in their adherence to old German ways by their clergy and by the rulers of the smaller kingdoms and principalities which Bismarck was compressing into his German Empire. Their princes and their priests often regarded America as a vast area sparsely settled by second- and third-generation English Protestants and secularists who would seek to destroy the traditional faith and culture of Catholic immigrants, especially the Germans. As early as 1847, King Ludwig of Bavaria pled with those who were leaving their ancient villages in his domain for America to "stay German, stay German! Do not become English!"

Father Colman Barry summarized the character of the people making up this second mass migration to America in these words: "They were, for the most part . . . a conservative force in the community. . . . They wanted the order and discipline of parish life as they had known it before coming to the United States . . . this deep love of the German fatherland . . . meant an attachment for living as the emigrant had lived in Germany . . . many of the German emigrants felt that if they could not practice their faith in the German way when they came to America, then they would not practice their faith at all. This was why the mother tongue was stressed, the *vereins* encouraged, and the traditions fostered."

During the last thirty years of the nineteenth century, American Catholicism was rent into two factions: one, called by their opponents the "Americanizers," was led by Archbishop John Ireland of St. Paul. Archbishop Ireland believed that the host of immigrants from old Catholic countries then arriving should be blended into American life as quickly as possible, and not separated into parishes where they would cling fearfully together, speaking their old language, while the wonders and riches of American life remained forbidden fruit. Ireland's antagonists were known as the Cahenslyites, after their leader, Peter Paul Cahensly, whose social work, particularly among German immigrants, had led him to believe that the German-American "Americanizers" were "ashamed of their German origin." Cahensly feared that "banning the German language from Church and school, and the establishment of English" would bring the result that "the children, with the loss of their German mother tongue, would lose good morals and the Catholic faith. . . . The bond between parents and children is broken, for they can no longer understand each other."[5]

It was perhaps, inevitable, that the already abraded edges of the German-American and Yankee-American communities in Minnesota should have been further roughened when Cahensly's views became widely known. Minnesota's Senator Cushman K. Davis denounced Cahensly on the floor of the United States Senate as an "intruder" who was attempting "to nationalize American institutions and plant as many nations as there are people of foreign tongues in our midst. . . . We are to his mind a nation upon whom the political intriguers of the European world are to operate all their own theories at their own sweet will. . . ."

In the previous year, 1891, a conference of churchmen meeting in Lucerne, Switzerland, asked the Holy See to fragment the Church in America into nationality groupings, each with its own bishop. In the 1880s and early 1890s Cahenslyism was at high tide and estrangement was most bitter between German immigrants and disillusioned Forty-Eighters on one hand and the previously amalgamated Americans on the other. But soon the path to amity opened. The pope, after a personal appeal by Ireland and a careful examination of the allegations against Americanizing, refused to pursue a Cahenslyite policy. As time passed, the controversy over Cahenslyism receded into the past, as if it were one of the casuistic quarrels of the Middle Ages. As Father Colman Barry puts it: "German Catholics eventually came to accept the position of the Americanizers. The mother tongue was dying out, American national habits were being assimilated, the United States was be coming recognized by them as a nation. No more protesting memorials were forwarded to Rome, since German parishes gradually became mixed parishes, national parishes slowly gave way to territorial parishes. . . ."

Feeling as strong as that prevailing among the German Americans in Minnesota during the Cahenslyite years inevitably affected domestic architecture. It would have been very strange if their houses built during the years from 1870 to 1895 did not show a self-conscious Germanness, and insistence that the cultural heritage of these embattled people was worthy of expression in the new land. In fact, the domestic architecture of the most intensely German sections of Minnesota did show an emphasis upon traditional German patterns of building which was not present in the first houses built by Germans in the state nor in those they built after their nativist ardor cooled.

After the Dakota War, the Germans returned to New Ulm and began to complete the transition from wood houses to brick which had barely begun when the Indians struck the town. Nearly everything had been destroyed by fire, and brick, a traditional German material, must have seemed particularly reassuring as new structures were erected among the charred ruins. But after 1870, the plain brick houses which might have been built like those of the Germans of the 1850s were succeeded by a new style which was self-consciously derived from the German Gothic tradition, as it was later described by the Eleventh edition of the *Encyclopædia Britannica*, "German Complete Gothic is essentially national in its complete character . . . From the first there is conspicuous in it that love of lines and that desire to play with geometric figures which in time degenerated into work more full of conceit and triviality than that of any school of medieval artists. . . . They are severely geometrical and regular in their form."

Brick was, of course, the traditional material of those portions of Germany which were under Bismarck's control and which sent to America the most vehemently nativist of the emigrants. Ornamented, geometric brickwork during this period abstracted the wooden ornament of American styles into equivalent patterns of brick. Three-dimensional carved shapes were flattened to two dimensions and presented as abstractions in contrasting colors.

At 423 North German Street in New Ulm, this process can be observed as it affected a Greek revival doorway which in German hands became a mere applied ornament upon a brick wall. Across town at 508 South German, Rudolph Kiesling built, in the early 1870s, a cubical house with a hip roof and windows set in rounded arches. In Yankee communities its roof, extended widely in the Italianate manner, would have been supported by ornamental brackets and the windows would probably have been capped with hood molds. In New Ulm, how-

ever, the brackets were merely indicated by dark brick shapes against lighter walls. The brick has now been painted white, with brown paint covering what was once darker brick.

L. W. Nieman House, New Ulm, c. 1890

German nativism in New Ulm is symbolized most eloquently in the great shrine of Hermann, the Teutonic hero who vanquished the legions of Varus and turned back the efforts of Rome to extend her conquests to the Elbe. The architect of that monument was Julius Berndt, designer of countless floats in the parades in which the citizens of New Ulm celebrated their German heritage. Only the home of distiller Henry Subillia at 504 South Minnesota can be ascribed to Berndt with certainty, and its brickwork has been painted over and a discordant concrete block wing added. There are, however, two other houses in the area in Berndt's style which were built during his lifetime: 827 North Minnesota, a piece of Gothic stage scenery in the eighteenth-century fashion, and 708 First Street North, built according to local tradition by contractor John Groann for a man named Schroeder who moved back to Germany leaving only the lower story of his castle completed. If these be Berndt's work, they would represent a group entirely without analogues elsewhere, theatrical and thoroughly German.

Simulated corner blocks in contrasting colors of brick can be seen on most houses built in this period of German nativism. As the nativists became more numerous and feeling became more intense, their houses increasingly took on the elaborately decorated style of their homeland. At 426 North State Street in New Ulm, Bernard Fesenmaier built a quoined brick house which stylized the decoration of the Gothic revival, replacing the decorated bargeboards beloved of wood-carving

Bernard Fesenmaier House, New Ulm, c. 1888

Yankees with a cusped pattern on light bricks under the eaves. A few blocks away, at 201 North State Street, Minnie Grausam added a bank of downward pointing bricks in place of a belt course to an array of brick decoration like that of the Fesenmaier house. Both structures, according to local tradition, were built between 1888 and 1896.

The house at 110 South German, built in 1885 by a man named Pfenninger, adds to the mansard roof and wrought-iron cresting popular in the 1870s, a series of sharp gables and dormers, hood molds linked by courses of light-colored brick and a broad front porch with elaborately carved posts. The mansion built by George Schmidt at 200 South German about 1898 later became the home of Dr. L. A. Fritsche, a pioneer physician, mayor and father of more physicians and another mayor. Later owners have painted over its brickwork, hiding the varicolored decoration which gave the house its distinction. Corner blocks, belt courses linking simulated hood molds, all the self-conscious medievalism of the era are there, but through the whitewash they can be seen only as shadows.

In 1865 and 1866, Herman Billing, Christ Virning, William Bergenhausen, Frank Yaeger, John Roch, Nicholas Meyer, Reinhart Stumpf, and Frank Konen led a group of colonists from the Catholic Rhineland provinces of Prussia to settle the rich prairie area of Morrison County, northeast of St. Cloud. Soon they named their town after Father Xavier Pierz, the missionary whose tales of the land's fertility and its salubrious climate had reached their ears in Germany. Like New Ulm, this was a German island in a sea of strangers. Unlike New Ulm, however, it clustered about its church. In the 1880s, at the peak of the Cahenslyite fervor, a great Baroque brick church was reared by these pious men and their descendants, its interior glowing with the bright colors of the German tradition. Red, gold, and blue, in frescoes and statuary still shine there, and around the church the small brick houses of the early settlers remain. Many of them have heavy hood molds and corner blocks and a few display the contrasting colors of brick which enrich the exterior of their church.

In Scott County, on the west side of US Hwy. 169 a half-mile north of County Road 19, is another German-built hip-roofed cube. Its windows, like those of the Kiesling house, carry the figure of hood molds in a brick lighter than the reddish-buff of the walls, and the style mark of German-American architecture in Minnesota during this Cahenslyite period appears: the simulation of corner blocks—quoins. Light-colored brick is set in clusters down the corners of the cubical structure in imitation of the blocks of stone which, in the old country,

*Gustave Lanz House,
Scott County, 1875*

had buttressed masonry walls. The land under this house was bought by Michael Lanz in 1863. His son, Gustave employed two German immigrants, Ernest Born and William Valbricht, to build the house, probably during the 1870s.

The greatest of Minnesota's German mansions is the magnificent house designed by Herman G. Schapekahm for the brewer August Schell and built in 1885. Its brick and stonework are as fresh, extravagant, and splendid as in the days when August Schell walked down the path from his brewery, through his gardens, up the steps and into his cool parlor. It is set off by pines which must have been brought in from the north to give it a Bavarian aspect, for they were not indigenous to the New Ulm area. Behind the house, Schell created a deer park which is still visited by hundreds of children when grounds are open to the public. The house itself carries the tendency toward a revival of German Gothicism to its highest expression in the area: there are the

August Schell House, New Ulm, 1885

quoins, no longer merely imitated but actually cut from blocks of stone; there are stone belt courses carrying a row of stone points thrusting downward into the brick. The hood molds and the piers between the windows are of stone as are the decorations under the eaves.[6]

August Schell had been in the party of immigrants from the Cincinnati turnverein which had founded New Ulm. He started his brewery in 1860 and by the time his mansion was completed was selling 4,500 barrels per annum. . . . (Mrs. McConkey would have been aghast.) A journalist of the community said in that year that the quality of Schell's beer was "known far and wide as being a first-class article." His house enjoys the same reputation and value to our state as a monument as do the Ramsey house, the Sibley house, and the Faribault houses in Faribault and Mendota, the Huff-Lamberton house in Winona, the Burbank-Griggs house, the Folsom house in Taylors Falls, and the home of Joseph R. Brown in Henderson. It marks the crest of Cahenslyite architecture in Minnesota, the ultimate effort by the German-Americans of New Ulm to assert the validity of their own heritage of language and custom.

4

The Greek Revival

AT THE MISSISSIPPI'S MOUTH, along the bayous, tall white pillars thrust upward through nights so thick with heat that the birds labor to swim through the air. Far, far to the north, where the Great Lakes freeze into ice floes, the pillars have shrunk into the frigid faces of white Grecian houses and pilasters shiver a bare few inches in the arctic wind. From the opulent Attic mansions of Blue Hill and Belfast in Maine to the spartan hostelries of Wolf Creek and Oregon City, the Greek revival prevailed. Talbot Hamlin, whose study of the revival ranks among the great classics of architectural writing, appraised its effect in these words:

> Never before or since, I believe, has there been a period when the general level of excellence was so high in American architecture, when the ideal was so constant and its various expressions so harmonious, when the towns and villages, large and small, had in them so much of unostentatious unity and loveliness as during the forty years from 1820 to the Civil War.

That unity was an outgrowth of the eighteenth century. The same broad concepts of beauty were accepted by most educated men, submerging all but the most insistent folk traditions. Small houses still showed national and regional differences, but when more ambitious residences were built of pinewood, brick, or stone, they were formed in a sedate colonial style. From the Appalachians to the sea, domestic architecture was free of ornament and blocklike in massing. Eighteenth-century Puritans in New England shared one thing, at least, with contemporary Virginia cavaliers: an architecture which reflected a commitment to the clean, clear outlines of the Age of Reason.

Rationalism, the most revolutionary force of the eighteenth century, was joined by Thomas Jefferson to nationalism, the explosive principle of the nineteenth century, and from that synthesis came the classic revival. In Jefferson's design for the Virginia State Capitol, he emulated the only classic building he had seen, the Maison Carré at Nimes, France.

While it was early established as appropriate for public buildings, the Greek revival was slow in finding domestic devotees. The Virginia Capitol was built in 1789, but Jefferson's first temple-form house was not built until 1819, as a faculty pavilion at the University of Virginia. It may seem strange that so appropriate an expression of their national pride should not have quickly appealed to Americans. A form which made no concessions to its site, which scorned the greens and browns and curving lines of nature, might seem a good expression of the will of a nation which was taming a continent and assured to dominance over natural forces. But it took political events to call the style to the attention of homebuilders, just as political independence had made it "official" for courthouses and town halls.

True independence from Britain did not come until after the second War of Independence, 1812–15. Only after Andrew Jackson redeemed the national honor, at New Orleans, did his countrymen feel independent, and even then, anxiously so. Then came the Greek War of Independence (1826–27), making the public aware of the ancient buildings which formed the background of a modern struggle which seemed much like America's own Revolutionary War. Jefferson's classicism, largely Roman in derivation, yielded to more Grecian forms by degrees so imperceptible that the terms Roman revival, Greek revival, and classic revival were used, as they are today, interchangeably. Ancient Athens gained new admirers as a surge of sympathy for Greece ran through America. In the 1830s and 1840s, Wisconsin, which was accepting its first great wave of settlement, named towns after Athens, Attica, Sparta, Ixonia, and Troy. Greek fashions in furniture, hairdressing, tombstones, and clothing were suddenly popular. James Marsden Fitch has pointed out "how genuine was this sympathy, and how deep beyond the educated classes it extended. . . . [This is] clear both from the political rallies and money-raising campaigns to aid the living Greeks and by the adoption of the cultural forms of long dead ones."

The tide of settlement reached Minnesota after the Greek revival had already lost its vigor on the Eastern Seaboard. In the East, industrialism was creating deep divisions in society, exalting some to great riches and degrading others. Urban mobs reigned in some places, debasing Republican institutions, as the vulgar pride of nabobs, purchasing legislatures and trafficking in senators, debased it elsewhere. American society was changing.

Minnesota did not suffer much from industrialism, from the division of society, from the erosion of common ideals, until after the Civil War. It was far at the extremity of settlement, far from the cockpit of the economy, far as well from the forces which were corroding and fragmenting the old America of farms and small towns. Before the Civil War it put forth a last dispensation of beauty in the flowering of the Greek revival. The soil from which that flowering grew was still rich with idealism, still uncluttered by urban sprawl, and still unpoisoned by industrial wastes.

Frederick Jackson Turner, in his speech dedicating the Minnesota Historical Society building, recalled what Harriet Martineau had spoken of the settlers' "high democratic hope, their faith in man. These men were emotional. . . . They had faith in themselves and their destiny. And that optimistic faith was responsible for their confidence in their own ability to rule and for the passion for expansion. . . . They felt both their religion and their democracy, and were ready to fight for them." This is not difficult to understand; men who set out for the fringes of civilization might be expected to display a more intense pride in their national ideals than more sedentary folk left behind; frontiersmen might be expected to hold more intensely to those attributes of their heritage which give them confidence and pride than would people who had only to look about them to see the town hall, the courthouse, and the policemen. Frontier idealism found its natural expression in the Greek revival. That idealism persisted in Minnesota while it remained agrarian and while the influence of the frontier was still strong. As late as 1865, Minnesota was still largely a land of independent farmers, producing for their own needs and for the villages nearby, not yet dependent upon the clanking machinery of an industrial society, upon national systems of food processing, credit, and transportation. In 1860, the largest city in the state, St. Paul, had only 10,000 people, three times the number in the second largest, St. Anthony, out of a total state population of 172,000. In 1865, outside of Ramsey and Hennepin counties, the census figures show that the next most populous was Fillmore County, which had 17,000 people but no town of more than 2,000.

So, on the agrarian frontier, the Greek revival had a late flowering, beautiful and doomed. It took three principal forms, of which the first, the porticoed mansion, is extinct in Minnesota, represented in the area only in Wisconsin. One of that state's finest examples, however, the Darling house, is just across the St. Croix River on Second Street in Hudson. Since the other two forms, the gable front and the broadside type, were derived from the full porticoed temple, it is there that the characteristics common to all three can best be observed.

Unlike the styles discussed in previous chapters, which came to Minnesota in the memories of settlers, the fashions in architecture described in this and succeeding chapters were transmitted by drawings and literary descriptions. The Greek revival was, in a sense, propaganda architecture, deliberately propounded to the masses in pattern books and builders' guides illustrating prototypes in great detail and stressing their appropriateness for patriotic Americans. Thus, while the entire model might not be reproduced, doorways, windows, and moldings could be selected as conditions permitted.

The mansion of dry goods merchant Frederick L. Darling was built in 1857 and 1858 by the master carpenters Ammah and Amasa Andrews who came from New York and almost certainly brought with them the pattern book from which their version of the Jeffersonian pavilion was taken. Jefferson's original form, in the faculty houses at the University of Virginia, became popular in western New York and then in Ohio, Michigan, and Wisconsin where structures very much like the Darling house were constructed in chronological sequence, moving westward. These houses have tall, two-story porticoes backed by carefully carved pilasters. To the side, the height of the columns is reduced to a single story, covering the front of a wing, as if recalling Jefferson's cloisters (walks under which students could find shelter as they moved from class to class, from pavilion to pavilion). The doorway within the portico has a rectangular transom divided into square glass panels by lead supports. Beside the doorway are small engaged columns and, between them, rectangular sidelights (vertical rows of windows). Above the pillars is a complete triangular pedimented gable. Sometimes gables on these houses enclosed a window or fanlight or a louvered opening to vent the attic. Across the bottom of the gable and

continuing along the sides of the house is a broad, flat board, sometimes decorated with subtle carving to simulate the ancient entablature. These, together with moderately sloping roofs and inconspicuous
chimneys, were the style marks of the Greek revival style.

Generally, however, the full two-story portico was too drafty for
midwestern use; it was intended for brighter sunlight and gentler win-
ters. On the northern prairies, tall white pillars glittered icily in sub-
arctic moonlight, and the floor of the porch accumulated billows of
windblown snow. Men more adaptable or less conscious of precedent
than Frederick Darling and the Andrewses reduced that portico to a
single, sheltering story, where it came to look remarkably like a French
gallerie. (Perhaps the shrinking process was encouraged by the presence of galleried French houses in the neighborhood, which demonstrated the virtues of cover in a snowstorm and of shade in summer.) A
structure similar to the Darling mansion in massing window arrange-
ment and in its Grecian doorway, known as the Erb house, at 628 NW
3rd Avenue in Faribault, built some years later, shows the completion
of this adjustment. Its portico has become a one story "verandah" below the gable, sheltering the doorway.

*Frederick L. Darling
House, Hudson,
Wisconsin, 1858*

Porticos were not only impractical in a northern climate; they were expensive, far beyond the means of men just moving up from a soddy or a tamarack hut. As a more modest substitute, still possessing the same symbolic significance, they built the gable-end Grecian house, without a portico but retaining Grecian style marks to suggest the full temple form: the pillars were recalled by wide planks set vertically at the corners, not quite pilasters but still adding to the gravity of the form. The pedimented gable still crowned some houses even after the portico had disappeared, but, more often, the hypotenuse of that triangle was merely suggested by carrying the entablature from each acute angle a foot or two across the front, forming what might be called a "hooked gable." Even when these refinements had to be abandoned, the stately doorway, with its transom and sidelights, remained.

Minnesota, in the period before the Civil War, was settled largely from the water. The Greek revival, therefore, is a riverfront style. Many towns retain fine small Grecian houses along the riverbank, away from the highway. "Angel's Hill," that portion of Taylors Falls largely settled by the parishioners of the old Methodist church, is still, after many remodelings and desecrations, an extraordinary collection of white clapboard New England buildings showing the strong influence of the Greek revival.

In chapter 1 we examined the French-inspired galleries across the front of the largest of these, the home of William H. C. Folsom. It also bears the marks of the Greek revival, with a pedimented gable and broad entablature boards.

The Methodist church was probably the work of the two master carpenters, Lenord and John S. Bullard. They were in no hurry. It is said that they waited two years for a white pine to be cut, up the valley, which could provide boards tall and broad and knot-free for the pilasters which flank the doors. Up the Government Road, a hundred feet or so, is their finest house, built for C. A. Winslow about 1853. Like the church, it lacks a portico, but the classic pediment and well-proportioned recessed doorway impart a ceremonial character. Under the eaves, within the gable, are fine dentils which reappear along the entablature at the sides and above the door. Almost hidden behind the house is a cabin which, apparently, preceded it, and which the Bullards carefully fitted out in Grecian detailing to match their new temple in front. There are other Grecian houses in the town: the home of Patrick

Fox, a block west on the Government Road from the Scott house, has been covered by grey shingles but its doorway retains its classic grace; a small house with a well-proportioned portico is marooned behind the Laundromat, and the distinguished home of Paul Munch, on the riverfront.

C. A. Winslow House, Taylors Falls, 1853

Patrick Fox House, Taylors Falls, c. 1853

A variant of the end-gable temple built at 1677 Gilmore Street, just off Highway 61 on the outskirts of Winona, was one of the oldest houses in the area. It was built around 1854 by George W. Clark, the

first man thereabouts to stake a claim for farming. Clark, who was born in upstate New York, arrived in Fond du Lac in 1851, walked across the state of Wisconsin to La Crosse and found employment with lumber dealer Silas Stevens. He arrived at Winona on November 12, 1851, to support Stevens's land claims. The population of the county reached twenty-one by Christmas; most engaged in the illegal cutting of timber on public lands. Clark, unlike the others, was not interested in speculating in town sites and repaired across a slough to build his Grecian house with oak beams cut on the place.

There are many gable-front Greek revival houses in Minnesota. A few of the more interesting are listed in the appendix to chapter 4. Two final examples may illustrate variations on the Grecian theme. In the lost community of Valley Creek, northwest of Afton, there is the house built around 1864 by Newington Gilbert. The rectangular mass of the "temple" has been surrounded by a one-story colonnaded porch, as if the great columns of the Parthenon had been reduced to a domestic

Newington Gilbert House, Afton / Valley Creek, 1864

scale. Gilbert himself may have designed the house, which is not unlike those he would have known in his childhood in upstate New York. The style of the porch may have come from nearer at hand. It is similar to the famous Walker Tavern at the Cambridge Junction, Michigan, on the route of the Yankee migration westward and to the porches on the Andrews brothers' houses up the St. Croix in Hudson. Valley Creek long remained what it was in the time of Newington Gilbert: a quiet place, settled by farmers and those who prepared farm produce for market. It never knew a boom and was relatively untouched by the great land rush of the 1850s.

Even before that land rush, during which the Greek revival reached its full achievement, some of the French-American fur traders demonstrated how they could adapt to the new world forming about them by taking the forms for their houses from the national Greek revival style, rather than from the French colonial tradition. Jean Baptiste Faribault, as has been noted, was the first to do so. His son, Alexander, did likewise.

Alexander Faribault was Henry Sibley's contemporary and had served as his secretary (succeeded by Hypolite du Puis) until heading southward to establish his own posts. In 1826, he had been at the Dakota Village of Tentonka Tonah, near what is now known as Cannon Lake. In 1835, his first major venture was trading at the confluence of two major Indian canoe routes, the Straight and Cannon rivers, where in one year he collected 50 buffalo robes, 130 martens, 100 minks, 633 raccoons, 25 lynx, 5 foxes, 2,050 pounds of deerskins, 125 pounds of beaver skins, and 39,080 muskrats. Game was less plentiful as the years went on, but in 1853 he built a large frame house on the site to which he had moved in 1844. This was after the Dakota treaties had replenished his purse through the customary government payment of "traders' claims." His relationship with the Indians (several of whose leaders were related to him through his mother and his sisters' husbands) was always one of mutual respect. During the Dakota War he fed and sheltered friendly Indians in the neighborhood to the acute displeasure of his white neighbors.

Faribault was prosperous: his house had nine bedrooms, a music room, parlor, sitting room, office, kitchen, summer kitchen, and sewing room, and was used as a polling place, town hall, and, in the early days, in lieu of a chapel, there Father Augustin Ravoux celebrated the Mass. As early as 1836, Faribault investigated farming in the area and later

raised livestock, bees, poultry, fruit, and grain. He was the proprietor *Alexander Faribault House, Faribault, 1853* of a sawmill and flour mill, but he did not take the proceeds of his many enterprises to his grave, for he gave generously to Indians and whites, relatives, neighbors, and strangers. Three thousand dollars went to the town's first resident priest to build his church, ten acres to Episcopal Bishop Henry B. Whipple (the most articulate critic of the Indian treaties of 1851) for his church as well as the grounds of Shattuck School, one of Bishop Whipple's favorite projects. Faribault, an ardent Catholic, also gave land to Seabury Divinity School established for the training of Protestant ministers. He served as a delegate to the Territorial legislature and managed to retain the friendship of both Henry M. Rice and his old mentor, Sibley, when the two had become personal and political enemies.

The windows on its street facade are paired to light the loft under a rectangular horizontal transom, with two more on the second story flanking a door which leads out upon the roof of the porch and below, within the porch, the conventional two windows and Greek revival doorway. The structure is informal, fresh, comfortable, and unconcerned about purity of style. Its interiors have been meticulously restored and filled with period furniture, including some of Faribault's own. Now open to the public, the address, once unnecessary, is now 12 NE First Avenue, Faribault.

George D. Snow House, Le Sueur, c. 1870

Most Greek revival houses in Minnesota were of the end-gable type, but a few followed the broadside styles, which wholly abandoned the classic portico and turned the gable to the side, leaving only the doorway and the entablature to mark the front facade as Grecian. Thus, in general aspect, these houses returned to the older Georgian tradition, where the entry was normally centered in a broad facade. The beauty of the two-story, five-bay, and end-chimney broadside house with Greek revival details is well demonstrated by the home of George D. Snow, built between 1864 and 1870 at 129 S. Second Street in Le Sueur.

It has had a variety of porches across its front and it is possible that the small Federal portico there now closely reproduces a larger original. George Snow came to Le Sueur in 1857 and speculated widely and successfully in farm and town real estate. When he built this house, it included a wing to the north running back toward a woodshed, storage rooms, and a barn. (Snow also built and owned a cubical Italianate house on the road to the Le Sueur golf course.)

A humbler example of the broadside Grecian structure is the Ard Godfrey house on University Avenue Northeast in Minneapolis. It is a one-story version of the five-bay symmetrical facade with the door in the center and classic detail. Godfrey was a pioneer lumberman from Maine whose home, built in 1848, was probably the first frame dwelling in Minneapolis. The Grecian residence of John H. Stevens was built in the next year just across the Mississippi, then moved by thousands of school children in 1896 next to Minnehaha Park; in 1982 it was moved into the park and is now open to the public. Stevens was

Ard Godfrey House, Minneapolis, 1848

John S. Proctor House, Stillwater, c. 1850

another town site promoter who acquired his interest in real estate from his employer, Franklin Steele, sutler at Fort Snelling. John Stevens was encouraged by Steele to secure a War Department permit to a claim on the west bank of the Mississippi before the land had been officially opened for settlement by the treaties of 1851. In return, Stevens pledged free ferry service should the military desire, in its wisdom, to use that whitewater stretch of river instead of more tranquil reaches above or below. Stevens's house, not so graceful nor symmetrical as Godfrey's, but similar in massing, was used as the Minneapolis City Hall until 1854. Stevens was a man of large visions: plans for the first State Fair were made in his parlor when most of the state was still wilderness, and in 1869 the legislature actually passed resolutions to move the State Capitol to a town site owned by Stevens and several friends in Kandiyohi County, but the project was scratched by a veto of the governor.

In the St. Croix Valley, Grecian details were added to several broadside cottages. One of the most ingratiating of these was built by a lumberman-turned-farmer, Andrew Mackey, in 1855 on the main thoroughfare of Afton. It hid its entrance in the corner of a porch cut out from beneath the gable, like earlier houses built in the Western Reserve of Ohio. It was modest in size, but the editors of the *Andreas At-*

las of 1874 tell us that "it was a palace compared with the usual frontier dwellings." In Stillwater at 220 South Fourth Street, overlooking the ravine that became Olive Street, is a house built for the fourth warden of the state prison, John S. Proctor. It may have been constructed as early as 1850 and shows the broadside cottage at its finest. Once again the early Georgian style is evoked—it has the shape of a number of the white weatherboard cottages restored at Williamsburg, Virginia—but there are Greek revival pilasters at the corners and, within its small portico, an austere Grecian doorway, bearing a rectangular transom unlike the urbane fanlights of Williamsburg. The broad dormers were probably added later to admit light and air to the attic, and to the rear, later owners have built on a succession of appendages.

At Marine-on-St. Croix, Asa S. Parker of Vermont created a variant

Asa Parker House, Marine-on-St. Croix, 1856

on the Greek revival form. To a cubical, hip-roofed house in the urban New England mode he added pilasters, a Grecian doorway, and a narrow, two-story portico. He had come to the sawmill town in 1839 as one of the partners in the Marine Lumber Company, and he celebrated his prosperity in 1856 by erecting his white pine mansion. The ungainly portico is borne by two huge, round, fluted pillars. Most pioneers, like Proctor, had to be content with box pillars of four mitered boards. The doorway would have looked more imposing without the beetling balcony above, but despite its flaws, the *St. Paul Advertiser* said in 1857 of the Parker house and its neighbor, the Orange Walker house (since destroyed by fire), that "for style of architecture and beauty of finish" they were "not surpassed in the Northwest." There are smaller houses in present-day Marine which better convey the conservative character of that community of New England emigrants, but the one built by Asa Parker is the grandest Classic revival house in the St. Croix Valley. It is not Grecian; its form and especially its portico are too attenuated for that. Some architectural historians have seen in houses which possess such verticality a Roman strain in the classic revival and have drawn attention particularly to a group of houses of this character along the Ohio River. Minnesota possesses another exemplar of this type, "Locust Lodge," completed in 1855 at Frontenac, for Evert Westervelt.

Westervelt had prospered in a fur-trading partnership with James "Bully" Wells (a relative of the Faribault family and delegate to the Territorial legislature, chiefly distinguished as a bare-knuckled fighter). Upon the stone foundation of their first trading post he built a residence in the shape of a cross. On each of its four faces is a pedimented gable, and there are heavy pilasters at the corners. The entablature board swings broad and clean around the cornice. There is a Lower Mississippi touch: a wrought-iron balcony in the center of the riverfront. The Grecian doorway is placed asymmetrically, and the mass stands higher, less compact than most Grecian houses. Westervelt is said to have brought the interior paneling from Cincinnati, and he may have found the plans there also.

A hundred years have passed since the Greek revival brought its brief glory to Minnesota. Its decline was so rapid that the technical causes of its passing which have been suggested seem too slow acting to suffice. Most architectural critics have agreed that the archaeologists who flocked to Greece and gave a great impulse to the revival by the ex-

Evert Westervelt House, Frontenac, 1855

amination of ancient monuments were themselves the agents of its decay. Direct study of Greek public buildings showed that the ancients were not, themselves, bound by the "orders" developed by Renaissance scholars seeking to make a "system" out of insufficient evidence. This was an explosive discovery. Men no longer depended upon their old authorities, the architectural rulebooks of the Renaissance, and there ensued a ruleless search for novelty. It led to a promiscuous use of old architecture of all ages: Greek, Roman, then Egyptian, Medieval, and, finally, at the end of the nineteenth century, Roman architecture was again pillaged for stylistic devices to titillate the jaded taste of the time. Talbot Hamlin suggests that the Greek revival's emphasis upon a pictorial effect was a symptom of "picturesqueness," the disease from which it died. "Progressively, as other styles developed, particularly the Gothic revival, all of them together developed a straining after effects toward claptrap, stage-scenery.... The desire for ostentation ... along with the desire for cheapness ... was the death of the essential qualities of the Greek revival."

The evidence in Minnesota, however, indicates that the Greek revival, there, did not die of technical causes. It was a casualty of the Civil War. That conflict destroyed the economic, social, and ideological circumstances which permitted the Greek revival to put forth its last, brief flowering: the rural, nonindustrial society, the absence of extremes of rich and poor, the high idealism of the frontier.

After the war there was a new spirit in the land; the nation had a new technology and a new literature, a new investment banking system and a new public morality, a new palette in its painting and a new distribution of power in its politics. Lewis Mumford eloquently describes the change in the opening pages of his *Brown Decades*, and adds, "the nation not only worked differently after the Civil War; the country looked different."

In Minnesota, very few men still built Greek revival houses. Though in the Old South the Greek revival had symbolized the antebellum world of slave-owning plantation operators, in Minnesota and in the Old Northwest Greek temples had been the homes of independent freeholders. After the Civil War many of these men returned home to find that work was only available in the employ of a new class of entrepreneurs, some of them war-rich speculators. A new phenomenon had appeared: as Talbot Hamlin observed, the "emergence of the millionaire ... [was] as fatal to the artistic ideals of the Greek revival as were the greed, the speculation, and the exploitation that produced him. For, if he were to enjoy his success, he must make his money obvious to all— and ostentation became a new ideal in design.... What [other] architecture was possible for such a man than eclecticism?" The architecture of the Greek revival could not survive in a society dominated by such men. And in the Upper Midwest it died. The independent householder was now overshadowed by a new class of very rich men, who built large, showy houses staffed by squads of servants. Before the war, in the 1850 census, Iowa reported only ten domestic servants out of a population of 200,000, and Minnesota 15 out of 6,000, most of whom, probably, were attached to the military. After the Civil War the proportion of domestic servants came slowly into line with the national average, about one out every twenty-eight persons.

The war had, of course, brought industrialism to Minnesota, vastly accelerating the growth of cities and the concentration of wealth. Even agriculture came to require larger and larger amounts of capital; the world of Jefferson's free and independent yeoman was beginning to disappear. Between 1860 and 1870 the number of manufacturing establishments in Minnesota quadrupled, and investment in farm machinery on the average farm had multiplied six times. Men grew rich making and selling machines.

Finally, the war worked a subtle spell upon the old idealism of the frontier. It was as if the spirit of high-minded devotion to the symbols and the substance of the Republic was shriveled in the heat of the conflict. Governor Alexander Ramsey was in Washington when Sumter fell, and, rushing to the War Office, he made the first offer of any state to supply a regiment of volunteers. Enthusiasm ran high at home and his rolls were quickly filled. From Duluth, Leonidas Merrill walked 160 miles to enlist at Fort Snelling, and Robert Jefferson traveled two hundred miles by canoe with his wife and baby to the same destination. The state's adjutant general, John B. Sanborn, who was paid a prodigal $100 per year for his services, provided the uniforms for the first regiment at his own expense.

At the beginning it must have been a glorious adventure in the spring sunlight: General Sanborn's uniforms turned out to include red flannel shirts, black trousers, and slouch hats. Drilling was brief and when the orders came to proceed down the Mississippi toward the scarcely credible war, it was a time for parades and celebrations. Colonel Willis A. Gorman of the First Minnesota "fairly howled with joy . . . the men hurrahed and hugged each other," and crowds lined the riverbank to cheer the departing heroes.

At Bull Run they lost 20 percent of their strength, the highest loss of any regiment; at Antietam, the Minnesota sharpshooters lost half their number; of 262 Minnesotans who began the fight at the Peach Orchard at Gettysburg, all but 47 were casualties. There is dispute about the Gettysburg statistics, but there is no doubt that as the years of war ground on, the parades and cheering of that first summer became a mocking memory. Letters written home by the Minnesotans recorded the slow growth of disgust and despair. After Ball's Bluff they were forgotten by the generals, to spend all of the rainy night standing in the streets of Alexandria. The thievery of sutlers was magnified to a national scale by profiteers. To men shivering in the trenches before Petersburg, Jim Fisk might have seemed the wise one, warm and distant, enriching himself and reporting, "you could sell anything to the government at almost any price you've got the guts to ask." Men were growing rich at home while Colonel Gorman's heroes were growing cold and weary and old. By 1864 the spirit of the early volunteers had gone. The draft was introduced. Of 14,274 men eligible in Minnesota, 11,234 were exempted, 272 bought substitutes, and 2,497 failed to show up at all. No attempt was made to find them.

The Dakota War had intervened, distracting both men and attention from the war against the Confederacy, but Indian wars had occurred before and had not caused any profound psychological changes. They were expected. They were the price of expanding a modern culture at the expense of a Stone Age culture. But the American Civil War meant that modern culture itself had demonstrated an incapacity to govern itself without bloodshed. The Constitution had been maintained, not by senators reasoning with each other amid statues of the ancients in marble chambers, but by the death and mangling of farm boys on the battlefield. A profound loss of confidence afflicted the nation. Pride, which had built itself temples, was replaced by a more anxious and invidious spirit.

The passing of the Greek revival marked the passing of the idealism of the frontier and the old arcadian simplicity of the prewar period. The Greek temples had symbolized this simplicity, this confidence in man, his reason, and his Constitution. The Grecian style spoke for the long glories of the Jeffersonian spirit, first stated in the Declaration of Independence. The style and that spirit could not last long after the old order collapsed in 1861.

5

The Gothic Revival

GEORGE STEVENS KNEW what life was like on the edge of the wilderness. He was born in Oswego, New York, and when he was sixteen his father had taken him on the western road. They arrived in Chicago in 1834, a frontier post which Henry H. Sibley in his *Autobiography* described as "a stockade constructed for defense against the Indians, but abandoned, and perhaps a half dozen dwellings . . . and a single store. . . . A more uninviting place could hardly be conceived of. Sand here, there, everywhere, with an occasional shrub to relieve the monotony of the landscape." When the Stevenses arrived the scene was somewhat more animated: three thousand Indians were there to receive their annuities, splashing about in the spring floods which had turned the sand and mud flats into quagmires. The two emigrants set out westward, traveling six miles through mire and water a foot deep. They settled for a while in Pontiac, Illinois. Food was short. They lived on cornbread, wild honey, and milk. After slowly accumulating some means as a frontier storekeeper in a series of squalid settlements, George Stevens arrived in Rushford in Fillmore County in the spring of 1856.

Southern Minnesota settlers were in those days in peril from animals, from Indian resistance, and from the weather. Only the hardy survived. Bears were still shot in the area. Rattlesnakes infested the hillsides. Franklin Curtiss-Wedge, the historian of Fillmore County, reports frequent rattlesnake hunts, panics started by rumors of Indian attacks, and tales of the floods which swept through the deeply eroded valleys. George Stevens bought a quarter section on the flats above the Root River, below high limestone cliffs. Then he laid up a log cabin like his neighbors. In July, his wife and baby daughter joined him there. The summer was lovely, the fall brisk, but soon after the corn crop was harvested, the winter began, the winter of the hard crust. The snow was deep and the crust so blown and hard that horses could not get through the stage routes to Dubuque or St. Paul. Snowshoes, skis, and sleds were improvised, but food ran so low that "everyone lived on johnny-cake." The deer had the same trouble as the horses, and it was found that "a good man on snowshoes with a stout stick could trail a deer over the crust until the animal tired, and then club him to death." Stevens, his wife and child, and the few other families, marooned in the valley floor, lived on corn bread and venison until spring came.

Three or four years later (the date cannot be fixed precisely from local records) he began building a large stone house. By that time he had multiplied his capital by real estate dealings and as the co-proprietor of a general store. What would be expected of a man who had suffered and endured so much of the rigors of nature? What sort of house would he build? Would we not predict that he, like most of his prosperous contemporaries, would celebrate his victory over the elements and set up a temple on his broad acreage, overlooking the rising town of which he was a proprietor? The likelihood increases when we recall that he was of New England ancestry and had grown up in upstate New York where, as Mr. Hamlin says, "the Greek revival most clearly set the character," in a time when "this triumphant Greek revival work of the 1830s in up-state New York was definite and polished, quite different from the tentative earlier approaches." But our expectations are confounded by the character of George Stevens, which was more than a synthesis of the factors which had conditioned him. He was a scholarly man, who read widely in the literature of his time, and, while the inventory of his library has been lost, we can be fairly sure that from that literature he acquired his preference for the Gothic revival.

The romances set in the Middle Ages, which entranced readers of the 1850s, were full of vivid descriptions of castles, abbeys, and granges. John Ruskin felt that deeds of daring done therein gave a "strange and thrilling interest" to such terms as "Vault, Arch, Spire, Pinnacle, Battlement, Barbican, and myriads of such . . . words everlastingly poetical," and to nineteenth-century houses festooned with facsimiles of these devices of the Middle Ages. In America men like George Stevens made use of the Gothic revival to permit themselves whimsical decoration and to assert a character beyond the workaday and the conventional. Stevens's Gothic house implied that he was more

*George Stevens House,
Rushford, c. 1859*

than a middle-aged frontiersman, keeping store and trading in real estate. He was an heir to another time, no less hazardous, certainly, but more courtly.

Two themes run through the Gothic revival in Minnesota: first,

Gothic houses were to be harmonious with nature. As Geoffrey Scott said of English cottages "the house is to take the colour of the country-side, to lie hidden in the shadows and group itself among the slopes . . . as almost to form part of the Nature that surrounds it."[1] Second, it places less emphasis on the facade, upon an exterior impression, than upon interior comfort and convenience.

The Gothic house could be harmonious with nature because its shapes were natural, its rooflines pitched in parallel to arching trees, its eaves carved like vines (these carved boards were called barge-boards), its chimneys prominent like those of ancient cottages, and its colors deliberately chosen to blend with the natural hues all about.

It did not sit, as a Grecian house did, glaring out upon its sur-roundings, daring a vine to touch it with a tendril. It invited nature to enshroud it, so that as the favorite author of Gothic revival builders' guides put it, "rural architecture and rural scenery . . . [were] harmo-niously combined." For a man establishing himself on the frontier in the 1850s, the antiquity of Gothic shapes and the carefully cultivated fusion of house and grounds had profound value. An aspect of long-established residence was part of the image he sought to present. The harmony of nature with the habitations of men is not an effect achieved overnight. It requires the slow working of the laws of vegetative growth or the assistance of a landscape gardener or both. The scars of con-struction, the marks of wagon wheels and shovels, the debris of the builders, the clay dug from the basement—all take time to disappear. Time invests a house with mellowness, softens its edges, makes it seem less of an intruder. The Gothic revival honored the ancient past. A raw, fresh society, conscious of its roughness and determined to acquire the cultivated manners of older societies, fused its social ambitions with its romantic recollections of novels and balladry and sought quickly to ac-quire the semblance of age.

It was to those sensitized by reading medieval romances that An-drew Jackson Downing, landscape gardener and chief evangelist of the American Gothic revival, made his appeal for nature "refined and soft-ened by art . . . [with] judicious transplanting, with seemingly infor-mal groupings of trees, with pleasant contrasts of rugged growth and close-shaven lawn, with contrasts of dark and light foliage, with grace-fully curving roads and parks." George Stevens actually practiced these precepts a short time after the winter of the hard crust, when another man might have thought nature was something to ignore as much as possible. Such was the power of the ideals of the Gothic revival.

Downing's creed reached the frontier in his books of patterns for houses. They not only suggested plans and appearances, but illustrated the soft greens, browns, ochres, and buffs, "the earth tones" he favored for exterior colors, instead of the "barbarous Grecian white." The colors and shapes of landscape were to be a part of architecture; nature was not to be conquered but taken into partnership. "We must not be surprised at lynch law and the use of the bowie knife, but when smiling lawns and tasteful cottages begin to embellish a country, we know that order and culture are established."

What did Downing mean by a "tasteful cottage?" He meant something vaguely medieval, something which produced pleasing sentiments in the breast of the cultivated man.[2] During the course of the eighteenth century in England, many a false ruin was built to inspire such reflections when a real one was not at hand. The most famous American Gothic house, Glenellen, built for the Gilmor family of Baltimore, was entered through the arches of a make-believe ruin. For literary men of this period, ruins, particularly medieval ruins, produced the same intoxication as medieval poetry. Medievalism in architecture expressed the same sentiments as medievalism in literature. In England, Horace Walpole wrote his Gothic novel, *The Castle of Otranto*, in a huge synthetic Gothic house at Strawberry Hill. His friend, William Beckford, followed hard with another Gothic novel, *Vathek*, and, since he was a man of vast wealth, could order his architect to create a house at Fonthill Abbey which, until the collapse of its jerry-built 376-foot tower, was the cynosure of the romantic world.[3] Finally, the most influential of all Gothicists, Sir Walter Scott, invested the proceeds of his Waverley novels and his Border Ballads in a Gothic house at Abbotsford in Scotland. Scott's novels were part of the same literary movement which produced those of Charles Brockden Brown, Tennyson's *ldylls of a King*, and much of the poetry of Samuel Taylor Coleridge, one of the murkiest of medievalists.

It was Scott whose influence reached into the libraries of thousands of men such as George C. Stevens, and shaped the architecture of many an American house and some American public buildings into the stage scenery of the Olden Days. Mark Twain, no admirer of the Gothic revival, complained in *Life On the Mississippi* of the Louisiana

State Capitol, "a whitewashed castle with turrets and things, materials all ungenuine within and without, pretending to be what they are not . . . Sir Walter Scott is probably responsible for the Capitol Buildings, for it seems unlikely this little sham castle would ever have been built had he not run people mad a couple of generations ago with his medieval romances."

Andrew Jackson Downing had no desire to litter the land with "whitewashed castles" (we have had to wait for the invention of the mass-produced hamburger for that) but he did recommend "an irregular cottage, in the old English style . . . abounding in carved vergeboards and pendants, clustered chimney tops," which he deemed more "domestic" than a temple. He also thought it more "honest," a house—somewhat fortified, perhaps—but beneath the battlements, a house. Structurally, of course, it was acknowledged to have "something of grotesqueness, or at least fantastic richness in its details—something indicating a certain license . . . not to be measured by the standard of the rule and square, or the strictly utilitarian view." The result was to cover over the basic structure of the house with peaked roofs, slice its windows high and narrow, often peaked or pointed at the top, and decorate it with elaborate carving along the eaves. Occasionally it was sheathed in board and batten to emphasize aspiring verticality.

The aspirations of the Gothicists were phrased in literary terms, and their critics derided them in equally literary language. Downing invoked "the sentiment of architecture . . . Merrie England . . . the hearty hospitality, the joyous old sports, and the romance and chivalry"; W. B. O. Peabody replied in the *North American Review* that "the sight of the well fed, portly citizen in chivalrous armor would not be more unsuited to our present habits of thought than the application of that style to the . . . homely cottage, which always seems uneasy . . . in such masquerades."[4]

James Fenimore Cooper persuaded his friend Samuel F. B. Morse to cover over his Grecian house in Cooperstown with a Gothic shell, and Washington Irving rejoiced in a Gothic Grange on the Hudson, but Edgar Allan Poe's *Broadway Journal* looked at Downing's grange at Newburgh on the Hudson and observed "two octagonal blind towers which have puzzled us exceedingly to guess at their uses. Perhaps they may be cases for depositing fishing rods. . . ."[5] The Gothic revival became the style associated primarily with men whose romantic inclinations had been confirmed by reading Waverley novels and balladry, and who had the means to decorate their houses with pleasant unnecessary Gothicisms accumulated from the pattern books.

In the 1950s, architectural critics began to take Downing's protestations more seriously and the third characteristic of the Gothic revival, its emphasis on informality and comfort, has received its due: Andrew Jackson Downing has been recognized as a precursor of Frank Lloyd Wright. James Marsden Fitch, writing in 1947, suggested that "insofar as the Romanticist movement, whether in print or in masonry, served to free building from the now-dead clutch of the Classic, it was progressive. Its liberating effect upon the plan was immediate and healthy, as was its new emphasis upon the out-of-doors." John Maass, writing a decade later, suggested that American Gothic houses "mark the real beginning of modern architecture. The Greek revival house was designed to fit behind a traditional facade, it belongs in a formal garden, is best viewed from the fixed standpoint of Renaissance perspective. The Victorian house [used as a synonym, here, for the Gothic house] broke free from this academic scheme. It is planned from the inside out; the broken, 'picturesque' exterior makes the most of sunlight, shade, and foliage. These are good houses to walk around, to view at different times of day and year. Inside, they have a happy, hide-and-seek quality of surprise."

Although in its more earnest Victorian years the Gothic revival took itself quite seriously, nonetheless this informality, this building for pleasure, was always a part of its charm. Whenever the Renaissance tradition (represented in the 1850s principally by the Greek revival) insisted on too crabbed a regard for architectural propriety, the Gothic revival was always there to remind householders that an alternative was available, more expressive of individual quirks and more adaptable to convenience. One can say with certainty that comfort was as important to proponents of the Gothic revival as harmony with nature and romantic medievalism.

The Gothic revival was literary architecture; so we are informed by the biographies of those who built the most significant Gothic houses in Minnesota. George G. Stevens is described by Curtiss-Wedge as "a deep student ... [who] ... owed his broad culture and wide fund of information to keen observation and close reading, rather than to years spent in the halls of learning; and that all within the reach of his influence might have the same advantages, he, with his good wife maintained a library for many years, finally donating books and building to the city." What of the others? Aside from Stevens they were William G. Le Duc, lawyer and proprietor of St. Paul's first bookstore; John B. Gilfillan, teacher of English, lawyer, regent of the University of Minnesota, and a founder of the Minneapolis school system; Isaac Atwater, his fellow regent, lawyer, and historian; Eugene St. Julien Cox, lawyer, orator, and judge; Henry M. Nichols, a scholarly Presbyterian minister; and William Dickinson, of whom, lamentably, we know next to nothing.

But, it might well be asked, what of Willard Bunnell, founder of Homer near Winona, a timber-cutter who disposed of rivals for the town site by "beating them bloody" and demolishing their claim shanties? How does he qualify as a colleague of these respectable gentlemen? And did he not, also, build a Gothic house?

Willard Bunnell House, Homer, 1858

Perhaps we should look more closely at Willard Bunnell himself, and at his house. He lived with the Indians along the Mississippi for ten years, built a log cabin along the riverfront, and sometime in the 1850s moved up the bank to build a house based on one of Downing's designs. It is rectangular, with a gable in the center of the broad side (this is the center-gable type), and sports a non-Gothic, two-tiered, French gallerie across the riverfront. The center gable and those on the ends carry richly carved "carpenter's lace." The windows are pointed in the Gothic fashion and the siding is as natural as Downing would have asked. It was never painted; the Winona County Historical Society, which restored the house, reports that the siding was brought upriver from an Iowa mill after being soaked in turpentine and linseed oil. Bunnell may have been moved by Downing's injunction that houses blend with the landscape or he may merely have been applying his common sense; the wood has survived more than a century without care and without visible decay.

Why would a "tough" like Bunnell have troubled so much to create a smiling cottage? It is true that he ran away from home when ten years old to serve as a cabin boy, that he made his living in the illegal traffic in furs and, later, in the illegal cutting of wood on government lands, but it is also true that he was reclaimed from the sea by his father, a distinguished physician, and that he was given a good education (his sister became the wife of the patroon Steven Van Rensselaer of Albany, New York). When Bunnell brought his own wife to Homer he was proud to provide the only place between Prairie du Chien and Mendota "with sheets on the beds and a white woman in residence." His brother, Dr. Lafayette Bunnell, who came west to Minnesota because its climate was thought to be helpful in combating his tuberculosis, became the first historian of southeastern Minnesota and was proud of his brother's fine manners and courtly ideals.

The model from which Bunnell may have taken his house, a Downing sketch, was more closely followed in 1871 by William Dickinson when he built what is locally thought to be the oldest house in St. Cloud. Dickinson, listed in the Andreas *Historical Atlas of Minnesota* as an engineer, bought a lot at 503 Fifth Street in the previous year from John S. Kennedy and James A. Roosevelt, absentee speculators, and built there a close reproduction of one of Downing's center-gable cottages.

William Dickinson House, St. Cloud, c. 1871

When the parishioners of the First Presbyterian Church in Stillwater met to select a design for their new manse, they, too, looked into Downing's pattern books and found there "Design XI—A Cottage for a Country Clergyman." The house they made ready for their new minister, Henry M. Nichols, in 1857 has less synthetic rusticity than Downing recommended: its porch, at the intersection of two wings, has straight, slender posts, not Downing's nubby tree trunks crisscrossed like Saxon leggings, and the Stillwater Yankees stripped away some of its crockets and finials and painted it white. But they also contributed some beautiful, lacily carved bargeboards to the steep pitch of Downing's roof, his prominent chimneys, and his carefully landscaped grounds. The house now sits proudly amid those gardens at 208 W. Chestnut Street, above the steps leading down the bluff to the church.

A Downing design for a more stately, castle-like house was employed in Hastings by General William G. Le Duc. Le Duc was born in Wilkesville, Ohio, in 1823, and studied at Howes Academy in Lancaster, Ohio, where his closest friend was William Tecumseh Sherman (whom he called "Cump"). After attending Kenyon College he studied law, was admitted to the bar in 1849, and arrived in St. Paul in 1850. He opened the first bookstore in town (and probably in the state) and published a *Minnesota Yearbook*. After attending the Traverse des Sioux Treaties in 1851, most of his energies were directed toward developing the real estate there acquired from the Indians. He secured a charter to build a Wabasha Street bridge southward across the Mississippi from St. Paul and platted the town of West St. Paul which lay at the other end of the bridge. In 1853, he witnessed the last Indian skirmish within the city limits of St. Paul and reported pursuing the retreating marauders as far as White Bear Lake where "provisions, liquid and otherwise" ran out.

Those were the days when railroad charters were thought to be passports to riches. Le Duc acquired several, none of which prospered, but he did better in flour milling in an uneasy partnership with Alexander Ramsey and in real estate around Hastings after he purchased, through Henry Sibley, that quarter interest in the townsite which had belonged to Alexander Faribault. He moved there in 1857 and soon began planning the building of a towered Gothic residence based on a plate in Downing's pattern book, *Cottage Residences*. Mrs. Le Duc reversed Downing's plan to allow the sunlight to flood into her parlor. Before the house was begun, the Civil War had started and Le Duc accepted a commission, directing the completion of his home by instructions from the camps and marches of the South.

Arriving at the front, he was pressed into service in the quartermaster corps where he was credited with saving " a considerable portion" of General McClellan's artillery during the retreat from the Peninsular Campaign by the creation of corduroy roads through swamps (like those commonly built in Minnesota). After Gettysburg he moved west with Hooker, whose supply lines he kept open by provisions carried on a steamboat he had constructed from scrap parts, an old engine, and raw lumber found at Bridgeport, Alabama. He accompanied his old friend Sherman to Atlanta, where he earned the gratitude of the inhabitants by his humane execution of Sherman's orders. (He was

given a civic reception in the town after the war.) Many of his later years were spent in public service; as U.S. Commissioner of Agriculture he reorganized the department at the request of President Hayes, a wartime companion. He was, according to Thomas M. Newson, a contemporary, "a tall, quick, active man, with positive convictions, fertile in expedients, with a restless brain and unbounded energy." He died in 1917, at the age of 95.

Le Duc's house in Hastings was donated to the Minnesota Historical Society by Carroll S. Simmons, and recently passed into the hands of the city of Hastings where it is now run as a museum by the Dakota County Historical Society. It clusters around the sharp vertical accent of a tower. Windows, pointed, under heavy hood molds, and eaves wearing carved tracery are in accord with Downing's picturesque ideals. The sunlit parlor in which the General read the Waverley novels to his daughters now looks out over the yard toward the asphalt of Highway 61 and the ice cream and hot dog stands of a different world.

There is only one other house in Minnesota of the towered Gothic style of the Le Duc mansion. It was built by the brilliant and tragic Eugene St. Julien Cox. Cox was the son of traveling Americans who gave him the exotic middle name after a stay in Switzerland. He grew up in Philadelphia, was well educated, studied law, and was admitted to the bar in Wisconsin in 1854. He came to St. Peter, Minnesota, in 1857 and established a thriving practice. He served creditably in the Civil War and in the suppression of the Dakota War, then returned to St. Peter where he was elected mayor. During these early years, he lived in a center-gable Gothic house (which was remodeled in 1873 by Joseph Mason and moved to its present site at 213 Broadway). In 1871 he completed a new, larger Gothic house on Washington Street with two wings meeting at a square tower bearing a peaked cap. There are small balconies under the tower's upper windows and, under elaborately carved eaves, there is a wooden rhythm of arcs. Precedents for this house are not easy to find in the pattern books, but E. St. Julien Cox was a man who found little virtue in precedent or in conformity. "He made many friends and likewise not a few bitter enemies," says one county historian; he was "affable and genial and always daintily dressed," says another. A polished speaker, he served in both houses of the state legislature, missed election to the U. S. Congress by very few votes, but won a seat as district judge in January of 1878.

A man of his talents might have made a great name on the bench, but St. Julien Cox did not. After a trial of five months and seven thousand pages of testimony, he was impeached by the legislature in 1882. The prosecution charged that he repeatedly had presided while "royally drunk," had played the melodeon in his court room, and had invited all the members of a grand jury to "have a drink on him." His popularity, however, did not diminish. Before his conviction four thousand of his

E. St. Julien Cox
House, St. Peter,
1871

friends signed a petition asking for acquittal and finally in 1891, the legislature passed a new ruling "vacating, annulling, and expurgating all the proceedings." But his career was broken. He lived in the Dakotas for a few years, returned briefly to St. Peter, and died in California.

Eugene St. Julien Cox was better attuned to the rowdy frontier than the close tolerances permitted in the civilization which was being bolted and welded together in Minnesota in the years after the Civil War. He was a man of great gifts; he might have sat beside two other lawyers who built Gothic houses in the area, who successfully survived the transition of the frontier into settlement, and rose to the Supreme Court and to the Regency of the State University. One of them, Isaac Atwater, was truly a man of the frontier, who had thrived in its rugged competition and its elastic legalities, and then had become the soul of respectability. The other, John B. Gilfillan, arrived at a time when settlement had already proceeded to a point where a scholarly young teacher of literature was in great demand. Finding his best opportunity in the law, he applied himself to that profession and prospered mightily.

Atwater was born in Homer, a town in Cortland County, New York, of parents in sufficiently comfortable circumstances to send him to Yale College and then to the Yale Law School. He practiced for three years in New York City and then set out for the new territory of Minnesota. He arrived in October 1850 and became a partner of the first lawyer in Minneapolis, John W. North, who was living in a house near the Falls of St. Anthony. Success came quickly; within a year Atwater was appointed a regent of the University of Minnesota and, six years later, justice of the Supreme Court of the state. He had also piled up a small fortune, like others who, as he put it in his scholarly *History of the City of Minneapolis,* were "making occasional deals in lots." A later historian, Marion D. Shutter, dryly pointed out that Atwater had erected a claim shanty in the Fort Snelling reservation on the western side of the Mississippi River several years before it was legally open for settlement and "staked out a claim before the Traverse des Sioux Treaty was ratified and proclaimed." He sold that property at a profit in 1852, then staked a new claim for 160 acres more and sold that to a fellow attorney, Hilary B. Hancock (twin brother of General Winfield Scott Hancock of Civil War fame) after solemnly legalizing his claim through the United States Land Office after it opened in May of 1855. The land records indicate that some time before his sale of this second property to Hancock (in May of 1857), he erected on it a Gothic cottage which can be found at 1607 South Fifth Street in Minneapolis. The date is uncertain, naturally enough, since it was built on government property by a regent and a leading attorney soon to sit on the state Supreme Court, but the house is charming and should be preserved as a monument to the versatility of a pioneer lawyer and judge. Atwater, having conquered Minneapolis, went to Nevada in 1864. He stayed only three years, found the practice of mining law lucrative, but also found the camps no place for a man of quiet, literary tastes. He returned to Minneapolis, joined Judge Charles E. Flandrau in a law partnership, and not only was a pillar of that thriving city but turned out its most readable and accurate history, in three thick volumes.

The Gothic revival house best known to Twin City residents is the John B. Gilfillan house at Tenth Avenue and Fourth Street Southeast in Minneapolis, near the University of Minnesota. The Gothic revival encouraged variation, and the Gilfillan house was built by a master carpenter of great individuality: B. O. Cutter, born in Sebec, Maine, and partner of Minneapolis's first resident architect, Robert S. Alden. He probably finished the so-called Gilfillan house in 1856, lived in it while he was working on buildings for the University of Minnesota, and sold it in 1869 to Gilfillan.[6]

B. O. Cutter House, Minneapolis, 1856

The editor of the *Evening News of St. Anthony and Minneapolis*, writing on February 28, 1858, indicates that Cutter made his reputation with this house, the most celebrated in the region. The description rhapsodizes on the "ornamental hanging foliage" of the balconies, the "ornamental sculptured mantles finished with enameled Oriental paintings," and the exterior "imitation of shaded stone, furnished by E. S. Brockway, so well done as to completely deceive the [short-sighted] eye a short distance from it." Donald Torbert has noted that "every termination of the steep roof planes and gables is marked by scroll-work, pinnacle and pendant. All the square-head windows carry heavy drip-caps."[7]

John B. Gilfillan, like Le Duc, Cox, and Stevens, was a cultivated man with an appetite for the classics. He was a farm boy from Barnet, Vermont, who came to St. Anthony to earn some money as a teacher to pay his tuition at Dartmouth College. He never returned to Dartmouth, however, for he was so adept at his apprenticeship in a law office that he went directly into practice; however, he retained an intense interest in education. He was the true founder of the elementary school system of Minneapolis and later served as a regent of the University of Minnesota. He was city, then county, attorney, served in the United States Congress for one term, was judge of the district court and president of the First National Bank of Minneapolis. He was handsome and courtly, and a writer of clear but colorful prose. Late in life, he moved from the St. Anthony district, which was declining in favor with the fashionable, to Lowry Hill, where he erected an immense brick residence in the then-popular transition style, midway between the Gothic he left behind and the Renaissance palace mode then coming into fashion.

He left his wooden Downingesque cottage to a succession of owners, including a bootlegger whose still remains in the attic. The house was finally rescued by an academic fraternity which was able to restore his library with its wonderful carving and the wainscoting of the dining room. The house remains as an expression of the scholarly Romanticism which did not outlive the Civil War. From houses like these went many men, full of medieval notions of chivalry and valor, in bright uniforms, with all flags flying. Many of them died in the flaming underbrush of the wilderness and in the trenches about Petersburg. (Perhaps chivalry had died earlier, with Jeb Stuart. It could hardly survive in the world of Ulysses S. Grant.)

Yet, the Gothic revival itself again revived a generation later on an escarpment high above Lake Superior. The forms of the houses, it is true, no longer came from Andrew Jackson Downing's pattern books, but they were animated by the same spirit as his earlier Gothic houses. They were sentimentally rustic, based on literary models, featured steep roofs, pointed windows, enshrouding greenery, and were set in a carefully informal, deliberately unspoiled, natural setting, just as Downing would have wished. How did they come there? The answer lies in the delayed arrival of industrialism and urbanization in the northeastern corner of Minnesota and the simultaneous presence there of men of means, sentiment, and literary bent who had a distaste for the grimy encroachment of the city upon the countryside.

The modern, industrial world came late to Duluth. In 1865 there had been a brief gold rush to the shores of Lake Vermilion. The Minnesota Gold Mining Company was formed with Henry Sibley as president.[8] The company sent three hundred men scurrying about the area, looking for gold they never found, and, after two years, abandoned the search. But a road had been built from the lakeside at Duluth, up the steep hills along Tischer Creek, through the pine forest to Vermilion. Soon after the mining camps became ghost towns, Duluth itself felt the impact of the collapse of Jay Cooke's banking empire in 1873 and lost its corporate charter in 1877. It was not until 1886 that it became a city again, and the iron boom began. Though iron had been found on the Vermilion Range in 1875, the Mountain Iron Mine on the Mesabi did not send its first shipment until 1892. For the next twenty years the hinterland of Duluth was not only the iron-mining center of the United States (as late as the 1930s two-thirds of the iron ore produced in the country came from northern Minnesota) but it also surpassed the Chippewa and St. Croix valleys as a producer of lumber. In 1902 more than a billion feet of pine were cut, much of it by the mills on the St. Louis River at Cloquet. The population of Duluth itself grew by 80 percent in the first five years of the 1890s.

But in Duluth, boomtown though it was, there was a conservative strain which was manifested in the creation of a residential suburb designed to be simple, restrained, and nostalgic. It was laid out along the old Vermilion Road in two sections, one called Hunter's Park, named by John C. Hunter, and the other called Glen Avon by his son-in-law, Angus Roderick Macfarlane. Hunter began as a trader operating "an emporium of the builder, sailor, fur-trader and Indian." He organized the Duluth Savings Bank in 1872 and went on to develop his investments in banking, real estate, railroads, and mining. Macfarlane had come to Duluth as a protegé of Hunter, worked in his bank and, ten years later, married his daughter. Together they laid out a suburb at the

end of the electric streetcar line, a suburb as full of the spirit of romantic literature as any of the neo-Gothic villages built in England seventy years before. Among the street names were Waverley, Abbotsford,
Melrose, Kenilworth, Wallace, Bruce, and Laurie. The lots were large,
and the pine and hard woods were left undisturbed. Ronald M. Hunter,
Macfarlane's brother-in-law, helped to design two houses in the area,
at 2317 Woodland, and 1702 Wallace Street, making use of the black
and grey igneous rock which cropped out through the pine duff. The
first of these houses is the most intriguing example of his late Gothic
style: twin pointed windows are set into the stone where it approaches
a half-timbered peaked gable. Larger blocks of granite are set as quoins
and around the lower windows, creating a fortress under the pines,
looking out upon a deep ravine. The deliberate quaintness should not
lead us to presume that their builders were not in earnest about their
symbolism. As soon as a few houses had been built in the area, a large

stone building was created which became the Craggencroft Classical Institute for Young Ladies, which modestly spoke of its setting where "work is done without depression and languor," in the Tennyson-Superior Drawing Room, the Elizabeth Browning Reception Hall, or the Lowell Library and Studio. "True, it is cold from December to April, but steam and clothes and blankets abound." The school closed in 1902 and three large stone houses in the neighborhood have been built of its remnants.

Temperature was always a matter of interest in Duluth, even to the heirs of hardy thanes, particularly when they were dependent upon the streetcar to get home. One evening, after a performance at the Metropolitan Theater, lairds of Glen Avon commandeered an extra streetcar, with the sympathy of their fellow citizens. As the mayor pronounced the next morning, they acted in desperation "after their trying experience of the night before, when some of the residents had to ride on the roof of the last car, when the wind . . . was blowing at the time, making the journey miserable, if not absolutely perilous. . . ."

Glen Avon and Hunter's Park were the last of Minnesota's picturesque suburbs. They represented a final expression of the spirit of Sir Walter Scott, a refuge from commercialism, a withdrawal from the urbanization which was changing the city below into the likeness of other cities to the south a generation or two older. Ronald Hunter's house at 2329 Woodlawn was the century's last tribute to Andrew Jackson Downing.[9]

(More Gothic houses in Minnesota are listed in the appendix to chapter 5.)

6

The Italianate Styles

WHEN MIDWESTERNERS FIRST WENT TO EUROPE, they went to admire. When they returned, a generation later, they went to acquire. In the first years of modest prosperity after the Civil War, those who took the Grand Tour were content to bring home memories of continental mansions which they copied as they could, shrinking the scale and substituting local materials. The great boom of the 1880s sent a wave of far more prosperous folk abroad. Full of pride and wallets bulging, they simply bought the models and brought them home. From 1890 until this day, it has not been unusual for rooms and, occasionally, entire structures to be crated up in Europe and reconstituted in American houses. Because of its former grandeur and its long prostration, Italy has been a popular place for travelers first to wonder at and then to ransack. Until recently, the grandeur could be purchased cheaply.

Italy was the homeland of an architectural fashion, called in America, "Italianate," "bracketed," or "the villa style," which flourished throughout Europe and America in the middle years of the nineteenth century. Its chief characteristics were extended eaves supported by decorative brackets, windows and doors set in rounded arches, and (particularly in sophisticated, urban houses) cupolas and towers. (Bracketed eaves and overhangs originated not only in ancient Italian prototypes but also in wooden buildings like Swiss chalets and the seventeenth-century colonial houses of New England. But by the time the bracketed styles reached Minnesota, they had become associated with the Italianate style—and English critics used the terms "American bracketed" and "Italianate" interchangeably; see Appendix to chapter 6 for further speculation on the origin of the bracket).

Like Greece a generation earlier, Italy at mid-century inspired the romantic imagination. It possessed a grand antiquity and was undergoing a present struggle for freedom against foreign oppressors. The heroism of Garibaldi succeeded that of Lord Byron. Probably the ruins appealed even more than the heroism, however, for these late romantics were not so prone to action as their fathers; they preferred literary nostalgia to politics. They doted on what Sir Kenneth Clark called "dramatized decay." Ruins were the natural circumstances of romance, thought many Americans, especially since their own country was so shiny, hustling, and new. Nathaniel Hawthorne was among many who followed the scent of mold to Italy, a "poetic or fairy precinct, where actualities would not be so terribly insisted upon as they are, and must need be, in America . . . a country where there is no shadow, no antiquity, no mystery, no picturesque and gloomy wrong, nor anything but a commonplace prosperity, in broad and simple daylight. . . . Romance and poetry, ivy, lichens and wall-flowers need ruin to make them grow."

It was, of course, not entirely necessary to go all the way to Italy, for the Italianate style could be readily derived from pictures. It was characteristic of the Italian revival that it was picturesque in the same sense that the Gothic revival was literary: romantics were enticed by the Italy of landscape painters, particularly by Nicholas Poussin and Claude Lorrain, who painted dryads and shepherds gamboling before half-ruined arcades and bracketed fragments of roofs and towers, presumably arousing pleasing sentiments in the breasts of their aristocratic patrons. Richard Payne Knight, the English philosopher of the picturesque who was the literary mentor of Andrew Jackson Downing, suggested that these "fabricks" (artificial settings for artificial rusticity) could serve as the basis for a new romantic architecture. Downing agreed, and recommended Italianate houses of "picturesque and irregular outlines" as alternatives to his Gothic cottages.

But it was not only the Gothic revival which broke the way for the Italianate fashion; the Classic revival led by a different route to the same bracketed villas set in bosky dells and to the same vineyards populated by nut-brown, laughing peasants. The antiquarians who measured and recorded every classic ruin in Italy were, of course, enraptured by the discovery of Pompeii and Herculaneum, with their frescoes providing fresh memorials of country life in classic times, and of the architecture of the Roman villa. The frescoes at Pompeii led to the recollection, by the learned, of a commendation by the elder Pliny of the pleasures of dining in a tower room, open to the breeze and the view. Once again, an image of an ideal past led to the development of an architectural form, in this case the belvedere (a tower or, at least, a cupola) from which to view the countryside. Belvederes soon soared above houses built in the old Roman manner in Germany, England, and America, houses which were informal and irregular in massing, with long-extended eaves supported by extended rafters and sheltering the walls and windows below from a searing sun.

Like the Greek revival before it, the Italianate style was international in its appeal. Villas appealed to the tastes of the middle class which was rising to affluence in western Europe and in America. Such houses had dignity, a good pedigree, and a picturesque quality affording opportunity for display. An Italianate house was built by the versatile Regency architect John Nash in 1802 at Cronkhill in England, and many more followed in Britain, including Queen Victoria's Osborne House on the Isle of Wight. Henry-Russell Hitchcock acclaims as "the international masterwork of the asymmetrically-towered Italian Villa mode" the Prussian Court Gardener's house at Potsdam, designed by Karl Friedrich von Schinkel in 1829–31, six years before the first American work in the style, Bishop George W. Doane's villa in Burlington, New Jersey.

Americans were unwilling to acknowledge that they shared the style with others; they were becoming self-conscious about their provincialism. They had been to Europe, they had been made aware of the polish and pedigree they lacked, and they wanted to assert their own claims as men of taste. So the Italianate style was modified and became the bracketted style (the number of t's was optional), "an indigenous style in architecture," according to the editor of the *Architectural Review and American Builder's Journal*, writing in November 1868. He went on to assert that "its appearance is pleasing to Europeans; and, indeed, it has many points about it superior to the domestic architecture of Europe. . . . Those prominent cornices, so highly ornamented, and those brackets, which, while they support them, give, at the same time, such a distinctive feature to this style, as to be known to English architects, as the American Bracketed Architecture; those umbrageous 'stoops'; those broad and shady piazzas, all now so peculiarly our own . . . go to make up this new style."

From these sources, then, came the elements which made up the American Bracketed style or Italianate style. There were really two styles: one, merely a traditional cube to which brackets and, occasionally, a cupola were added, and a second, very different in intent and aspect—the true, irregular Italian villa. Let them be called first, the bracketed house and second, the villa. Both had brackets and both were frequently called Italian for this reason, but the bracketed house is severe with a low hip roof; the villa is jumbled, informal, towered, with a roofline broken by dormers, false gables, and, later, a steep mansard. One is a somewhat corrupted child of the Renaissance. The other, to be examined first, is a waif with a vaguely medieval look, seeking acceptance by stressing its willingness to enter domestic service.

Minnesota possesses two of the most splendid and carefully tended villas in the nation: the Burbank-Griggs house in St. Paul and the Huff-Lamberton mansion in Winona. James C. Burbank built his great limestone mansion in 1865 at 432 Summit Avenue, now a thoroughfare, then a cart track through an oak wood. This was a peak year for the riverboat trade and the stagecoach business for Burbank, who profited nearly every time a passenger or a package moved in Minnesota by water or by road. He laid up his mansion of massive blocks of local grey limestone three stories high and surmounted it with a cupola which with its spire adds fifteen feet more. Four-foot brackets support the eaves. About the windows are smooth blocks of stone, imparting an urbane aspect which is missing from the squat, rough facade of the Ramsey house, built during the same period of the same materials but wholly different in effect.

The front hall has not, apparently, been changed since its construction except that it is now lit by tall leaded windows which may have been installed later. This is the most magnificent room built in Minnesota during Burbank's generation. It is paneled in hardwood, carved into small arcades to repeat the rhythm of the windows and the arches of the verandah, and the doorways are as fine as any of the chambers into which they open. Those rooms are not original; they were imported by Mrs. Theodore W. Griggs after 1900: a French drawing room; an Elizabethan study; an elaborate, paneled Italian dining room; a long marble corridor leading down to a mirrored ballroom. About the balcony which overlooks the hall from the second floor is a group of bedrooms which also were removed from European houses and reinstalled. The interiors, therefore, while grand, represent the cosmopolitan taste and capacity for acquisition of a generation which came to affluence in recent decades rather than the character of Burbank, who built the house three years after the Dakota War in a river town which had no paved streets and was still risky on Saturday night.

*James C. Burbank
House, St. Paul,
1865*

Burbank must have been a man of extraordinary taste. Instead of building among the fashionable folk in Lowertown, he found a site on the edge of the bluff overlooking the town and the river. There he built St. Paul's grandest house. Why he chose the Italian style, we cannot tell; perhaps he had been impressed by villas he had seen in his travels, perhaps he merely worked from pictures. Burbank had come to Minnesota from Vermont in 1850 and founded an express business, carrying mail and supplies from Galena, Illinois, to St. Paul. The steamer *Nominee* carried the merchandise until the river froze and then it went by Walker's stage line down the old fur traders' road by way of Prairie du Chien. In 1856, "disgusted with the wretched service" provided by Walker, Burbank and his partners organized their own stagecoach operation to Dubuque, which had just been reached by the railroad (thereby hastening the decline of Galena, which had been the point of shipment for nearly all northern goods). Originally they moved only freight, but soon carried passengers as well and ultimately "pushed Walker's slow coaches out of business." They secured the downriver mail franchise in 1858 and, to expedite service, built a road down the west shore of the Mississippi as far as Winona, cutting down bluffs and bridging streams. By changing horses every fifteen to eighteen miles, the distance of 105 miles could then be made in twenty-four hours. The next year, they added the Stillwater and Superior lines and then bid successfully for all government mail service in Minnesota. Their Minnesota Stage Company covered 1,300 miles by stage and 300 miles by pony routes, employed 200 men and 700 horses by 1865. Burbank was also a partner in a company which, in 1858, had been appointed by the Hudson's Bay Company to ship their merchandise to New York or Montreal by way of St. Paul instead of through York Factory on Hudson's Bay. To carry the four to six hundred tons of merchandise covered by this contract, the partners operated two steamships on the Red River and a system of Red River carts to St. Paul, until they found "that the interest of the Hudson's Bay Company and their own interest were not identical." In 1864 they sold out this venture to a new Hudson's Bay agent, Norman H. Kittson, who had been operating a stage line between St. Paul and the Red River since 1843. Burbank, however, continued to be an important figure in the river traffic until the advent of the railroads ended the reign of the steamboat.

It was not an unprofitable business; Henry M. Rice, Hercules L.

Dousman, and Henry H. Sibley had been among the organizers of the Galena Packet Company which in 1855 cleared $44,000 on the operations of the steamer *War Eagle,* which had cost them $20,000. The *City Belle,* which had cost $11,000, cleared $30,000. There were, of course, risks. That year Louis Robert had added the *Globe* to his fleet, and in October sent her up the Minnesota "carrying Sioux annuities consisting of goods and $90,000 in gold. She struck on a rock . . . and the merchandise being placed on the banks of the river, the dry grass was carelessly ignited by the Indians and the merchandise with fifty kegs of powder, destroyed." All that gold. Apparently blown to smithereens. Undeterred by such risks, indeed, perhaps, fascinated by them, Burbank reorganized the St. Paul Fire and Marine Insurance Company and became its second president after the Civil War.

The Burbank-Griggs villa is without equal in grandeur in Minnesota; but as a monument to enterprise and audacity it is rivaled by that built by Henry D. Huff in 1857, in the very latest style, amid a straggle of shanties on a sandpit on the edge of Indian territory, five years before the Dakota War. Henry Huff, more than any other man, was responsible for building that riverfront village into the city of Winona; he could visualize boulevards where ran only ruts.

Huff grew rich creating a city on a town site he had bought for a few thousand dollars from speculators more easily discouraged than he. Huff had learned the joys and profits of real estate speculation in Kenosha, Wisconsin, and in 1853 was led westward to a sandy plain beside the Mississippi which was without a single tree. Barren, windswept, and threatened by floods every spring, it was then called Montezuma. Huff assessed that title as too exotic to attract investors and had it changed to Winona, after the sister of Chief Wabasha, who had acquiesced to the loss of the area to the whites two years before. In 1855, Huff bought the platted area of the town and started a new newspaper to extol its beauties. In 1857, he added a hotel, the Huff House, built a flour mill, and soon afterward promoted a transit railroad. But his house is his permanent monument, conjured up on as unprepossessing a town site as could be found on the river. It pivots around an enormous Vanbrughian tower at one corner, its essentially cubical mass broken into pavilions and bays.[1] The eaves, supported by brackets, rise up in strutting gables, and there is a separate gabled pavilion in the rear.

Huff-Lamberton House, Winona, 1857

In 1873, Huff, having proved his point, retired to luxurious ease in Chicago, selling his mansion to Henry W. Lamberton, a railroad land agent who dabbled a bit on his own, and whose fortunes blossomed when iron was found under some of his stumpage near Chisholm, Minnesota. Lamberton's wife is said to have been an opera singer from St. Louis, and she engaged the Italian craftsmen who were laboring on Wisconsin's state capitol to come to fresco the ceilings of her husband's mansion. Later, she added the Moorish gazebo and porch which festoon the front of the house. Despite her ministrations, it is Henry Huff whose mark is strongest upon this great house, the most arresting landmark on the river between the Hercules Dousman's house at Prairie du Chien and the rough limestone mansion of James C. Burbank in St. Paul.

As the century grew older, the villa style became more and more picturesque, sprouted towers and dormers, lengthened its brackets, sported more and more jigsaw work about its verandah. Especially, however, it emphasized its tower. Men do not persist in building a certain form in their houses over a prolonged period merely to follow fashion. That form must impart to them some desired feeling; it must have psychological value. Towers began to be used upon larger Gothic houses, like those of William Le Duc and E. St. Julien Cox, and they became increasingly popular as adjuncts to the villa. First they popped out as cupolas or belvederes, then grew as time went on into full-scale towers. Their popularity was sustained through the mansard interlude; then they remained prominent in the complex patterns of what will be called in this book the American Picturesque. Finally, towers furnished the axis about which moved the rounded forms of the disciples of Henry H. Richardson.

It is possible, of course, that towers were merely thought to be arresting shapes against the foliage and the sky and that they provided vertical accents in design. But why so ubiquitous for so long? It seems more likely that they answered a yearning in the spirit of an anxious generation after the Civil War. A fortress tower had been, for a millennium, a symbol of safety, a strong point to which men might repair, a refuge which stood secure above the roofs and narrow streets of the town; and a church tower, symbol of spiritual security. It was so constant a motif in domestic architecture between 1860 and 1890 that it must have become once again, for some at least, a symbol of security.

Neither James Burbank nor Henry Huff built around a tower, but most of the builders of smaller villas who came after them did. There are several good examples in the Hastings area, the best preserved of which was built by a pioneer lumberman, Allen E. Rich, in the late 1860s at 117 E. Seventh Street, based upon another Downing design. The interior is graced by a spiralling walnut staircase, and was carefully restored by Mrs. Walter Walbridge.[2]

The best example of the villa style in the St. Croix Valley was also derived from a handbook. It was built for Captain Austin T. Jenks in 1871

at Fifth and Pine Streets in Stillwater. Captain Jenks was a colorful character who owned a fine 110-foot stern-wheeler, the *Brother Jonathan*, and with it towed log rafts on the St. Croix and the upper Mississippi. As he progressed from captain to commodore to financier, his reputation grew, and his red-brick villa set a fashion. The style was carried to a higher pitch by the Tucci family of Stillwater a few years later when they built a more elaborate brick house with a campanile a few miles west of Stillwater on Highway 96.

By that time, however, many Italian villas had acquired a French cast. Already the flat roof of the campanile had begun to bulge upward; the Downing pattern used for the Rich House had been insufficiently vertical even for Henry Huff, who had placed a mansard roof with dormers and a wrought-iron crest atop his tower, and the Jenks house had an even more steeply pitched "cap" on its tower. The tendency reached its fullest expression in the Sprague house at Third and Hill Streets in Red Wing. (This is probably the most important architectural intersection in the state: the Lawther Octagon is at one corner, and Purcell and Elm-

Philander Sprague House, Red Wing, 1868

slie's Hoyt house of 1914 is on another.) Philander Sprague was an early grain merchant and miller in a town which has had a taste for exotic architecture since its first permanent structure, an Alpine chalet, was built there by Swiss missionaries in 1836. Sprague and his wife, Hanna, were social leaders of the town and added a complete mansard roof to their red brick villa in accord with the French Imperial fashions of the day. The house was completed in 1868 and is more elaborate and more vertical than the cottages Downing had suggested: the wings are shorter and the tower appears higher. It is also more palatial: there are groups of round-arched windows set under stone hoods, a spiral walnut staircase winds upward into the campanile, and the fireplaces are inset with painted tiles and faced in marble.

The Sprague villa and the Le Duc Gothic house were built in the same period and, superficially, they look somewhat alike. But William Gates Le Duc, though he outlived Philander Sprague by a half century, was a man of the old order, and Sprague was of the new. Le Duc's house was a citadel of the romantic Gothic movement. Philander Sprague built an Italian house with a French roof, aspiring to grandeur. The dominant instinct of the last half of the nineteenth century was to pile masses higher and higher, seeking an effect which finally could have been appreciated only by the birds.

The second strain within the Italian revival was called the American Bracketed house by English architects: a good, short description. It merely added brackets to the traditional cubical house with a hip roof and often reinstated the popularity of the old New England captain's walk or cupola on the roof. Houses of this sort were very common in Minnesota. One of the finest, a frame mansion, was built in the 1870s by Henry G. Page at 219 Whitford Street in Fergus Falls. Page came from Polo, Illinois, and arrived in Fergus Falls early in the 1870s. He acquired land beside the falls which had first been reported as a good mill site by Joe Whitford, the town's founder, to his employer, James Fergus, of Little Falls. Fergus named the falls, Whitford, the street. Page built a water-powered flour mill and soon replaced the log cabin Whitford had constructed in 1858 (the first building in town) with his own cubical, hip-roofed mansion which has a spreading wing to the rear. It is white, four-square, self-assertive. Its owner became the first president of the First National Bank, and later president of the village council.

Henry G. Page House,
Fergus Falls, c. 1875

Cupolas could be seen on the skylines of most ambitious Minnesota towns during the 1860s and 1870s. In St. Paul, the cupola and campanile truly came into their glory. Like the medieval burghers and nobles of San Gimignano in Tuscany who built fifty-six towers, each seeking to surpass the other, the merchants, riverboat owners, and speculators of this metropolis of the region vied with each other in building large cupolaed houses from which to view their bustling wharves, warehouses, stores, and streets.

The *St. Paul Pioneer and Democrat* of September 2, 1860, said of one of them, built by a "Mr. Bass" (who may have been the saloon keeper of that name) that surmounting its third story was "a spacious observatory, large enough to hold a company of twenty or thirty persons inside, and on the outside as many more. The view from this is unsurpassed." Two years later, Henry Sibley moved into St. Paul and placed atop his new house on Woodward Avenue a belvedere as large as Mr. Bass's. From it, he could see the cupolas of his compeers, Norman H. Kittson, Horace Thompson, John L. Merriam, William F. Davidson, and, atop the bluff, of course, James C. Burbank.

Far to the south, near La Crescent in Houston County, a railroad contractor named Daniel J. Cameron erected a farmhouse with a cupola large enough to serve, today, as a living room for one of the apartments into which the house has been divided. Cameron arrived from New Jersey in 1859 after building the Hoosac River Tunnel, thus establishing a reputation which led him under most of the great mountain ranges of the country during the next twenty years. He tunneled Boston Mountain in California, Buckbone Mountain in Arkansas, and laid out the stretch of roadbed which penetrates the granite cliffs past rocky bays east of Port Arthur in Ontario. When he returned to La Crescent in 1881 he came out into the sunlight, admired the view from the cupola over his fields to the river and, according to local tradition, "indulged his passion for fast horses." The town has since grown up around it and has given it an address at 429 S. Seventh Street.

Cameron's farmhouse is a good introduction to the great brick mansion that Patrick Henry Rahilly constructed on his twelve-hundred-acre domain west of Lake City. (It is at the end of an avenue of elms on County Road 15, which leaves Rt. 63 three miles west of the city limits.) Rahilly was born in 1833 near Limerick, Ireland, came to the United States when he was sixteen, worked in Pennsylvania as a farmhand for two years and then, in 1854, arrived in Rochester, Minnesota, where he found a job with W. D. Lowery, an early capitalist. Rahilly proved capable; Lowery put him in charge of his farming interests, then brought him into his mercantile and banking operations. Rahilly moved to Mt. Pleasant near Lake City in 1860 and began to accumulate land holdings. First, he built a large Greek revival house, but when it burned in March 1879 he drew out of his memory the red brick mass of the Brackenridge mansion which had been the pride of Rochester in the days of his impecunious, immigrant youth. (Covered with a Georgianesque shell in the early years of the twentieth century, the Brackenridge house is now unrecognizable.) The house he then built is very like old pictures of his model: tall, stately, with high ceilings, an arcade of windows set in rounded arches and surrounded by a dignified piazza. It was restored by Mr. and Mrs. Stephen A. Osborn.

Midway between the old, severe, cubical form of the American Bracketed house and the capricious Italian villa was a gable-roofed, bracketed house which evolved into an L-shaped and more picturesque version. As has been noted, most houses built in America during the eighteenth century adhered to the style we call Georgian: symmetrical, sparing of decoration, generally hip-roofed with three or five bays in the facade. Some of these added for variety a gable in the center of the front, and a few thrust forward the whole area below this to form a pavilion. In the nineteenth century, conservative folk often used this form, merely adding brackets to comport with fashion.

A good example of this style is the white frame house built about 1870 by Mark Hill Dunnell in Owatonna. Dunnell was a legal scholar and educator with the restlessness of a frontiersman. He arrived in Owatonna in 1867, after long years of roving. He had been born in 1823

Patrick H. Rahilly House, Lake City, 1880

Mark H. Dunnell House, Owatonna, 1870

in Buxton, Maine, graduated from Colby College, had taught in a school in Maine, become its headmaster and then state superintendent of schools. In the evening he had studied law and passed the bar in 1856. In that year he was still school superintendent, was serving in the Maine legislature, organizing the Republican Party in the state, and became a delegate to the party's first national convention which nominated John C. Fremont for president. In 1861, after seeing action at the first battle of Bull Run, he was sent, with the honorary title of Counsel, by the War Department to stop an influx of arms to the Confederacy through Vera Cruz, Mexico. Shortly thereafter the Mexican governor of the district departed for the hills—the Mexicans were resisting the army of the Emperor Maximilian, who had been foisted upon them by Napoleon III of France—and Dunnell became *de facto* governor of the province, which must have made his mission for the War Department somewhat easier. He then was recalled to inspirit flagging recruiting efforts in Maine. After the war, he moved to Winona, where he was elected to the Minnesota legislature, soon moved again to Owatonna, where he became superintendent of Minnesota's schools and, subsequently, was elected to the United States Congress, where he served for twelve years. In Owatonna, his house at 357 East Main Street is crowned by a pinnacled, bracketed cupola. Above the windows are hood molds now dramatized by dark paint. There is a tall double front door within an arcaded verandah and in the center of the front cornice is a small false gable, supported by thin pilasters which suggest, barely suggest, the coming of the center pavilion which was to dominate later houses in this mode.[3]

The largest house of this pavilioned, gable-roofed type in Minnesota was built in the early 1870s by Dr. Edward S. Frost at 321 West Seventh Street in Willmar. Dr. Frost, a man of considerable means who became the first surgeon in the area, built a rambling mansion of thirty-five rooms. The wing containing the library, billiard room, and ballroom was later separated and remodeled to serve as the residence of his grandson, Mr. Charles E. Frost, who reported that "little presently remains of the original inlaid floors, decorative plasterwork cornices and marble fireplaces which once graced that part of the house now used for apartments." The remaining portion of the old red house, next door, has a hexagonal tower at one corner, a double verandah, large brackets, and a center pavilion so far thrust forward that it becomes almost another wing.[4]

The two-story, L-shaped, bracketed form evolved out of the pavilioned style just described by sliding the pavilion to one side and creating the more casual, asymmetrical shape which appealed to a generation increasingly seeking variety and animation in architecture. The most dignified and splendid of this species is in southeast Minneapolis near the University of Minnesota at 424 South Fifth Street. It was built during the Civil War years by John A. Armstrong. Armstrong was a New Englander, born in Ellsworth, Maine, in 1831, the son of a tanner. At twenty, he and a brother shipped out for the California gold fields, by way of the Isthmus of Chagres, which they crossed by foot. On the Pacific side they "embarked . . . in an old steamer whose unseaworthiness was a little less dangerous than the cholera which attacked the crew and passengers in a virulent form." Surviving the voyage they arrived in San Francisco and made their way to the placer mines along the Feather River, where, "having accumulated a few thousand dollars in dust, deposited it in two banks, which soon failed, leaving them penniless." Back to the river they went. After four more years, they had acquired a second "stake" and returned to Maine. John Armstrong was restless, however, and in 1856 set out again for the wilderness, this time the pineries of Minnesota. He arrived in St. Anthony with enough capital to establish a lumbering operation, presumably up the Rum River Valley, which was then swarming with loggers. Armstrong contracted to cut and haul timber, managing his operations from St. Anthony. He was a powerful man and quick in a fight; in 1858, he was elected marshal, then deputy sheriff, and, in 1860, sheriff of Hennepin County. The spotty title records indicate that he began his house in that year. He had become a large enough factor in the affairs of the region to attract the notice of James J. Hill, who invited him to join E. N. Saunders, C. W. Griggs, and Hill to form the Northwestern Fuel Company. From 1867 onward, much of what earlier settlers had left of the "Great Woods" was cut down to supply stove wood for the rapidly growing cities of St. Paul, Minneapolis, and St. Anthony, most of it cut by Armstrong and his associates. He did not long enjoy his prosperity, however. He died of pneumonia in 1878.

The most striking feature of the Armstrong house is the elaborate cast-iron hood molds which surmount its windows, emphasized by dark brown paint against the buff brick of the walls. As the nineteenth century progressed hoods became larger and more elaborate, and the aspect of three- or five-bay houses came to acquire something of an arcaded effect, emphasized by their round-arched verandahs.

Emphatic hood molds, elaborate brackets, cupolas, and campaniles might have been impressive to some, but most men who built in the bracketed styles eschewed such extravagances and built simply. They preferred quiet houses under hip roofs, wearing their brackets with diffidence. In the St. Croix Valley, particularly, the New England tradition was strong, and, in Stillwater, there is a group of white-framed, simple

houses which, in a haze or at twilight, look very much like the town houses of small seaside towns in Maine or Massachusetts, despite their brackets: 122 West Linden (1856), 220 Chestnut (1871), 107 East Laurel (1875), and just below the Lowell Inn on East Myrtle, the beautiful brick home and office of Dr. Henry Van Meier, built before 1881 with an arched Federal doorway and arched windows.

John A. Armstrong House, Minneapolis, c. 1870

This tradition of cubical, bracketed houses persisted longer than any other in Minnesota. It was extinguished, along with its picturesque rivals, by the overwhelming success of the Classicistic movement at the Chicago Columbian Exposition of 1893. Thereafter houses of the cubical type were, it is true, still constructed, but they were self-consciously based upon learned antiquarianism.[5] The living tradition of the American Bracketed style was dead.

7

Architecture at Mid-century: Experiment and Emulation

DURING THE MIDDLE DECADE of the nineteenth century, while the Greek and Gothic and Italianate styles were achieving elegance, two subcurrents were running through American life which produced their own, generally ungainly, architectural results. These were the experimental strain, exemplified by the cement house in the shape of an octagon, and the snobbish strain, prostrating taste before imported fashion, uncritically accepting the mansard magniloquence of the court of Napoleon III.

One of these aspects of the American personality was inquisitive, innovating, and irreverent of precedent. The other was blinded by the authority of contemporary crowned heads of Europe. An amused Mark Twain created characters representing each of them. The Connecticut Yankee, returned to Twain's America, could happily have inhabited a gravel-walled octagon, and the Duke and the Dauphin never bamboozled Huck Finn's friends any more than Louis Napoleon's architectural furbelows dazzled the fashionable folk of their time.

Orson Squire Fowler, author of *A Home for All: or the Gravel Wall and Octagon Mode of Building*, was a sort of Yankee peddler himself. A salesman of many nostrums, the chief evangelist of an octagon house expressed the hope that it would be filled with innumerable mechanical contrivances. He had three great enthusiasms, each of which he evangelized to great effect and profit: phrenology, sex, and the octagon house. Since this is a work confined to architecture, let it be said only in passing that his publications on phrenology were bulky and admired by thousands, and that his second enthusiasm produced a 930-page volume called *Sexual Science*, three wives, and many children, of whom three were sired after he had passed his seventieth year. A review of state architectural histories indicates that his contributions to architecture can be observed in 126 octagon houses still standing in New York State, 19 in Wisconsin, 4 in Ohio, 6 in Indiana, 6 in Iowa, 4 in Illinois, at least 3 in Michigan, a dozen or more scattered elsewhere as far as California, and 6 in Minnesota. Of these, the grandest are: "Nutt's Folly," a Turkestani extravaganza octagon in Natchez, Tennessee; the four-storied octagon mansion on the Hudson River once owned by the historian Carl Carmer; and the John Richards house in Watertown, Wisconsin, which has fifty-seven rooms (more or less) in its four stories.

Fowler was, apparently, a charming man who felt that the prevailing revival styles with their carvings and cornicings were designed only for the delectation of the rich, and that what was needed was a scientific, simple "machine for living." (The phrase, of course, is Le Corbusier's, but it could be Fowler's) He espoused the octagon form because eight walls could enclose more space than four of the same length, because the carving of rooms like the slices of a pie left less space wasted in hallways, because the disposal of wastes would be concentrated in a single, central soil-stack, and because such a shape simplified the distribution of central heating and of running water. These fresh approaches to housing were highly attractive to his generation. Fowler demonstrated that they were practical in his own house at Fishkill, New York, which had central heating, gas lighting, hot and cold running water, and indoor flush toilets in 1853, a full generation before these conveniences were generally available. He observed the frequent association of diseases with the use of tainted public water supplies, and recommended the use, instead, of individual cisterns for rainwater in each house.

Fowler spoke for many of his countrymen, then and now, in extolling the delights of mechanical ingenuity. What a menu is to a Frenchman, a hardware store is to an American. We love gadgets. We are at the mercy of hucksters at county fairs and in automobile showrooms. We have had a popular tradition of experimentation which has led to a myriad of inventions to dazzle neighbors, and which have, on occasion, dazzled the world. In the decades before the Civil War, American ingenuity was widely diffused and particularly fruitful. Then were developed Samuel Colt's repeating gun, Walter Hunt's fountain pen, fire alarm, ice boat, and safety pin, McCormick's reaper, and John Deere's plow. An aspiring actor named Isaac Singer pooled the patents for sewing machines; a successful painter named Samuel F. B. Morse sent the first telegraph message. A rising young lawyer patented a method for sinking and raising boats by bellows and signed the documents "A. Lincoln, May 30, 1849."

The 1840s were a particularly good time to apply this love of experimentation to architecture. The nation was not only willing to listen to new ideas, but to adopt them passionately. Norman Ware has called this the "hot-air period of American history" and points out that "there were enough freaks abroad to warrant some derision. Phrenology flourished, alongside the 'Water-cure.' The Grahamites had a vision that was later to commend itself to Bernard Shaw and Upton Sinclair, and whole wheat bread. The 'Disciples of Newness' left Boston for a played-out farm. Robert Owen flitted back and forth across the Atlantic, catechizing prince and the pauper in the true law of life. There was the ever-recurrent 'new woman'—at that time in bloomers. Temperance reform, the wrongs of Hungarian liberals, Association, capital punishment, and slavery, all gave birth to 'movements.'"

This positive impulse toward innovation gained strength from a contemporaneous rejection of its opposite—revivalism—in all its forms. Revivalism had benefited from scientific inquiry into the forms of the past, but now science exacted its price. Research into the realities of the Hellenic and Middle Ages informed antiquarians of the social circumstances within which the architecture of those periods developed and made it seem a little absurd to try to plant that architecture in the soil of Jacksonian America. As Talbot Hamlin, the great expositor of the Greek revival, wrote later: "Archaeology and history were now rapidly becoming respectable sciences, not mere opportunities for wish-fulfillment dreams. As a sense of the actual historical past as *past* increased, so also did the consciousness of present as *present;* the time element was becoming of ever greater importance; the *now* was triumphant. Once this self-conscious feeling for the present had developed, the day of the revivals in art was over; the differences between the life and needs of the past and those of the present were too great to be bridged."

But what was to be the alternative? Could Americans develop their own architecture? A few artists and architects thought so, among them the sculptor Horatio Greenough. To him, Jefferson's classical Virginia State Capitol, "claims pity for its degraded majesty" and Richard Upjohn's Trinity Church was "the puny cathedral of Broadway." Ralph Waldo Emerson exhorted the American architect to consider "the climate, soil, the length of day, the wants of the people, the habit and form of government . . . [and] create a house in which all there will find themselves fitted."

It is an error to dismiss Fowler too lightly as a persuasive peddler of architectural snake oil. He stood in a long and honorable tradition of inventors and popularizers of inventions whose great exemplars were Benjamin Franklin and Thomas Jefferson. Like them, he was confident in the power of reason, intrigued with mechanical contrivances, and determined to make ingenuity socially useful. As Richard W. E. Perrin has said in describing Wisconsin's particularly generous crop of octagons, they "marked the beginning of inventive and experimental architecture by which it was sought to organize and enclose space to meet particular needs according to reason and logic instead of inherited tradition alone." Fowler was not, nor did he profess to be, the inventor of either the octagon form or of cement-wall construction. He combined them, convincing several hundred householders to break away from habit and follow his example.

The octagon form has ancient lineage: the Greeks built an octagonal Temple of the Winds at Athens about 300 BC. A page from William Kent's *Designs of Inigo Jones* of 1727 attributes a design for an octagonal structure to Jones. Thomas Jefferson's home at Poplar Forest was an octagon housing octagonal rooms and octagonal furniture. Charles Bulfinch, designer of the Boston State House and redesigner of the National Capitol, and Robert Mills, the first native-born professional architect in America, both designed octagonal churches.

While learned men were exploring the variations of the octagon form, it also attracted the interest of craftsmen who worked solely upon problems to which it provided readier answers than traditional box-like buildings. Near Lake Michigan in Ozaukee County, Wisconsin, a German carpenter named Clausen built many octagonal barns, presumably to better resist the strong winds coming from Lake Michigan. There are many other octagonal barns in Wisconsin and in Minnesota. These structures could enclose large spaces without the columns or interior bearing walls that might obstruct the maneuvering of a hay cart.

Fowler, with the instinct of a popularizer, took the academic tradition, with its emphasis on beauty ("the most perfect form is the circle, and the octagon is the closest approach to the circle which can be practically constructed"), the folk tradition with its emphasis on economy and utility (less wall to surround more space, concentration of water, waste, and heat), and popular delight in novelty, and combined them into his *A Home for All, or the Gravel Wall and Octagon Mode of Building.*

"The Gravel Wall" was to be cement, grout, or "pebble dash" as it was known in early Minnesota. Each of these words has an imposing pedigree: Cement was a word the Romans used to describe a binding material they made up of mortar and rough pieces of stone (*caedimentum*), and used to cover over the brickwork of their houses and the stone of their monuments. During the Middle Ages the Roman formula was forgotten; despite the best efforts of men to make effective mortar out of such elements as pitch, eggs, wax, and sulphur, the results were not impressive. However, when the forests from which men had been building houses were almost depleted in many parts of Europe, in the early days of the Renaissance, an intense effort produced a mortar which, once again, went into common use.

The building of stone houses covered with cement became traditional in many places. Whitewash was introduced to keep off the frost and it is likely that Minnesota would have had many whitewashed, cement-and-stone houses if wood had not been so plentiful and so cheap. Those completely of cement and pebbles are rare. General Israel Garrard built a cement house which still stands a few hundred feet south of St. Hubert's Lodge at Frontenac. Two early "pebble dash" houses can be found on the south side of Walnut Street in St. Peter, and articles in the popular press suggested a "newstyle house" of mud, sand, and gravel. One such recommendation, in the April 7, 1855, edition of the *St. Paul Pioneer,* is locally credited with suggesting to John T. Cyphers the construction of his remarkable "grout house" in Lakeland, Washington County, in 1858. Its walls are nearly two feet thick, apparently laid up by pouring the "grout" between wooden forms, leaving the door and windows to be framed in wood. The arch over the door must have required careful bending of the form. Were it not for its unusual material and its low-sloping roof, this house might be classified within the Gothic revival, for its eaves are richly decorated with carving, its gables are wooden, etched to simulate stone, and the small dormers carry more carven cresting. Possibly the house is not to be classified sty-

John Cyphers House,
Lakeland, c. 1858

listically at all; it is the individual creation of a man interested in practical construction, easy upkeep (its outside walls need only to be sluiced with a bucket of water and brushed) and also in decoration.

John Cyphers apparently required only the stimulus of a newspaper column to experiment with concrete construction. There were others in the Upper Midwest like him, ready to discover how easily "a mix" could be composed and how solidly it hardened. It is reported in an unpublished thesis by Lucille M. Oliver, titled "The History of Princeton, Minn.," that Dr. E. C. Gile "had the shingles removed from the roof of his house and had a solid cement roof laid over the house in place of the shingles. The doctor soon discovered the roof he had laid cracked up and he had it taken off and shingled again."

Limestone lies just beneath the surface of much of southern Minnesota, and lime kilns can be found under the banks of many streams where the water was close to the rock. There farmers could burn the limestone, keeping it hot enough to drive off the carbonic acid and produce lime they could slake with water from the creek to make slaked lime which, combined with sand and pebbles, made mortar.

One of these early users of cement was Joseph Goodrich of Milton, Wisconsin. Fowler reported that on a lecture tour in 1850, "near Janesville, Wisconsin, I saw houses built wholly of lime, mixed with coarse gravel and sand found in banks on the western prairies and underlying all prairie soil. I visited Milton, to examine the house put up by Mr. Goodrich, the original discoverer of this mode of building and found his walls as hard as stone itself, and harder than brick walls. . . . He erected a blacksmith's shop, and finally a block of stores and dwellings; and his plan was copied extensively. And he deserves to be immortalized, for the superiority of this plan must certainly revolutionize building, and especially enable poor men to build their own homes. All the credit I claim is that of appreciating its superiority, applying it on a large scale, and greatly improving the mode of putting up this kind of a wall."

Fowler had greater success in propagating octagon houses than in convincing others to use cement on a large scale for residential construction. Only one of the octagons built in Minnesota was of cement, and it, at 317 Walnut Street in Winona, built in 1857, has since been covered with stucco and completely remodeled, so that no pebble-dash surface above the foundation is exposed. The builder is unknown, and, indeed, it is characteristic of these houses that their builders have either been forgotten or that we know little beyond their names. It is as if they were all cast into the shadow of the giant, Orson Fowler.

The best preserved octagon in this region is across the St. Croix River, in Hudson, Wisconsin, where Judge John S. Moffat built a

John S. Moffat House, Hudson, Wisconsin, 1855

wooden octagon in 1855, with a cupola and paired brackets under flaring eaves. The verandah, which surrounded nearly all octagon houses built in this region, bears hexagonal columns much like those of the Greek revival houses built in the same town by the Andrews brothers, and one suspects that they had a hand in this one as well. Another octagon house, in Afton, Minnesota, burned down in the 1950s, but there remains a former Baptist church of eight sides a few miles to the north in Lakeland, converted into use as City Hall. At Second and Spring Streets in Hastings, on a lot J. F. Norrish bought from Alexis Bailly and

Henry H. Sibley, he built a stone octagon in 1858, which, though now stuccoed and remodeled, still sustains its jaunty air.[1]

J. F. Norrish House, Hastings, 1858

James L. Lawther erected his brick octagon at Hill and Third Streets in Red Wing after a visit to the metropolis of Dubuque, where the patriarchal Edward Langworthy had completed the grandest house of the type on the Upper Mississippi, offering inspiration, presumably, to

James L. Lawther
House, Red Wing,
1857

those who lived in rawer, smaller towns. Lawther's was built in 1857. A wing was added in 1870.

Back from the river, at the intersection of County Roads 0 and 7 in Eyota, just off the route between Winona and Rochester, Truman Mattison built a small, one-story octagon in the middle 1860s with a pile of barn siding he had accumulated, laying the planks vertically. It has since been shingled, and is now divided into two apartments.

In Clearwater there remains the shell of a grand octagon built in 1857 by Artemius Stevens. Stevens was the owner of timber tracts and a sawmill along the Clearwater River, and built his house in the center of a red cedar grove overlooking his property. Clearwater was as large as St. Cloud, proud of its hotels, its mills and factories. It has lost population and industry since, but has had the good fortune to lie across the Mississippi River from the main highway between St. Cloud and the Twin Cities and is a popular junction for those vacationers heading "up north" to the lakes region. As has been noted earlier, it contains a half-dozen structures of the 1850s clustering below the bluff as they did a century ago. Artemius Stevens built his house on

the prairie above. Isolated from its neighbors, it has been altered be-yond recovery.

The last of these Minnesota octagons, and the latest, is to be found three miles northwest of Granite Falls. Its owner in the 1960s, Mrs. Gladys Fredrickson, reported in a letter to the author that "it was built by a Mr. Holt between the years 1875 and 1879." Beyond this, local records are silent. Like most other octagons, it has acquired a variety of porches, bays, and projections over the years. Considering its com-fortable size and the marble fireplace which graces its sitting room, it seems likely that this was the house of a prosperous citizen, perhaps even of the Honorable Henry Hill, founder of the town, who built a sawmill there in 1872. He might have acquired a taste for octagons during his law school days in Ohio during the 1850s, or even in New Hampshire, where, according to the county chronicler, he received his "academical education." None of the reference works of the time speak of a "Mr. Holt" in Granite Falls in the 1870s, so it was probably "Hill." Anyway, octagons testify more of their evangelist, Orson Fowler, than of their owners. Wisconsin has made a monument of the Richards house in Watertown. Of the Minnesota houses inspired by Fowler's lectures and books, only the Lawther House in Red Wing and the Holt House near Granite Falls could still be salvaged intact.

Before turning to the influence of Louis Napoleon upon Minnesota residential architecture, however, we should examine a house superficially like those recommended by Fowler, built by another innovator similar in spirit and septuagenarian vigor. Whereas the octagon represented the adjustment of the circle to the requirements of carpenters and masons accustomed to working on flat planes, the Hurricane House of J. B. Johnson was the home of a man who adjusted very little to any convention and admired bees.

Johnson arrived in Osakis, Minnesota, from Illinois about 1855. He operated a general store, trading in "raw skins taken from local areas," and owned a grain elevator. Mrs. Johnson founded the first bank in Osakis, of which she later permitted her husband to become president. A local historian reports that "he and his wife rode a bicycle built for two when both were at an age that made this activity remarkable." In Osakis, townspeople inform passersby who inquire about a remarkable structure on the north side of Highway 52, that it was built by Mr. Johnson soon after the great tornado of 1886, that its interior framing is taken from the wooden tea boxes from his general store, and that the down-drooping corners were designed to present no sharp angles under which another tornado might catch up the house and fling it about. However, Mr. Johnson's nephew, Clyde W. Long of Lincoln, Nebraska, states that "the local name 'hurricane house' is a complete misnomer as it was never called that . . . it was not built or designed with the intent to resist a hurricane. Mr. Johnson was an ardent admirer of honey bees and always had an apiary in his yard. He enjoyed studying the habits of bees and undoubtedly got the idea for his six-sided rooms from the cells constructed by bees." The house was built on the block now occupied by the Osakis Public School, and was moved either once or twice before reaching its present location. It was certainly a great source of pride to the Johnsons: they reproduced a photograph of it on the checks prepared for their Bank of Osakis. These documents show the structure in its pristine condition before it acquired a single-story addition, like a bustle, to the rear, and before it was perforated by small windows on the upper story. Along the roofline there was a parapet. Pinnacles matched the pendants still remaining, emphasizing the vertical bays at the corners, two windows above and two below. Where the hurricane-proof corners bent down the siding followed, making a diagonal pattern giving variety to the conventional horizontal weatherboards running across the rectangular panels. This is a house which can readily be scorned by those whose interest runs toward pure derivations from accredited styles. It is no thing of beauty. But it manifests fertility of invention and freedom of expression, virtues which have validity quite apart from the things they produce. Like the octagon houses, it is a social document worthy of respect.

The few remaining houses in Minnesota built in the Second Empire style of Louis Napoleon are social documents of an entirely different sort. Their chief feature is the mansard roof, tilting up sharply from the cornices, then easing gently back into a lower pitch toward a peak or a short ridge line. Minnesota's last remaining full embodiment of the style in its full wedding-cake splendor with tiers of applied columns, porches, pediments, pilasters, and balconies, the Conrad Gotzian house in St. Paul, was destroyed in 1964. But mansarded houses were built in nearly every town which had men rich enough to afford them. At the time of its vogue (roughly 1862 to 1873) the style was known as "General Grant," despite the fact that the old warrior's own home in Galena, Illinois, built during this period, was not in "General Grant" style. Perhaps that term has some validity however, since it represents in architectural terms the Grant Administration and its chief beneficiaries who built in that style and who had grown rich during the Civil War, Cyrus McCormick and Jay Cooke.

The popularity of the style represented no mark of respect to General Grant. Instead it demonstrated the abandonment of architecture which, like the Greek revival, embodied American idealism, or, like the Gothic revival, manifested a respect for a long tradition of civility and learning. The mansard style showed clearly the colonial status of American architecture, deferring to European fashions however ugly and impractical. It was appropriate to an age of extravagance, which, having lost its bearings during the Civil War, substituted display for commitment to any durable standards.

The mansard was truly ceremonious as employed by the architects of Napoleon III in 1852 when they extended the Hotel de Ville and the Louvre, immense projects which amazed visiting Americans. Many were in Paris on the Grand Tour, spending the profits derived from the expansion of industry and sutlering during the Civil War. American architects had just begun to go to Paris for training, and they, too, were much impressed both with the upward-swelling grandeur of the mansard roof and its sculptural possibilities. It was exhilarating to consider the opening of another dimension for display.

To the layman, the mansard became the symbol of opulence and fashion. Cooke, the greatest capitalist of the age, built a mansard palace in 1866 (for a reported $2,000,000) at Ogontz, outside Philadelphia, to which his pensionaries from Minnesota, New York, and Chicago would repair for instruction and replenishment. It was Cooke who paid Ignatius Donnelly to "represent the working men of Duluth" by lobbying for the expansion of his Northern Pacific Railway. Cooke created the towns of Pine City, Long Branch, and Forest Lake along the route of his railroad and destroyed the towns of Chengwatona, Alhambra, Franconia, and a string of others long forgotten, by passing them by. Duluth, which proudly called itself "Jay Cooke's town" was once visited by this fabulous figure, who distributed dimes, nickels, and pennies to men, women, and children, in that order. He was the man to whom others would turn for example; after all, the government of the United States had put into his hands the financing of the extraordinary expenses of the Civil War, for a commission.

McCormick, whose reapers had replaced the men drawn from the farms to fight that war, put some of his vast profits into a grand mansard house which was the pride of Chicago.

The Second Empire style lasted until the middle 1870s. The causes of its decline are obvious: Bismark put his boot through the papier-mâché imperium of Napoleon III, leaving France to the short-lived Commune of 1870 and to the Third Republic, which lacked the glamour to set a style. The example of Cooke and his fellows was less attractive after the Panic of 1873 brought many of them down upon the heads of lesser men. Cooke's personal failure caused the bankruptcy of most of his Minnesota ventures: the population of Duluth dropped from 5,000 to 1,300, half its business firms closed their doors, and the city allowed its charter to lapse. Cooke's house showed America's architectural "colonialism," his career, Minnesota's economic "colonialism."

At its best, employed as a sculptured form atop a massive structure like Alexander Ramsey's house, the mansard roof style achieved something of the beetling grandeur of the buildings in Paris from which it derived its form. At its worst, it made small houses look like boys struggling to look out from beneath their fathers' hats. An example of this strenuous and unsuccessful effort toward monumentality is the house of Ivory McKusick, built at 504 North Second Street in Stillwater. McKusick was a member of a pioneer family in the area, and waxed

Ivory McKusick House, Stillwater, 1868

suddenly rich on Civil War contracts. Downriver, in Red Wing, Theodore B. Sheldon built one of the last of the mansard mansions, in 1875, at 805 Fourth Street. He had accumulated a fortune during the nineteen years he had spent in the prospering port city, transporting lumber and grain, trading in wheat, promoting railroads and banks. He was a leading citizen, proud of his own opulence and of the community he had helped to build, and he celebrated both in the materials he employed in his house. The roof was of colored slate and tile, the railings and drip-moldings of cast iron, and the walls of yellow brick, all locally produced. This testament to the man, and to the town, is now decaying.[2]

We can rejoice in those few builders who seemed to parody the architectural pretension of the lesser Napoleon as Offenbach parodied his politics. In Stillwater, Jacob Bean, partner in a thriving lumber business with Roscoe Hersey, had grown rich but kept deferring the erection of a fitting testimonial. His wife finally waited no longer and built for her own amusement a cottage which is the apotheosis of the mansard style. She intended it for the playhouse of the mansion they never built. It is known today as "Grandma Bean's playhouse," at 1224 South Third Street. At 415 South Garden in Lake City, there is another little house with the same antic spirit, wearing a borrowed mansard pulled down about its ears, windows crowned by heroic moldings, and a Lilliputian tower bearing aloft a triumphant television antenna. We have lost the name of its builder, who must have had a sense of humor.

8

Tory Style and American Picturesque

ARCHITECTURE AND ECONOMICS moved closely in concert in the last thirty years of the nineteenth century. Architecture always mirrors the images in the mind of a man; whether his thoughts are full of pomp or prayer, civic grandeur or domestic quiet, or simply of a profusion of things, architecture will shape itself to make solid and tangible what are, in the mind, bubbles of thought. In the years from 1870 to 1900, it seems that most men thought mostly of the things that money could buy. Faith no longer occupied their lives as it had in the Middle Ages, nor did Reason hold sway as it had among the thoughtful in the Age of the Enlightenment. The Romantic Era had intervened, emphasizing emotion and feeling, and the Civil War had shriveled romance in powder blast. Things, however, remained—the residue of life without reason, faith or feeling, and things are the materials of economy.

Men could focus upon them without distraction in these years; there was neither great war nor widespread famine, and a vast and fertile land was yielding its first abundant fruits. A long peace prevailed between 1865, the end of the American Civil War, and 1914, the beginning of a war which rended Europe's dynastic order. Minnesotans heard tales of Indian skirmishes over the western horizon and witnessed a few outbreaks within the state itself; a few participated in the quick and easy victory over Spain. But through these years, the energies of most people were occupied in getting or seeking to get rich.

Professional architects were virtually unknown in the state, and therefore there were few of the distortions which borrowed images and academic preconceptions would later introduce. Some immigrants during this period still persisted in their native traditions, but most were caught up in the great confident American tide, abandoning nativism for the extravagant fashions of the day. A few Yankees, particularly in their St. Croix Valley enclave, still built chaste, white, clapboarded houses, but, in the end, they too joined in the onrush of the picturesque. Since human character in Minnesota in these three decades was predominantly materialist, architecture showed little else than a celebration of materials and a delight in the accumulation of details.

Though the progress of the economy was not a long, unbroken, upward sweep, it moved in an upward-tilted sawtooth. There was the precipitate fall into the Panic of 1873, then a slow recovery followed by an accelerating boom which broke in 1892, and then another collapse. In architecture, the early years of despondency and dependency (or as it was called in the last chapter, "colonialism") called forth still another imitative fashion, the Tory style. As prosperity and confidence returned, the elements of this style were torn away in a carnival spirit, combined, recombined, multiplied, and varied in wilder and wilder whirling circles. All the architectural attics of the world were pillaged for oddments to add to fancy dress costumes tirelessly invented for a dance of prosperity in a festival of materialism.

This was the general history of the years from 1870 to 1900, but, of course, neither life nor architecture moves by dull, drilled sequence from event to event, everywhere at once; in this period some areas of the state were still depressed and colonial while others were gaily independent and celebrating their prosperity. Nonetheless a certain sequence can be observed, first in the progress of the economy and then in architecture.

In the 1860s and 1870s, Minnesota was still culturally and economically a colony. Its colonial elite looked for capital, for canons of conduct, and for fashions in architecture to the Eastern Seaboard and to Europe. When a chief repository of this trust, Jay Cooke, fell from the ranks of the rich and impeccable in 1873, Minnesota's economy, which had been heavily dependent upon his ventures, received a heavy blow. Already this generation had been struck by the Dakota War and by the Civil War; in the 1870s depression was accompanied by a succession of natural disasters. There was the grasshopper plague of 1877 and in the next year, the rust and blight. 1878 was also the year when nearly half the milling capacity of Minneapolis was lost in the explosion of the Washburn A Mill. Wheat production in 1877 and 1878 practically stopped. The price of wheat had already fallen from $1.50 a bushel in 1866 to less than $.80 in 1870 and average yields from 22 bushels an acre in the 1860s to 9.61 in 1876, as the soil of the older wheat-growing areas showed signs of exhaustion. The railroads were crippled: just 7.5 miles of track were laid in the panic year of 1873; 350 had been laid in the previous year, before the fall of Cooke. In 1874, only 40 miles were laid; 10 in 1875; 29.5 in 1876.

But after a pause, the upswing came quickly. James J. Hill threw his prodigious energies into railroading in 1878, pacified the Dutch investors who controlled the St. Paul and Pacific Railroad, took the road from bankruptcy to net earnings of a million dollars in 1879, and a decade later it was across the Rockies. It reached Seattle, 1,816 miles from St. Paul, in 1893. Hill's peer, the titan among the millers of Minneapolis, Cadwallader C. Washburn, rebuilt his A Mill and restored its capacity in a year. By 1880, production had doubled, and in 1882 Minneapolis became the leading flour-milling center in the United States. Refinements in milling had proven that Minnesota spring wheat could be ground into flour fit for human consumption, and the Scandinavians who were pouring ashore in New York and Philadelphia were not deterred by bugs or blight from heading westward toward the wheat lands. The six Red River Valley counties grew in population from 21,000 to 71,000 in the decade after 1879. Minneapolis burst its seams; from 47,000 people in 1880 it became a city of 165,000 in 1890; real estate brokers were in a state of euphoria; three of them did $4.3 million in business in 1880 and they were joined by fifty-one new colleagues to do $27 million annually just three years later.

Lumber built the houses the farmers needed; lumber provided shelter for the inrushing city dwellers. St. Paul grew too, not so much as Minneapolis: from 41,000 to 133,000 in the decade during which the two cities often consumed more than 200 million board feet of lumber a year. In 1887 Minneapolis consumed 6 million feet of lumber to build sixty miles of boardwalk. Thomas E. Tallmadge put it: "The forest died giving birth to the city." Out on the treeless prairie, sidings would fill up with fresh lumber and it would be gone in a week; the railroads themselves were built over wood—more wood in trestles and ties than steel. In 1890 a single trestle at Two Medicine Pass in Montana took 2 million feet. Grain elevators were going up, as typical of the Midwest as

Crusader's castles in Lebanon: the Peavey Company, for its grain storage, filed a single order for 2.5 million board feet from Bovey and De-Laittre of Minneapolis.

These were the boom days along the St. Croix, in the downriver mill towns like Winona and Dubuque, Hannibal, Clinton, and Rock Island, and, increasingly, beside the Falls of St. Anthony. There, early in the decade, Minneapolis became the world's largest market for lumber as well as flour milling. In 1879, for the first time, a million logs went down the St. Croix. In 1890, 452 million feet swung down that great sluice past Stillwater; after that, the cut declined until the last boom went down in August 1914.

The architectural expression of the gloomy, early years of the period was the Tory style, brought to the attention of the public or those of the public who had time and resources enough for fair-going, at the Philadelphia Centennial Exposition of 1876. Though the Exposition was to celebrate American independence, in architecture it showed instead how dependent we still remained.

The Centennial Exposition was America's first World's Fair, and things were done on a grand scale. Philadelphia, which had only recently been the capital of Jay Cooke's ruined empire, recovered itself to welcome the people of the provinces and established a new style. Machinery Hall, the center of attention, covered four times as much ground as St. Peter's in Rome, and, of the thousand paintings which filled the fifteen rooms of the Art Building, those which drew the crowds and took the prizes were vast landscapes by Thomas Cole, Albert Bierstadt, Thomas Hill, Frederick Church, and others of the group we now call the Hudson River School. There was a tragic quality in this admiration for sunsets and glens and clear mountain lakes, for scenes of rainbows viewed by appreciative stags and mountain sheep. Though Fairmount Park which surrounded the Exposition was bosky and green, down below the Schuylkill River was already polluted with industrial waste. The Hudson itself was lined with scraggly mill towns and the tracks of railroads which threw clinkers, trash, and soot into the glens. In faraway St. Paul, Trout Brook, below farmer Dayton's Bluff, had begun to poison cattle, and where it ran into Lowertown, it was so foul that adjoining property owners were moving out. The shores of the upper St. Croix, once as beautiful as the Hudson, looked like a battlefield, strewn with stumps and slash; it was "lumbered out."

Landscape painting in the 1870s depicted a vanishing wilderness. The artists were conjuring up dreams of America's youth.

The flight of city people to the seaside resorts, which was a corollary of the artists' interest in unspoiled landscape, had led to the discovery of old colonial towns. *Harpers Magazine* followed the vacationers to these vestiges of preindustrial America and reported on such places as Newburyport, Newport, East Hampton, Marblehead, and Portsmouth in a series of nostalgic articles. Several of the states rediscovered their arcadian villages thought of sending seventeenth-century houses to the fair but rejected the idea, presumably on grounds of economy. Although one of the Centennial Exposition's most popular exhibits was a kitchen of 1776, in the 1870s Americans were not quite prepared for a "colonial revival." Their own past did not seem a worthy source from which to dig architectural precedents; their backward impulse took them toward the seventeenth century. They were not yet sure enough of themselves to abandon European precedent and seek in the American vernacular a tradition worth emulating.

The Philadelphia Centennial popularized a revival of the architecture of the seventeenth and eighteenth centuries, but it was not the "salt box" or "Cape Cod cottage," but instead, the vernacular of the English counties of Surrey and Sussex where, in that period, a picturesque transition style (like the Italian villa and, to some extent, the mansard) which developed out of the morganatic marriage of bucolic medievalism and the aristocratic urbanity of the Renaissance during the reigns of the Tudors and the early Stuart kings. It was half Gothic and half Classic, appearing without plan as manor houses grew, addition by addition, in picturesque disarray, during a long period of stylistic indecision. In Victorian England, the fashionable architect, R. Norman Shaw, had designed a number of rambling country houses reviving this manner of building, which were much admired both in England and in America. (Shaw later developed a style reviving the severe, urbane, symmetrical early Georgian which had been current in England in the reigns of Queen Anne and George I. By a curious, uncritical retroactivity, his earlier, informal country house manner came to be known as Queen Anne, a term which then was to be diffused to cover the whole gamut of picturesque architecture which grew out of it. The term is misleading and obsolete, and were it not so widely employed it would deserve a footnote rather than a parenthesis.)

Shaw's early country houses used false half-timbering, a grid of timbers separated by decorated plaster, richly carved (or pargetted), often over a solid brick wall. They were also characterized by steep roofs, tall clumped chimneys, decorated bargeboards, and vast expanses of looming gables, often hung with slate scales. His work was widely known in America through such publications as *Building News*. In 1869, Alexander J. Cassatt, president of the Pennsylvania Railroad, built a Shavian house on the "Main Line." In 1874, Henry H. Richardson produced his own variant of the theme with his Watts Sherman house at Newport, Rhode Island, and, two years later, the British themselves erected two buildings to house their delegates on the Philadelphia Exposition grounds which brought the style to the attention of thousands who were searching for an ancient manner akin to their own colonial but bearing a proper European pedigree. American efforts to work variations upon Shaw's revival of the Sussex vernacular were so associated with the Philadelphia observance of America's independence, and were such an ironic commentary on the nation's continued cultural colonialism that it seems just to call it the Tory style.

The *American Builder* reviewed these structures fulsomely and concluded with the hope "that the next millionaire who puts up a cottage at Long Branch will adopt this style, and he will have house ample enough to entertain a Prince, yet exceedingly cozy, cool in summer, and yet abundantly warm in winter, plain enough, and yet capable of the highest ornamental development." Millionaires in a dozen Long Branches sprang to their checkbooks. One who was wealthy enough to adopt this style was Henry Shipman. We know nothing about him except that he arrived in St. Paul in 1877, that he came with ample resources, that he departed again in 1883 having found, it is said, that the climate was not so salubrious as advertised. While he was in the city he began building a house in the Philadelphia Exposition style, at 445 Summit Avenue. It is Minnesota's most perfect specimen of the Spirit of '76—1876. A Tory spirit it was, celebrating the centennial of political independence from Great Britain by adopting what the *American Builder* called "the national architecture of Great Britain." High on the front gable are the slate scales which British houses had employed to keep the weather off lightly plastered surfaces between timbers and which Shaw had made a hallmark of his early style; Richardson, in Newport, had initiated the American practice of replacing them with wood shingles, but the mysterious Mr. Shipman (and real estate speculator Herman Greve, who completed the house) apparently was intent upon authenticity. A native touch (following Richardson's lead) was added by substituting blocks of yellow limestone for the brick Shaw generally employed in his lower floors.

The porches and the interiors show another influence which Americans first encountered in Philadelphia but had long been at work in England, the domestic architecture of Japan. In Europe, Japanese art had been inspiring painters as various as James McNeill Whistler, Henri de Toulouse-Lautrec, and Paul Gauguin since the 1860s. Japanese wallpapers were being sold by Jeffry and Co., and Anglo-Japanese furniture by William Watt. W. Eden Nesfield, Shaw's partner, had made use of Japanese decorative motifs in his country houses. In Philadelphia, the Japanese themselves appeared, contributing a "typical" house

Henry Shipman–Herman Greve House, St. Paul, 1883

and a Bazaar which caused a sensation. Geometrically carved screens and latticework immediately began to appear on American verandahs and in the Shipman-Greve house these are particularly emphasized by carved panels over doorways. Vincent Scully reports that at the Japanese house at the Centennial Exposition there was "a bird . . . handsomely carved in bas-relief on the wooden panel between the top of the front door and the overhanging porch." In Mr. Shipman's house each major room is introduced by a carved sign: the mahogany-paneled library by an owl in foliage, the dining room by golden oak fruits, carved fowls dangling in readiness for plucking over the passage to the kitchen and a lyre over the doorway to the music room (which was remodeled in the ivory and gold Louis XVI style a few years later, possibly by the mysterious genius, Harvey Ellis, of whom more will be said in a subsequent chapter). The stair hall is lit by a great window of stained glass, composed of birds and foliage in soft colors (subtler than the hard, clear jewel glass of later years) and the stairway itself winds down in the same grand, open manner as Richardson's for the Watts Sherman house in Newport, Rhode Island.

A fresh look at the exterior of this distinguished house reveals another aspect more Japanese than Shavian. Except on one of the gables, the false half-timbers are not laid in Shaw's characteristic diagonal or curving patterns (which emphasized not structure but the shapes of the areas upon which they are imposed). Instead, they assert a rectilinear pattern, a grid or basket. Here was the statement of structure in an abstract but direct way; it did not actually support anything but it showed that, underneath, there was a grid of lumber which supported the exterior sheath. In the Japanese tradition, structure—actual skeleton structure—showed clearly, for paper panels which made up walls were set between wooden frames. While the Shipman-Greve house does not present true half-timbering, it does suggest in a rectilinear way that the successor to half-timbering, the balloon frame, is at work underneath, just as Japanese houses showed how they were built in rectangles of wood.

There were very few structures built in Minnesota which so clearly demonstrated the influence of the Philadelphia Exposition as the Shipman house, and most of those which appear in the building magazines of the time have long since been pulled down. They were in residential neighborhoods in the larger cities where their owners could walk to work, and they have been overwhelmed by the expansion of commercial property. Until 1965, Linden Place in Minneapolis still contained two, in collapsing condition, and Virginia Avenue, just off Summit Avenue in St. Paul possesses two examples, both considerably altered.

There are, however, a succession of houses which show the loosening of the Shavian Tory pattern as it was whirled about, faster and faster, by the increasing pace of prosperity and exuberance in the late 1870s and 1880s and, finally, its breaking apart at the end of that period as its elements flew off and pursued careers of their own, in combination with exotic elements and in strange, disproportionate recombinations with their old partners. The decomposition of the Tory style occurred during a time of carnival spirits, when its sober traditionalism no longer satisfied either the amateurs and the master carpenters who designed nearly all of Minnesota's houses, or the small but swelling group of professionally trained architects whose influence was beginning to be felt.

It is a curiosity of Minnesota's architectural development how frequently her architects returned to false half-timbering; beetling gables; clustered, high chimneys; and banks of leaded-glass windows. Cass Gilbert, who by then was building the revived Federal style or whatever Renaissance fashion was current, returned to the Old English cottage for his own house at One Heather Place in St. Paul, about 1890. Clarence H. Johnston and Harry W. Jones worked the lode again fifteen years later, and a score of able architects came back to it again in the 1920s, lining Summit Avenue between Lexington Avenue and the Mississippi River in St. Paul, the residential hills of Rochester, and the escarpment above Duluth with quaint, half-timbered houses. It was as if the Tory style were dying like a fever, in weaker and weaker spasms, until it ceased about 1930.

But that fashion for picturesque Shavian manor houses of the rather gloomy sort made popular at the Philadelphia Exposition began to pull apart almost as soon the Shipman-Greve house was completed. Part of the decomposition was due to the absence of professional architects who might have been somewhat concerned with consistency of style, but much of the centrifugal force was generated by a popular desire for extravagance and drama in architecture which the relative sobriety of the Tory style could not provide.

This trend was illustrated at 506 Eighth Street South in Moorhead, the center of the fruitful wheat farming of the Red River Valley. There, in 1883, Solomon Comstock built a Tory-style house which had been designed for him by Kees and Fisk of Minneapolis. It displays false half-timbering, steep roofs, and clustered chimneys. In its original form, which can be observed in old photographs, it implied its wooden frame and its wooden sheathing in contrasting colors, an effect which has been bleached out by its recent paintings in monochrome. It has had some remodelings, too, but not enough to rob it of the confident, almost truculent demeanor which it had when it was the showplace of the three-state area in which Comstock's word was potent. Solomon Comstock was born in Argyle, Maine, in 1842. He graduated from the Law School of the University of Michigan in 1869, moved west, and became county attorney of the then virtually vacant Clay County in 1871, the year the Northern Pacific Railroad reached Moorhead. With the railroad came a flow of settlers; the population more than trebled in the late 1870s and 1880s. Comstock very early saw the importance of tapping the region with railroad spur lines and colonizing the prairie with people who would then ship agricultural products out and trade goods in. This was the sort of man who appealed to James J. Hill, and when Solomon Comstock came to St. Paul to represent his constituency in the state legislature in 1876, he and Hill established a close working relationship. By 1888 he was engaged in locating town sites for the Great Northern Railroad and was "interested in locating and promoting" eight in North Dakota and several in Montana. His hometown of Moorhead sent Comstock to the United States Congress in 1888, but according to a local historian, he was too important in townsite development to remain long in Washington and soon returned to his labors in the northern plains. He was the most significant political and economic figure in the Red River area, barring of course, James J. Hill himself and Norman Kittson, Hill's early partner, who was aging in the 1880s and tended to be less of a factor in the affairs of the region. Comstock's house, looming above all others in the town, is his memorial. It is now a state historic site managed by the Minnesota Historical Society, restored and open for guided tours.

In Duluth, cadenzas were performed on the Tory theme with great verve and skill by a gifted architect named I. Vernon Hill. Probably his finest work is a home at 2220 East Superior Street which he built for his own use about 1902. After his death in 1904 it was sold to Pentecost Mitchell, manager and, later, president of the Oliver Iron Mining Company.

It has a beetling gable above a beveled bay, a roof cascading past other gables and out onto a curved buttress. Some of Frank Lloyd Wright's earliest houses in Oak Park, Illinois, have roofs like this, and there is something, too, of the spirit of Norse stave churches in these

I. Vernon Hill House, Duluth, 1902

Duluth houses. Vernon Hill died in his thirties, before his work had crystalized into a personal style, but another of his youthful houses at 2306 East Superior was executed in 1901 for F. A. Patrick by Fawcett and Pearson, contractors. Here the front gable is split, for variety, and the roof slides down to the porch roof supported by a broad stone arch. Duluth has many interesting Tory-style houses; there is one, with a particularly pleasant sheltered bay of windows on the second floor, at 2210 East Superior built in 1905 for F. E. House.

In the work of I. Vernon Hill, and of most of the leading architects of this period, the chief focus of interest was the expanse of the gable. It provided a surface upon which the architect, carver, plasterer, and carpenter could display their talents. What began as an attribute of the Tory style of 1876 became, in the hands of Bruce Price, McKim, Mead and White, and Frank Lloyd Wright, one of the archtypes of American architecture: an ornamented triangle.[1] Observe, if you will, some Minnesota examples.

If one walks to the side of the house Clarence H. Johnston remodeled in the late 1880s for Charles P. Noyes's partner, E. H. Cutler, at 360 Summit Avenue in St. Paul, one passes a series of angular projections and bays and then comes upon a huge paneled gable with three varieties of shingling and strong carved brackets. It was the work of Leroy Buffington and designed shortly after the Greve house. The gable alone, taken from a plan he prepared for Mr. Cutler in 1882, was added to an earlier house, which Johnston remodeled again—around the gable.

A more craggy gable was presented as the prime attraction of the mansion built by railroad contractor Donald W. Grant at Sixth Street North and Third Avenue in Faribault in 1890. Grant used Faribault as a base for far-ranging ventures, including vast reaches of farmland. His house was designed by J. Walter Stevens of St. Paul, and was described by a Faribault newspaper as follows: "Gables project to the south, east and west . . . [and are] provided with oriole windows [sic] fitted with colored glass. A front gable is furnished with ornamental shingles and dove cote windows. . . . There is very little of a gaudy or 'gingerbread' style of ornamentation, but the general effect is rich and substantial. . . ."

The neighborhood of the Stevens house in Rushford is a museum of variously decorated gables, all of them of the style of the last two decades of the century, except that Gothic veteran and its cousin the Parker house. A comparison of the true Gothic revival and the American Picturesque is there more clearly presented than anywhere else in the region. George Stevens built quaintly but quietly, in accordance with a language of symbols bespeaking an ideology; on the other hand, the high wooden houses of the 1880s have no ideological content. They are pleasant, hollow, and a little noisy.

Admirers of the picturesque gable find it at its best amid the pandemonium of the 1880s, in such examples as the great red wooden house of Albert J. Lammers at Marsh and Third Streets in Stillwater. Its giant surfaces display an extravagance of woodcarving. It seems probable that the work was done by Scandinavians, for along the roofline are the upswept dragon heads of a Viking ship. The Lammers house celebrates wood, as it should, since it was built in 1889 when Stillwater was in the midst of its lumber boom.

The emphasis upon large gables as billboards for the skills of the building trades was one of the chief elements of the Tory style, persisting throughout the 1880s and early 1890s. The articulation of structure—basketry—was the other. The Sussex vernacular, in the hands of Norman Shaw, and the Japanese vernacular were the primary contributors to the fashion for basketry during the earliest, integrated phase of the Tory style. As Toryism loosened into the picturesque, the American vernacular joined in and imported a pattern providing some unity to architecture in the 1880s and early 1890s.

Vincent Scully has pointed out that since the 1840s, Americans had been articulating structure over the entire surface of houses. Coining the term "stick style" to describe houses built in this way, he described them thus: "Asymmetrical and free in plan, varied in massing, the wooden houses disseminated by the pattern books of the mid-century were distinguished most of all by the articulation of their thin wooden members and by the skeletal qualities derived from their frames."

In Minnesota, probably because a sub-Arctic climate did not encourage thin, articulated walls for year-round homes, the popularity of this stick style was largely limited to lakeside houses, appearing only occasionally in city dwellings. One example remains as it appeared before it was cosmopolitanised by Tory and Japanese elements, a summer cottage built in 1879 at 303 Lake Avenue in White Bear Lake. Charles P. Noyes, a patron of Cass Gilbert's most refined academism for his city residence, acquired this picturesque house soon after it was built. (Next door was a similar cottage, now vanished, erected by Governor William R. Merriam.) By the lakeside, Noyes enjoyed a genial life in this red wooden house under a long-sloping green roof, with a two-story living room surrounded by a balcony and lit by plates of colored glass set in an oriel window. That window, on the exterior, is sheltered by a decorative wooden truss and a carved plate which emphasizes the easy curve of the gable. The rooms to the side are low and pleasant, beneath exposed beams. This cottage is one of the last of its kind, and it deserves preservation as an example of one of the most uninhibited and cheerful periods of American architecture.

The stick style, working together with Tory and Japanese elements, contributed an element of continuity to the American tradition, as well as an element of unity to the composition of domestic architecture as the 1880s went forward. Builders who quailed at the elaborate artifice of half-timbering could get something of the same effect by employing broad wooden members to mark, against an exterior wall, the boundaries between interior spaces. Boards could be set at second-floor level, and, below, in parallel, at the first-floor ceiling level. They could indicate the framing of windows and the occurrence of interior partitions. As the decoration of projections and bays became more picturesque and elaborate, as carving and spindles, lattices and shingles, dormers and gables, molding and false pargeting encrusted surfaces, simple rectilinear members formed units to impart scale and afford repose to an eye wearied by all this activity.

Scale and repose were qualities badly needed in the architectural carnival of the 1880s. The structural capacities of wood had been learned, and never had its decorative possibilities been so happily exploited. Everywhere could be seen the carpenter's delight in structure and carving—a delight manifested in monumental form in the home of Rudolph McBurnie at 259 West Wabasha in Winona. McBurnie had good reason to be pleased with lumber. He had been manager of the great Laird-Norton Company and was one of the Winona representatives in the Mississippi Lumber Company syndicate formed by Frederick Weyerhaeuser in 1893 to purchase timberlands covering a large enough expanse of Wisconsin and Minnesota to ensure a supply to the downriver mills and fix prices. The McBurnie house, probably built in 1886, was distinguished not only for its "basketry" but for the carved panels between.

Another example of the imposition of a stick-style grid upon a picturesque form is the house Mayor Jacob Austin of Fergus Falls built in 1883 astride his real estate holdings on Guttenburg Heights. Austin refined away extravagances from the Italian villa style, truncated its campanile, and inserted before his door a small polygonal porch. The basketry of the stick style is there to remind the viewer of its balloon frame.

The late 1880s were a strutting time, accelerating in confidence and prosperity. If houses in its earlier years clearly showed the hand of the carpenter, in the last years, before the Panic of 1893, many look as if they had been designed by a confectioner. At 275 Harriet in Winona is a shining, extravagant, white palace typical of those years, in a location which tells a good deal about the history of the area. First on that corner there had been the house of the early land speculator and railroad promoter William Windom, who was a U.S. representative, then a U.S. senator, then secretary of the treasury under Presidents Garfield and Benjamin Harrison. After Windom moved to New York in 1883, his house was torn down and replaced by a grander dwelling for railroad operator John Blunt. When, in 1890, W. A. Hodgins was ready to celebrate his prosperity, he tore down the Blunt house, hired the architect Charles G. Maybury, personally selected the lumber, and erected an apotheosis of residential timber. His firm, Youmans Brothers and Hodgins, had milled the lumber which was floated down from the Chippewa and St. Croix, and had very early perceived the importance

W. A. Hodgins House, Winona, 1890

of the "line yards" established along the sidings of the new railroad pushing westward from Winona which supplied building material to the towns rising on the prairie. After Hodgins's death, his widow sold the house to a lumberman turned financier, William Pliney Tearse (whose initials led to his being known as "White Pine" Tearse by many). One who observes only the lower story might think it a fairly conventional white frame mansion. But the second and third stories make up a joyous encampment of towered and gabled pavilions, some enclosed by shingle, some opening in arcades. Turrets are sliced below their caps to admit windows, leaving teetering cones above, and slender posts surmount the peaks, ready for pennants. The entire concatenation is united around a central chimney stack, whose brickwork catches the upward thrust of all the other components.

With the Hodgins-Tearse house we come into the presence of the final phase of the American Picturesque style, which abandoned all formal precedent to assemble a loose, exultant combination of whatever oddments might please the owner or the builder. It was the outward sign of an interior disorder which some critics might think wanton and vulgar, but which represented the character of its owner far more clearly than do the architect-designed and decorator-filled aseptic containers inhabited by many people today. Everyman had his own Smithsonian, into which the attic overflowed. Rooms bore on their tasseled tablecloths whatever their owners were collecting at the time. The living room of one of the most pleasant of these houses, the Pennsylvania mountain retreat of the great conservationist Gifford Pinchot had a twenty-foot war canoe on one wall; Barbizon School paintings on another; spears, rifles, and etchings on a third; and books everywhere. Theodore Roosevelt's house at Sagamore Hill, on Long Island, was much the same; it may have been a mess, but it was his mess, and not that of a hired arbiter of taste. The same could be said for many Minnesota houses of the picturesque period; they were not very beautiful but they were interesting and varied. Their inhabitants were acquisitive. They were energetic. So, in a real sense, were their houses. And, for the while, they were uninhibited by academic tut-tutting.

When traveling Americans discovered the Taj Mahal or the masterpieces of Saracen architecture in Spain, and found that they could not be bought, they reproduced parts of them at home or, to put the matter more precisely, they added Saracen details to their collections. The

Moorish window or balcony, which can be identified by an inverted horseshoe arch, was featured on the wooden house of brewer Otto Schell in New Ulm, near his brewery. The same ornament festoons a humbler house which was moved from Park Avenue in Minneapolis to 2500 Portland, in the same city, about 1898. It has two Bedouin tents, stained glass, and a small balcony for the muezzin. The seraglio and gazebo added by Mrs. Henry Lamberton to the Huff mansion in Winona (see chapter 6) may have suggested a similar gazebo to the unknown builder of a house at the south end of Main Street in Lanesboro which has oriental pavilions and a tower-like Tamburlain's helmet, bearing aloft the horn of a unicorn.

Southern Minnesota can boast no more enthralling museum of the devices of those years than the house of George W. Taylor, built in 1890 at Second and Bridge Streets in Le Sueur. Taylor was born in Toronto

George W. Taylor House, Le Sueur, 1890

in 1840, orphaned at three, and became independent at nine. He came to Le Sueur in 1865, was employed as a clerk in a dry goods store, married the daughter of the proprietor of a competing emporium, joined his father-in-law in 1877, and bought him out in 1893. He was a stockholder in the Farmers' Bank and one of the early presidents of the Minnesota Valley Canning Company. His house was rescued from neglect by Werner Heinsohn, who repaired it, restoring its great stained-glass windows and its vast expanses of carved woods. The exterior is decorated by molded panels and cross-hatched siding, portcullisses under false gables, hammer-trusses supporting nothing, brackets, grids, and crockets.

Earlier houses were frequently given a new screen of decoration during this period, new dormers, new bays, new spindled porches. Gothic houses lent themselves to such modernization most readily: the house built in the 1850s at Government Road and Plateau Street in Taylors Falls by an early surveyor named Royal C. Gray was exploded in the picturesque period into projections and bays, and given a new porch. One suspects that the same treatment was given a much earlier Gothic house by Nicollet County Probate Judge Henry Moll on Washington Street in St. Peter. Moll, a small, spare man with elliptical steel glasses, manifested again the propensity of literary men for the Gothic style. The son of a harnessmaker, he went to work for F. A. Donahower in one of the retail establishments that St. Peter's dominant banker had acquired. Moll was elected city marshal in 1881. Ten years later, he successfully campaigned for sheriff; in 1888, he opened a bookstore and in 1902 was elected judge of probate court. Probably during his period as a purveyor of literature he added an array of steeples, spindles, towers, shingles, and porches to the earlier house. Only the Gothic gable peeps out from above this froth, nearly engulfed, but still reminding the viewer of an earlier and somewhat less extravagant era.

At the end of this period came a group of picturesque mansions, stylistic smorgasbords, tossed salads of oddments from many periods and styles. Their walls were frequently of soft red sandstone carved into fantastic shapes, but architects of the time were unafraid to mix stone with brick and terra-cotta. The greatest designer of these houses, and probably the greatest architectural intelligence to work in Minnesota in the nineteenth century, was Harvey Ellis. His mansions for Fred C. Pillsbury and Samuel C. Gale in Minneapolis, and for John L. Merriam in St. Paul, have all been destroyed, but admirers of his work can still see it in nondomestic form in the Taintor Memorial civic center in Menomonie, Wisconsin, and two buildings at the University of Minnesota: Pillsbury Hall and Nicholson Hall. No design drawings have been found of the mansion of George W. Van Dusen, at 1900 LaSalle, in Minneapolis, but it might be attributed to Ellis stylistically and by his very close associations with its architects of record, Orff and Jorelmann. It has much in common with his remaining domestic work in St. Joseph, Missouri, and Rochester, New York.

The Van Dusen house is composed of heavy masonry, but not the red sandstone in Richardsonian forms which Ellis had used in the 1880s. It employs blocks of pink Luverne jasper, sculpted into the rough suggestion of an early Renaissance French chateau, but as is true of Ellis's work, it is really a free, imaginative evocation of a dream castle, building upward, higher and higher from gable to turret to spire and then to a huge chimney stack. Ellis was a vagrant draftsman who drifted from one architectural office to another in the Upper Midwest from 1884 to 1893, and readers whose curiosity about his erratic genius is piqued by the Van Dusen house may want to read something more of him in the Fall 1966 issue of *Minnesota History*.

The picture books of the 1880s (like *Picturesque St. Paul*, published in that city in 1890) contain dozens of huge stone piles, assembled of various styles and looking like ruins from the moment of their completion. They were more scenery than housing. They were built to amaze the beholder and remind him of the wealth of the inhabitants. Many have fallen before the wrecker's ball, have become institutionalized, or have taken in boarders. Kitchenettes occupy closets, drawing rooms are partitioned, woodwork has been painted, and frescoes covered with wallpaper. Even those which are sustained as single family residences have often been amputated down to practical sizes. Summit Avenue in St. Paul displays the state's largest collection, possibly because St. Paul has remained prosperous enough to maintain them but not so prosperous as to tear them down for replacement.

The character of these houses which sets them apart from the international styles which preceded them and the decorous and academic fashions which dominated the scene in the 1890s was their unrepentant individuality. They were gaudy, perhaps, but never dull. They set forth the confidence of a generation which had tamed a vio-

*George W. Van Dusen
House, Minneapolis,
1893*

lent climate and a recalcitrant terrain. And they did not take themselves too seriously. Playfulness is part of the spirit of the 1880s and in some places, for special reasons, it persisted as late as the First World War. Two final examples of that playful, prideful spirit may serve to illustrate not only this period and its temper, but also the problems which are posed by an effort which too earnestly pursues the power of influences. The first example is found in Minneapolis, the second in Fergus Falls.

Swan J. Turnblad (born Sven Manson) came to America with his parents when he was eight years old, settled in Vasa, Minnesota, and changed his name while he was in high school. He purchased a flagging Swedish-language newspaper in Minneapolis and built it into a flourishing journal with broad distribution. In 1910, he completed a mansion at 2600 Park Avenue in Minneapolis which cost $1.5 million and made it clear to the Anglo-American and German-American nabobs whose houses had lined that street since the 1880s that the Swedes had arrived. It contains twenty-three rooms within walls of smooth grey limestone. It was, and is, a proclamation, not a restoration of anything Swedish. It seems likely that Turnblad intended that it would ultimately become what it is now—the American Swedish Institute, a center for Swedish culture in the region—but it was too late to draw unselfconsciously upon Swedish nativism. Instead, it is the house of a wealthy Swedish American, housing many precious Swedish heirlooms, but like most other mansions of the time it cannot be fixed on the architectural map. The architects were not Swedish: Christopher A. Boehme was born in Minneapolis in 1865 and had been joined in partnership by the Polish-born Victor Cordella. Donald Torbert, who has studied the house carefully, suggests it is a potpourri of details from many sources and that the "decorative treatment of the tower machicolations would suggest that the primary source of inspiration for the design lay in the sixteenth century mannered Gothic manor-houses of Poland and the Baltic region where architect Cordella was educated."

The interior of the building is full of Swedish items: there are carved Viking figures supporting the great hall fireplace (the carver was a Pole, Albin Polasek) and one of Turnblad's favorite paintings in the National Museum in Stockholm is reproduced in Swedish stained glass on the stair landing. (It depicts the "Sacking of Visby" as if it were a visit by a trade mission.) Many of the rooms have Swedish porcelain stoves, Swedish rugs cover the floors, and the major rooms are paneled and furnished with an opulence which might have been seen in a very eclectic Swedish nobleman's house of a generation or two earlier. Turnblad, his wife, and daughter did not live very long in the house; it was large and expensive and not very cozy. They finally moved to an apartment across the street. One could be reminded of Lord Chesterfield's famous lines about the mansion of General Wade: "As the General could not live in it to his ease, he had better take a house over against it and look

at it." In Turnblad's case, the house was probably never intended for a dwelling, but as a testament and, possibly, as the achievement of the childhood dream of Sven Manson to own a castle.

The Norwegians dissolved into American society more readily than the Swedes. They occasionally remained together in their own communities, but often joined the polyglot population of the lumber camps long enough to earn enough to purchase a farm. There is a strong possibility that Norwegians, who knew well how to work in wood and had for centuries substituted carving and shingling for color in their own wind-buffeted villages, may have contributed to the emphasis upon wooden ornament in Minnesota's residential architecture of the 1870s and 1880s, but a task force of doctorate applicants would be required to establish that possibility as a theorem. Nonetheless, houses like the marvelously carven Lammers house on Third and Marsh Streets in Stillwater, where Scandinavian wood-carvers worked, can be happily scrutinized by laymen with some knowledge of Norse ornament.

But influence-seeking is perilous. The casual classifier would be easily deceived by the Clement house at 604 Burlington Street in Fergus Falls. Clearly Norse in spirit, like a stave church, it rises in a succession of heavy, roofed masses to a tower which itself bears a steep, shingled roof in two stages: the first the short, projecting pent roof common in Norway (to shed water from the wall), and the second at the top, bearing a spire. Carved wooden panels repeat the pattern of the windows, and the walls are covered with alternating shingles and siding. The porches are decorated with an angular fringe like a raised portcullis, unlike the scroll-saw work of most American houses of the time. Yet there is no evidence that the house was touched by a Scandinavian hand and, despite appearances, it was not a product of the 1880s. The occupant in the 1970s, Mrs. Wendell Huber, writes that it was built in 1870 by a Yankee master carpenter for his own use. "Charles C. Clement was an early settler of English origin who came from Lowell, Massachusetts . . . a carpenter by trade, his granddaughter has in her possession a walnut box lined with velvet which she said was his graduation thesis from his status as apprentice . . . to master carpenter. . . . Most of the wood used was white pine and believed to have been obtained locally; however, wood used in the fireplaces and circular stairway was likely imported."

Swan J. Turnblad House,
Minneapolis, 1903-10

Charles C. Clement House, Fergus Falls, 1870

The Clement house was built ahead of its time by a man who was serving a personal whim; the Turnblad house arose after its time because its builder had come late upon the scene and wanted to mark his presence in a way which could not be ignored. This full-throated individualism became rare after 1893. It modulated into a new decorum, very restrained, very conscious of precedent, and representative of a new spirit which settled upon the land.

9

The Architecture of Propriety

THE BRIGHT, DISORDERLY AMERICAN PICTURESQUE reached a paroxysm in the late 1880s. Whole neighborhoods looked as if they had been created by an explosion at the lumberyard. In the 1890s there was a reaction; the public, seemingly embarrassed by its late indiscretions, recoiled into caution.

This reaction took two related forms: classicism and antiquarianism. Classicism bore the same relationship to the classic revival of the 1840s and 1850s as Hellenistic art had once born to the Hellenic; it was later, looser, luxurious, tending toward a flatulent monumentality. Mere size became admired: huge pilasters, cliff-like porticoes, vast palladian windows, goiterish details of a vaguely classic origin grew upon masses too small to support them. In the 1890s, this was, however, not joyous extravagance. It was conservatism without taste. It represented a seeking-after-classic precedent by a generation of clients and architects who had lost their sense of proportion. Antiquarianism yielded results, dull but meticulous, as a growing number of well-trained technicians during the 1890s and the first decades of the twentieth century created a set of reasonable facsimiles of Italian Renaissance palaces and English country houses.

The expressions in Minnesota of this new concern for decorum will be detailed in these final chapters. So, too, will be the ambiguous Richardsonian influence which competed with them and the revolt of the Progressives against them. But neither the prevailing styles nor the work of the dissenters in Minnesota are intelligible unless they are placed in context. They reflected a habitat composed of economic, metabolic, social, and intellectual forces.

The parallelism between economics and architecture in the 1890s followed a course by now familiar: The panics which seized American economic life during the nineteenth century generally followed periods of exhilarating expansion and speculation. Depression came after panic, sobering artistic life (which was hardly its most significant result from the point of view of those who suffered and survived). We have observed the architectural symptoms of economic depression in the years 1873 to 1879. Their recurrence in 1893 is a neglected but interesting aspect of our social history.[1] The Panic of 1893 had an immediate effect upon the economy and psychology of Minnesota, though the blow was softened in the northern part of the state by new discoveries of iron bringing wealth to Duluth and the Iron Range. Elsewhere as early as 1891, "there had been a surprisingly large number of commercial failures. Foreign investors were liquidating American holdings because of depression in Europe. The threat of free silver was driving gold into safekeeping. Overspeculation, inflated credit, and over investment in capital in risky enterprises foreshadowed disaster. . . ." Railroads went into receivership. Banks closed their doors. Farm prices plunged to low levels. By the first of July, lumber production had fallen sharply, and it took five years to recover. Homesteading of farmlands dropped from 241,000 acres per year to 158,000, and then crept only slowly upward again. On the Iron Range, prosperous as it generally was, the great Eastern financiers led by John D. Rockefeller and Henry W. Oliver rose to uncontested control over the ruins of the fortunes of local magnates like the Merritt brothers and Reuben and Alonzo Whiteman. Small entrepreneurs were shouldered aside by great trusts, and many were forced to enter syndicates to survive. "The Mississippi Lumberman's Association quickly gathered and agreed to reduce their cut 25 per cent; they agreed further to close all mills by the twentieth of September. The agreement was effectively enforced. . . ." Is it any wonder that under these circumstances the small-town capitalists and speculators who had celebrated the easy affluence of the 1880s with picturesque architecture, with flags flying and encouragement to the carpenter to "let her go," should now have been ready to accept a more restrained mode of building, endorsed by those captains of finance whose word was becoming the directing force in the economy?

The Panic of 1893 struck powerfully at the confidence of the people of Minnesota, a confidence further sapped by the action of laws more fixed than those of supply and demand. Human life has its own term, now somewhat lengthened, but still not far from the biblical "three score years and ten." The generation which had built Minnesota, which could look about and see the work of its own hands in the transformation of a wilderness into a thriving society, the generation which had seen what could be wrought by human will and energy, was passing from the scene. In its place emerged a second generation, better educated but less aspiring, wealthier but warier, who lacked the reassurance of an autobiography of accomplishment and lived in the shadow of their fathers. Such a generation responded to those who suggested that the taste of their ebullient parents was vulgar. In the way of children, they needed to assert their own character, and that character could be found in a new protocol, a new cultivation, a new caution and decorum. This is no discredit to them. The old world of the pioneer was filling up. The vast open arena of the personal dramas of Sibley, Brown, Le Duc, and their colleagues was now cluttered with civilization, industry, cities, railroads, mines, and the farms these pioneers had created. There was little room for more. The new generation pulled in its elbows, deferred to the accepted arbiters of taste on the Eastern Seaboard and sought the security of architecture certified as correct.

It is remarkable how few of the houses observed thus far in this book were built with inherited wealth. Only hereafter will the taste of the second and ensuing generations predominate. Many mansions built during the 1890s and the first decades of the twentieth century express the caution of inheritors, horrified of committing a "gaffe," dedicated to decorum.

The depressing effect of the Panic of 1893 upon the architecture of the Middle West was increased thereafter by the concentration of wealth during the era of the trusts into a few, conspicuous hands, who exerted not only financial but also style leadership. The iron-mining industry had made northeastern Minnesota into a colony of Pittsburgh. The railroads had long been subject to the counsel and dependent upon the capital of investment bankers, particularly J. P. Morgan and Company. These Eastern oligarchs were now inhabiting neo-Renaissance palaces: Morgan on Murray Hill, the Vanderbilts along Fifth Avenue and at Newport. It was not strange that Minnesotans of the second generation wanted to live in the same sort of houses. Architects were ready to furnish appropriately plagiarized Renaissance palaces just as picture buyers like Lord Duveen and Bernard Berenson were ready to supply taste for hire. It became the convention of the day to flatter bankers by comparing them to Medici and to speak of the oligarchs who ruled many cities as if they were Renaissance patrons of the arts. Patrons could think themselves, by purchase, Sforzas and d'Estes and built palaces to suit. The cold granite facades of these structures replaced the gay wooden, brick, and sandstone walls of picturesque houses. A classic hush fell upon the land.

The leading architects of classicism had studied at the great architectural schools, such as MIT or the École des Beaux-Arts in Paris. The École was more than a place to study. It was a shrine, and stylistically authoritarian. It venerated the past and required submission to precedent. Men of genius could refine their own talents within such an institution; lesser folk were crushed by the weight of its authority. It is possible to trace this antiquarian effect back to the graduation, in 1855, of Richard Morris Hunt from the École des Beaux-Arts. Hunt, the first American to complete his training there, returned to become, in Frank Lloyd Wright's description, "the darling of the '400.'" Hunt designed marble palaces for Vanderbilts, Goelets, and Belmonts at Newport, New York, and Asheville. He was a great craftsman and a profound scholar. His influence, however, was baneful. His insistence upon authenticity encouraged lesser men to assemble impeccably authentic early Renaissance details into new palaces giving a semblance of the old.

Hunt had no direct disciples in Minnesota. The great wealth and the social setting his work required was not yet available there in the 1880s. His younger colleagues in the academic reaction, Charles F. McKim, William R. Mead, and Stanford White, had many followers. McKim, Mead, and White set the standards to which most Minnesota architects aspired during the closing decades of the century. Cass Gilbert and Thomas G. Holyoke worked for the firm; Clarence H. Johnston studied in their shadow and himself attended the École. Edwin Hawley Hewitt, a younger man who, with Gilbert, Johnston, William Channing Whitney, and Jones, was among the most fashionable of architects working in the state, studied with Gilbert and attended both MIT and the École. This catalogue has significance. It enumerates a series of relationships which led to the creation of a classicist establishment. Finally, as a consequence of all these changes, the homeowner came to be a spectator to the creative process. No professional trained at the École des Beaux-Arts would have permitted the intrusion of a layman upon his learned researches and recombinations.

It was not strange that an architect who had deeply inhaled the intoxicating air of the École, who knew that he had been visited by genius, might take a patronizing view of his client. During the 1890s he was actually encouraged to do so by the client himself. Businessmen began to feel that they should remain within their specialty, the accumulation of wealth, leaving art to the artists. They permitted themselves to be relegated to the role of machines, to be plugged into the economic order in the morning and unplugged hours later. They were becoming familiar with mass production and mass distribution, with its segregated categories of producers and consumers, and, so far as art and architecture were concerned, they were consumers.

This acquiescence to the lopping-off of great portions of human personality on the part of the victims themselves was the consequence of an economic revolution, emphasizing specialization, of a shift of power to a second generation grown careful, and the arrival of a profession imbued with ideas of genius and pedantic pride. Among the victims of this unhappy confluence of forces were the practitioners of vernacular architecture and the talented amateur.

High among the glories of American architecture have been the contributions of amateurs of genius and of the nameless thousands who developed the vernacular tradition. In the 1890s even a man of great talent, like Louis W. Hill, whose designs for the hotels at Glacier Park are among the most interesting buildings of the period, did not feel confident that he had sufficient authority to design his own house. Industry demanded the specialization of tasks, and intensified commercial life deprived many men of repose for creative activity outside their trade. The very terms "dilettante" ("one who delighted in the pleasures of life and civilization") and "amateur" ("lover of the arts") ceased to be complimentary and acquired a tinge of preciousness. Thomas Jefferson, the great amateur, could be a statesman, farmer, architect, and dilettante of the violin, and his compeers thought him a gentleman; William Thornton, doctor of medicine, won the design competition for the Capitol of the United States over a group of professionals and no one thought it odd. Thus, in early America, men of all professions took a profound amateur interest in architecture, especially the architecture of their own houses. This tradition was continued by William G. Le Duc and Henry H. Sibley, by George Stevens and Henry Huff, but it began to run out in the 1890s as the businessman became a man of business. Period. An article in the *Western Architect* in 1904, describing the mansion of Charles M. Harrington at 2540 Park Avenue in Minneapolis, expresses well this attitude toward architects and their clients: "The twentieth-century businessman, whose affairs are conducted upon large and strenuous lines, becomes so engrossed in the work of money getting that it is fair to absolve him from any genuine devotion to the purely ideal or artistic in life. . . ."[2]

The Greek revival and the Gothic revival had owed little to the authority of professional architects, though their popularity was broadened by builders' guides. Amateurs working closely with master carpenters had created anonymous felicities, the bounty of the vernacular. Later, the picturesque period produced many houses delightful to inhabit and expressive of their owner's character. Picturesque houses often provided entertainment for the passerby and, for the occupant, surprises, places for children to hide, crannies, inglenooks, attics, dramatic balconies, ceremonial staircases with railings to slide down, space, carved wood, and colored glass. They were untidy but provided a joyous human habitat.

The Renaissance reaction brought an end to all this. It instated correctness as the chief virtue and the pedant as the arbiter. The client, exhausted by trade, contented himself with gadgetry and mere magnitude. The architect seldom sought to ignite this client's creative capacity. As one sage of the 1890s saw them, "The artist has to live, the rich man's intellect to be nourished, and the gratification of the latter provides for the physical needs of the former."

Minnesota architecture of the 1890s tended toward the proper whereas homebuilders in the previous decade liked the picturesque.

In recent years, another explanation for all this has commended itself to academics, putting emphasis on architectural style rather than context. Progressive architects suffered from the academic reaction, and after 1893 found their work less highly valued than white classicistic cubes and neo-Renaissance palaces. Frank Lloyd Wright and Louis Sullivan laid the blame upon the Chicago Columbian Exposition of 1893, which provided the occasion for architects from New York and Boston to overwhelm the innovators of the Chicago school, suffocating not only the excesses of the picturesque but also the freedom and novelty which it had carried along. This is an appealing thesis, has some elements of truth, and deserves to be set out, as much as possible, in the words of those who most passionately believed it. This we shall do, reserving for subsequent pages an assessment of how much of the truth it tells.

At the Chicago Exposition the official style was the Roman classic, executed in plaster and staff on temporary wood-and-steel frameworks and painted a dazzling white. Upon filled land, where there had been the lakeside swamp so gloomily described by Henry Hastings Sibley fifty years before, the nation's most celebrated architects created a dazzling Xanadu of vast buildings prefaced by porticoes, surrounding shimmering lagoons, in which they set titanic, if temporary, statuary. Wright asserted that all this was the product of men who would turn architecture into antique dealing, taking "ancient buildings verbatim. Whenever they found the buildings they admired, they copied them, enlarging the details by lantern slide. Used them straight." Lewis Mumford, agreeing with Wright, said that the resulting buildings in Chicago were "correct in proportion, elegant in detail, courteous in relation to each other . . . nevertheless, only a simulacrum of a living architecture."

Sullivan presented the Fair's effect upon the nation's architectural tastes in these bitter words:

> The crowds were astonished. . . . They went away, spreading again over the land, . . . each of them permeated by the most subtle and slow-acting of poisons; an imperceptible miasma within the white shadow of a higher culture . . . a higher and more dexterously insidious plausibility. Thus, they departed joyously, carriers of contagion, unaware that what they had beheld and believed to be the truth was to prove, in historic fact, an appalling calamity . . . a naked exhibitionism of charlatanry in the higher feudal and domineering culture. . . . The virus of the World's Fair, after a period of incubation in the architectural profession . . . began to show unmistakable signs of the nature of the contagion. There came a violent outbreak of the Classic and the Renaissance in the East, which slowly spread westward, contaminating all it touched. . . . Thus did the virus of a culture, snobbish and alien to the land, perform its work of disintegration; and thus ever works the pallid academic mind, denying the real, exalting the fictitious and the false. . . . The damage wrought by the World's Fair will last for half a century from its date, if not longer.

A glance across the architectural map of Minnesota in the years immediately after the Fair reveals scores of white classicistic structures. Many were clearly the product of the Chicago Exposition. In the year of the Fair, my great-grandfather, William B. Dean, built a white porticoed mansion, considered very modern, at the tip of Manitou Island at White Bear Lake, designed by Cass Gilbert. (As chief of the State Senate's Building Committee, Dean selected Gilbert's Renaissance design for the Capitol, and a little echo of it in the house he gave his son as a wedding present at 514 Grand Avenue, where my childhood was spent.) Mr. and Mrs. James D. Bronson of Stillwater went to Chicago on their wedding trip and returned to build, a decade later, a porticoed house at 1309 South Third Street, cornered in magnified pilasters. In Red Wing, in 1905, John H. Rich commissioned Clarence H. Johnston of St. Paul, who had designed many of the ceremonious buildings along the main esplanade of the University of Minnesota, to create for him a miniature White House at 1015 Fourth Street. A year earlier, Louis W. Hill, son of the Empire Builder, himself president of the Great Northern Railroad and conceiver of Glacier National Park, erected a great red brick mansion later expanded and given a portico serving as a vast porte-cochère, at 260 Summit Avenue in St. Paul, next to his father's mansion. One of the most beautiful of houses built in the classicistic style is now the Buckeye Nursing Home at 124 sw First Avenue in Faribault. Its first owner, Cassius M. Buck, began his business career when he was seven years old. He had been left fatherless, and accumulated small amounts of capital in the Horatio Alger tradition, organized a bank at Howard Lake, then a larger bank at Dassell, then a still larger bank at Annandale, and finally, in 1895, moved to Faribault where he became president of the Citizens National Bank and built his white-columned mansion. "In politics he is very prominent, being a staunch Republican," says the county historian.

The white portico became a symbol of the propriety toward which the architects of the Chicago Exposition aspired.

But the Fair had more than one architectural expression. Chicago itself was not only a showcase of the works of classicist reaction. The thousands who came for the Fair saw in the city the wonderful innovations in office and theater buildings Louis Sullivan and his colleagues had wrought. As a matter of fact, even at the Fair, Sullivan had seen to it that its ceremonious style was not so uniform as all that. His own contribution, the Transportation Building, was as novel as his skyscrapers. The eager people who flocked to Chicago, therefore, were exposed to both the classicist and what might be called the kinetic approaches to architecture, both to the embalming of precedent and to

Louis W. Hill House,
St. Paul, 1903

Cassius M. Buck House, Faribault, 1895

the celebration of ingenuity. The skyscrapers of Chicago were objects of wonder, sharing the interest of the visitors with the Exposition itself, and skyscrapers made the reputation of Sullivan, John H. Root, and Daniel Burnham, not the Eastern academicians. At the Fair, the building which attracted the largest crowds was not the New York Building, McKim, Mead, and White's version of the Medici Villa in Rome, nor was it the Minnesota Building, another Italian Renaissance palace, but the Transportation Building designed by Sullivan, with its celebrated Golden Door. The École des Beaux-Arts of Paris gave its gold medal for only one building at the Fair, an award which met with the almost unanimous agreement of European critics: it went to Sullivan, for the Transportation Building. This was not only the verdict of the professionals, but of many laymen.

In later years, when Sullivan became tired and cranky and alcoholic, the small towns of the Midwest kept him alive with commissions for banks, stores, office buildings, and residences. Yet, as the 1890s moved on, Sullivan found himself without clients and the classicists were busy with multiplication. Hugh Morrison has suggested that Sullivan was "ill-attuned to the spirit of the generation he lived in." The spirit of that generation was no more uniform, as the next chapter seeks to demonstrate, than was the architecture of the Exposition, but its dominant strains were not hospitable to a man cantankerous in character, derisive of precedent in architecture, and outspokenly radical in politics. The Fair may have had some influence in accelerating the displacement of picturesque informality by a stodgy academism but that tendency, characteristic of the generation of the reactionary 1890s, can best be explained in terms of deep currents within the economic and social life of the region, not merely as a fad started at a fair. These forces had begun before the Fair to affect the results which Sullivan attributed to that gathering of an awed and susceptible populace. In particular, the architectural record shows that McKim, Mead, and White were already exerting their style leadership upon men of genteel tastes in Minnesota, especially in St. Paul, before the gates of the Columbian Exposition were opened.

St. Paul, as has been noted, was always conscious of the New England heritage of a few of its leading families, and as bustling Minneapolis passed it in population in the mid-1880s, it stood upon its status as an older community and wrapped about its shoulders a mantle crocheted with the motto: "the Boston of the West." It became desirable to establish clear title to an ancestral home in New England. Charles and Daniel Noyes came to St. Paul from Lyme, Connecticut, with sufficient capital to join in a successful wholesale drug business with Edward H. Cutler, a Bostonian. The Noyes were men of imposing demeanor, married to wives who were well educated and gracious. In 1889, Charles P. Noyes commissioned Cass Gilbert to design for him a large frame house on Virginia Avenue, just off Summit. Gilbert caught the spirit of his client and the times with that facility which later made him one of the most successful architectural businessmen in the nation—by neatly cribbing its neo-Federal design and many details from McKim, Mead, and White.

McKim and his partners had rediscovered houses of this sort when they made their celebrated tour of New England during the 1870s. These classically trained men naturally avoided the heavy-gabled, dark, jumbled, picturesque medievalism of the seventeenth-century

Charles P. Noyes House, St. Paul, 1889

colonial in favor of later houses, built when the Georgian became prim in its final Federal phase, before the heavy, lapidary Greek revival replaced it. In 1886, they designed their famous version of a large Federal house, "magnified by lantern slide," in Wright's phrase, for H. A. C. Taylor at Newport, Rhode Island. Gilbert reduced the scale again for his Noyes house.

The Federal revival, upon which McKim, Mead, and White briefly rested on their way to a full Renaissance style, was their more sophisticated essay on the same theme as the white-porticoed cubes which less able designers of the uniform ceremonious style presented at the Chicago Exposition. The great New York firm did not remain Federal very long, but the endorsement given by these arbiters of taste to magnified versions of classic styles induced others to try it throughout the Midwest: for example, at 2316 East First Street in Duluth, William J. Olcott, president of the Oliver Iron Mining Company from 1909 to 1928, is locally said to have spent $140,000 in 1904 to create a house carrying what surely must be the most overwhelming gambrel roof in

the region, below which a two-story portico, more than thirty feet high, seems to be slightly apprehensive. (The Olcott House was given to the University of Minnesota in 1939, and was later sold to the Golden Hour Evangelistic Association.)

William J. Olcott House, Duluth, 1904

By this time, however, McKim, Mead, and White had moved on to their full Renaissance manner, abandoning all American traditions for European antiquities more to their taste. The most influential Renaissance houses built in America in the 1880s and 1890s were probably the group they created across Madison Avenue from St. Patrick's Cathedral in New York, in 1883. Their client, Ferdinand Heinrich Gustav Hilgard, vagabonding journalist, had lately become Henry Villard, promoter and president of the Northern Pacific Railroad. Only a trace of his Rhenish accent remained. He had put the first northern railroad across to the Pacific, while its rival, the Great Northern, had been moving cautiously westward, sending out rhizomes to pick up little towns and grain depots and cattle pens. The Northern Pacific had rushed through from Duluth to Tacoma without bothering too much with details. Villard was in a hurry. He was a sophisticated, eloquent man who had quarreled with his father while he was at the University of Munich and departed for America. He became a freelance newspaperman, covering the development of the West in the 1850s, writing in his new language, then serving as one of the most respected battlefield correspondents during the Civil War. In 1871, he went back to Europe to restore his health, and struck up an acquaintance with certain German bondholders who were agonizing about an evaporating investment in something called the Oregon and California Railroad Company. Villard agreed to investigate their problem, appraised the situation so well that he arranged a settlement, then, finding railroad finance to his liking, became receiver in bankruptcy of another failing road, the Kansas Pacific. In possession of that system, he stood off a raid by Jay Gould, organized another company to build eastward from Portland, Oregon, encountered a rival in the Northern Pacific, and then, by means of the famous "Villard Blind Pool," persuaded friends to help him acquire control of that road in 1881 by pledging millions for a purpose which he could not then fully disclose.

Villard was, like E. H. Harriman, primarily a financial genius, not a constructor of railroads. He built too fast, missed the best grades and the closest routes, extended himself too much. In the halcyon year when his road united the Northwest for the first time, he made a triumphant procession through his domain, with a giant reception in St. Paul, and came home to New York to commission McKim, Mead, and White to build a group of houses for him around a central court, residences for princes. A year later, the Northern Pacific was in receivership, Villard was nearly bankrupt, but his houses had established a new standard and a new style for American architecture.

Stanford White (the erratic genius whose murder by the jealous Harry K. Thaw later provided the occasion for a new standard and a new style for American journalism) had started the plans and exteriors for the Villard house and departed for a trip to New Mexico leaving the completion of the work to Joseph Morrill Wells. Wells substituted elevations derived from those of the Cancelleria Palace in Rome, which was then believed to be the work of the great Renaissance architect, Bramante. For the first time in America, a Renaissance antique was fabricated. There were to be many more. As Vincent Scully put it, these houses are "the apotheosis of the 'adapted' over the invented, of archeological exactitude over intrinsic growth . . . in their design method they were book architecture: flat, two-dimensional, anti-plastic—essentially academic paper work." All this was true. And for the academic architects, then ascendant, this was no indictment. They scrambled to go and do likewise, and Renaissance palaces began to appear in large cities across the country.

St. Paul architects did not wait long to make their own adaptations of Italian Renaissance monuments. In 1893, the earliest of the palaces still extant in Minnesota was laid up by Reed and Stem, an adaptable firm quick to take on a new style.[3] Their essay is at 340 Summit Avenue in St. Paul; lumberman Thomas B. Scott spent something more than $40,000 on the house and on the gardens which fall in terraces down the hillside to the servants' quarters below. Horace E. Thompson, son of a pioneer banker, commissioned Green and Wick of Buffalo in 1904 to derive from the Villard houses a mansion at Summit Avenue and Avon Street, in the light brick which might have approached Wells's original color. The St. Paul Central Library was built even more closely upon the pattern of the Villard houses.

At 344 Summit, next to the Scott house, Thomas G. Holyoke completed a vast mansion for Watson P. Davidson which he had designed nearly a decade earlier, before the World War. Holyoke had been Cass Gilbert's draftsman and, at his employer's urging, had gone to learn the new style from McKim, Mead, and White. The Davidson house extends backward from the street to form four floors of steel and concrete, containing 20,000 square feet, some of them allocated to such amenities as a gymnasium. The front entrance, with its heavy gates of glass and wrought iron, is as handsome as any neo-Renaissance work in the region.

Watson Davidson was the son-in-law of the commodore who, by co-incidence, bore the same last name and who had erected a magnificent bracketed and cupolaed house on the bluff near the Indian Mounds across the city. The progression in styles is instructive: the old riverboat operator was one of the last in Minnesota to build a mansion in the *continuous* American Renaissance vernacular. The next generation, working in a new age of railroads and intricate corporate finance on a continental scale, took its models from New York as New York had taken its from the École des Beaux-Arts. Watson Davidson was a capitalist, like his neighbor Scott. He owned 20,000 acres of farmland in the Red River Valley, office buildings in St. Paul, and had persuaded Louis W. Hill that the old carriage-road land grant owned by French bankers across the state of Oregon could be purchased at a good price. Together, they promoted farm and timber land and initiated the greatest lumbering boom in central Oregon, drawing in their friends the Brooks and the Scanlons of Minneapolis.

In 1904, two yeasr after Kees and Colburn had created the Charles M. Harrington house, they built a very similar structure on a smaller scale at 2309 East First Street in Duluth for Joseph Bell Cotton, the local attorney for United States Steel.

Ernest Kennedy, who composed many mansions for Minneapolis men of this generation, made his finest contribution to the Renaissance fashion in the Edward Gale house at 2115 Stevens Avenue, now owned by the American Association of University Women. It was built in 1913 and harmonizes well with McKim, Mead, and White's Institute of Arts across the park. Gale was the son of a pioneer attorney and real estate owner, and son-in-law of Governor John F. Pillsbury. In the same year, his associate John P. Snyder, whose father had served as the president of the Board of Regents of the University of Minnesota for half a lifetime and was a pillar of the city's economic life, followed the second-generation practice and built a Renaissance palace at 2118 Blaisdell. It has had additions to extend its use as a nursing home, but it and the Gale house are still the best examples of the style in the city.

The most appropriate use for houses derived from designs commissioned by Florentine financiers like the Medici and the Pitti, and favored rather self-consciously by later financiers like J. Pierpont Morgan (whose mansion in the style on Murray Hill in New York now houses his splendid library and art collection) was to make banks of

them. Fortunately this was the fate of the Frank B. Semple house at Blaisdell and Franklin in Minneapolis now used by the Franklin National Bank. There are 20,000 square feet in the main house, 5,000 more in the carriage house. The red carpeting and crystal chandeliers are still in place, and the concept of F. B. and L. L. Long (who produced the plans for the great hardware merchant in 1899) has finally been fully realized. Tellers' cages have been decorously inserted in the salon and loans are made in the smoking room. The uniformed guard looks perfectly at home.

A minor variation of the academic tradition had adherents in Minnesota: the "Elizabethan" primarily associated with the celebrated Boston firm of Ralph Adams Cram, Bertram G. Goodhue, and Frank W. Ferguson. Cram himself was a latter-day evangelist of the Gothic spirit, but the residential work of his firm moved only part of the distance back toward the Middle Ages from the Renaissance. In Minnesota, they replicated in miniature—relatively—great country houses built in England in the seventeenth century. During that period the Renaissance had imposed symmetry upon facades, but within the rooms were still grouped about high-beamed, Gothic great halls, lit by bays of tall windows. The exteriors of Minnesota houses modeled on these examples were almost always of brick, though in Cram's finest work (such as his additions to West Point in New York in 1904 and in churches like the House of Hope at Summit and Avon in St. Paul) the exteriors were of stone. Cram's firm was commissioned in the years just after the First World War to design a mansion for Paul Watkins at 175 East Wabasha in Winona. It has a fine reception room, a paneled dining room, and a vast great hall. It must have been drafty in the winter; photographs of the time show that it was furnished with a profusion of wild animal hides and thick rugs.[4] Watkins was the nephew of the founder of a patent-medicine company which still operates in Winona. The original elixir was purchased by the elder Watkins from a peddler in Indiana; produced for a while in Plainview, Minnesota; and then made into the staple of a diversified line merchandised by Paul Watkins. Cram, Goodhue, and Ferguson had worked in the Elizabethan mode for many years before they received the Watkins commission; their influence was shown more than a decade earlier in Duluth. In 1906, Chester A. Congdon's "Glensheen" was completed at 3300 London Road, designed by Clarence H. Johnston. It is Johnston's masterpiece. Genius did, in this case, come to roost on his shoulder, not so much in the grand reception rooms, the libraries and parlors, nor in the ceremonial dining room, as in the beautifully crafted detail of the glass-enclosed breakfast room, almost oriental in its fragility, and in a score of small felicities of detail elsewhere: the stained-glass doorway into the service wing beautifully represents the fin-de-siecle love of sinuous line; the carving and plasterwork are masterful. Outside, below the great terraces looking toward Lake Superior, was a pier for yachts. The garages and stables could accommodate a motorized battalion or a troop of cavalry. Congdon was an attorney who arrived in Duluth during the Iron Boom of the 1890s and soon was handling the acquisition of properties for the United States Steel Company. Occasionally he acted on his own account, and began accumulating what came to be vast holdings of mineral-producing properties in Minnesota and elsewhere.

Another notable work done in the same style and time is William Channing Whitney's house for lumber magnate Horace Irvine at 1006 Summit Avenue in St. Paul. In an earlier generation houses of this size would have been stamped with the character of their owners. But by 1900 they merely represented the craftsmanship of their architects and the wealth of their clients. Watkins, Congdon, and Irvine were all interesting, intrepid, and intelligent men. One gathers nothing about them from their houses except that they were rich and hired competent architects. The Irvine house became the governor's mansion in 1965.

It seems strange to encounter the towering figure of Henry H. Richardson in this company of antiquarians, but, if one examines not his purposes but only his influence upon Minnesota residential architecture, that is where he belongs. His powerful opening interior space

Chester A. Congdon House, Duluth, 1906

around a central hall, and his disciplined but flowing use of simple forms found no disciples in Minnesota. The two men who studied under his direct tutelage, Harvey Ellis and Harry W. Jones, have lost all their best residential work to the wreckers.

Richardson's architecture was easy to misunderstand; the disparity of judgments rendered upon it indicates that it was too easily absorbed by men who could master its manner without comprehending its spirit or its purposes. Speaking in 1922 for the establishment, Ralph Adams Cram said that Richardson's influence was "deplorable." From architecture's left wing, Frank Lloyd Wright said of Richardson that he was "just what America deserved most but should have had least . . . a powerful romantic eclectic." Yet Lewis Mumford, an admirer of Louis Sullivan and Wright, called Richardson "a colossal man . . . who almost single-handed created out of a confusion which was actually worse than a mere void the beginnings of a new architecture."

Richardson stands as the pivot of this story, looking backward toward academic and antiquarian revivalism, and forward toward a free use of interior space and a celebration of what the Wrighteans came to call "the Nature of the Materials": rocks, shingles, brick (not the "materials" in the sense of the ragbag of ancient odds and ends pasted together to form the picturesque mansions of the 1880s). Perhaps it is because he was Janus-like, looking both ways at once, that he is so difficult to classify. After delighting in Norman Shaw's Sussex revival, he moved on to develop what Vincent Scully has called "the shingle style": houses covered by a continuous skin, not disrupted by basketry or jagged bays and gables, but solid and direct, often in massive buildings encased in masonry emulated by countless imitators, some of them practicing in Minnesota. The style did make use of decorative detail which he had admired in the surviving buildings of the Romanesque period in southern France, Italy, and Spain, but details were not the essentials of the style. Richardson's work at its best unified enclosing material with form. While the nineteenth century had seen many revivals, Richardson went beyond style, into the deepest past, leaving the antiquarians behind. What he was doing can best be appreciated if terms like Richardsonian Romanesque are abandoned and Richardson buildings are examined. In the F. L. Ames Gate Lodge in North Easton, Massachusetts, of 1881, for example, there are no fragile, frantic sticks, no carpentered gables, no screen of verandahs, no vague shimmer of stained glass. Instead there is a round tower of boulders—a form more ancient than any Romanesque tower. There is a huge arch. Academicians once looked for its origins in southern France, then in the drawings of medieval Syrian churches which Richardson is thought to have studied in the 1870s. But this arch is simply a method of piercing a rock wall without diminishing its strength, adding, in fact, to its impression of weightiness and permanence. Richardson's rock is not merely a surface. It is the structure. The Ames Gate Lodge is a cave turned inside out.

It is true of course that Richardson employed precedents he found useful, as if he were constructing new walls from ancient rubble. The tower of the Palazzo Vecchio appeared upon the Hampton County Courthouse in Connecticut, portions of the Cathedral of Salamanca reappeared in Boston; Pisa, Ravenna, Rome, Florence, Arles, Avignon —all contributed shards from which he fashioned new work, as Haydn and Bach borrowed their colleagues' creations to enrich their own musical vocabulary, only occasionally with thanks. But what Richardson could do with such materials his less talented contemporaries could not. They were collectors. He was a creator. Always searching for novel antiquities, they were delighted with his discoveries, and employed round towers with conical caps, heavy arches of stone (or wood, careless of structural veracity) and quarry-faced masonry. They took the curious label which runs across the front of Richardson's Crane Library, a long stone horizontal terminated by short verticals, and made it a style-mark written on their buildings as if they were saying "Romanesques-QED."

The Richardsonian use of masonry was more natural to massive public buildings than residences. Only houses of vast scale could be made up of Richardsonian boulders without looking like a rock pile. When the structure's size was suitable for the material, the result was most impressive. Only one such accomplishment still stands in Minnesota. It was in 1889 that James J. Hill began construction of his mansion at 240 Summit Avenue in St. Paul. The architects were Peabody and Stearns of Boston, who vied with Shepley, Rutan, and Coolidge of the same city in carrying on Richardson's manner. For Peabody and Stearns, seaside resorts provided opportunity for freedom and experi-

ment, and very rich clients in the large cities provided occasions for less venturesome grandeur. For James J. Hill they designed a big house: eighteen bathrooms, thirty-five fireplaces, a billiard room, and a sky-lit, two-story art gallery which housed, among other things, twenty-two Corots. John Kirchmayer, a Bavarian woodcarver, spent nearly a year at work on the paneling and stair railings of the first floor. William Yungbauer designed and built much of the furniture.

The Hill house is Richardsonian in its use of heav, rock-faced masonry and in the heavy Syrian arches of the porte-cochère. Facing the gardens and the bluff to the south are cloisters and porches with heavy Romanesque columns. It is a strong composition, much simpler than those being constructed about it during the still vigorous picturesque period. The two pavilions which flank the great porte-cochère are balanced, solid, commanding, unequivocal. Edwin Lundie, a distinguished architect who knew the place well while Mr. Hill was in residence, has suggested that Peabody and Stearns took much thought to their client when they laid up his mansion. It is heavy, hunched, and craggy, as he was. It sits upon the site grasping the earth and glaring out upon the city which he, more than other man, had built. It expresses power, not polish, the confident, candid ruggedness of a man who never apologized.

James J. Hill made many men rich. He was a builder of railroads, of cities, of an educational system, an art collection, a fine private library, a bank, of systems for the breeding of cattle, the planting of wheat, the quarrying of stone, distribution of domestic fuel, and the mining of iron. He lived by daring and intelligence, loving power. James J. Hill was, in a sense, the last of the frontiersmen: physically formidable, he could help dig out a snowbound train in his sixties or push a three-hundred-pound desk out a window to save its contents from a fire. He was a fearsome figure who was regarded as a great natural force to be given a wide margin and not, under any circumstances, to be confronted directly.

Frank B. Kellogg, another sort of man, made use of another Richardsonian style. Kellogg was a man of the world. When he built his house, in the same year that Hill began his, he was already the beau ideal of a new generation. He had been born in Potsdam, New York, in 1856, was admitted to the bar in 1877 after a boyhood on a farm near Rochester, Minnesota, and a legal apprenticeship in that city. He became, first, a well-known trustbuster, employed by the Justice Department to prosecute the paper and Standard Oil trusts, taking a hand in the famous Northern Securities case which upset one of Hill's combinations, and investigating the Harriman railroads for the Interstate Commerce Commission. Then, establishing a course which has been frequently followed since, he applied his knowledge of the field of corporate finance to the service of the great enterprises of which he had lately been the scourge: he became counsel for the iron mining and railroad industries. In 1889, at the height of his prosperous legal practice he erected a house at 633 Fairmount Avenue in St. Paul, which evidences not so much Richardson's rugged masonry style as his more suave, shingled domestic work, with its rounded forms and flowing lines.

Kellogg was handsome and articulate, full of certainties, imbued with the confidence in progress and in the capacity of law to constrain

violence. In 1916, he was the first United States senator to be elected from Minnesota by popular vote. Mr. Folwell, abandoning the detached stance of a historian, permitted his affection for Kellogg to color his description of the next campaign. Kellogg, he says, "had a good right to expect" reelection, but "the Farmer-Labor combination gave him leave to return to private life." But not for long. The next year, he represented his country at the Conference of American States in Chile, then was named ambassador to Great Britain, and, from 1925 to 1929 was secretary of state. In 1929, he was awarded the Nobel Peace Prize. In this era, with Kellogg a celebrated international figure, Pierce Butler leading the conservative wing of the United States Supreme Court, and William Mitchell serving as solicitor general, the legal profession in St. Paul knew its proudest hour.

There are other Richardsonian houses in Minnesota, masonry laid up in what were deemed to be Romanesque forms. William Channing Whitney created one for H. C. Akeley at 2300 Park Avenue in Minneapolis in 1901, with two round barbicans at the corners of the facade with a false gable between. One of the turrets was perforated to create a double loggia, and, over to the side, there is Peabody and Stearns's porte-cochère. In 1890, Mr. Whitney had used but one tower and a false gable in designing a house for C. Alden Smith at 1403 Harmon Place, across town. Smith (whose silent partner was John S. Pillsbury) was Akeley's prime competitor. They were the first- and fourth-largest millers of lumber at Minneapolis in 1897, cutting 80 million and 52 million board feet, respectively. In 1889, Smith caught up to Akeley, cutting the same incredible total: 108 million board feet. Akeley was typical of the men who made Minneapolis the largest lumber market in the world in that year: he followed the falling timbers westward from Vermont, through Michigan to Minnesota. It was said that "he said nothing but he sawed wood"—most of it cut in Itasca County.

In Duluth, there is a curious black basalt house which, in a sense, is more Richardsonian than all these, for it is an extension of the rock on which it is poised. It is composed of boulders blasted from the volcanic outcrops over which the city grew. The black basalt gives the house (at 2505 East First Street) a primitive roughness lacking in the polite Romanesque houses built in the Twin Cities out of soft portage entry sandstone. The round corner tower with a conical cap, the steep tile roof, the inevitable false gable in the center of the facade, the arched porte-cochère with the battlemented top, were all clichés of the style by the time that architects Bray and Mystrom received their commission from H. H. Myers in 1908. It may have been Myers himself, an investment broker, who suggested the use of the local stone, for he had much experience with blasting it out of the way for the inclined railway which he had promoted to carry passengers up Duluth's escarpment.

In Minnesota, Richardson's influence was that of another fashionable architect who returned from the École des Beaux-Arts, emulated with little success by a host of midwestern practitioners who mistook him for another antique dealer. McKim, Mead, and White purveyed Renaissance palaces to the oligarchs of the East, Ralph

Adams Cram lamented the passing of the Middle Ages and built painstaking replicas of Elizabethan buildings. Richardson's true significance as an innovator was lost on nearly all his contemporaries except Louis Sullivan.

In the final chapter we will turn to the work of Sullivan, Wright, William Gray Purcell, and George G. Elmslie, who approached architecture as social document as well as an art.

10

Progressive Politics and Architecture

WILLIAM R. MERRIAM, banker and real estate promoter, was elected governor of Minnesota in 1889, the last in a continuous line of businessmen and businessmen's lawyers devoted to a rapid reaping of the fruits of farm and forest, enjoying the post–Civil War boom, nearly all untroubled by doubts about the economic and social order. Merriam and his friends inhabited mansions just behind the site where the vast neo-Renaissance State Capitol rose. By then their associates were already building vast neo-Renaissance palaces along Summit Avenue and on Lowry Hill, or equally vast neo-Renaissance manor houses or neo-Renaissance fortresses. It was an era of big business and big houses, expressing the orthodox ideology suggested in the previous chapter.

Throughout the countryside, however, doubts had already given way to denunciation: Grangers, Farmers' Alliance members, Knights of Labor, Populists, and a multitude of more violent radicals were speaking out against the concentration of wealth, low farm prices, high processing costs, monopoly, Wall Street, and the Trusts. Down in Kansas, Mary Elizabeth Lease was telling them to "raise less corn and more hell" and "Sockless Jerry" Simpson was inveighing against "the buccaneers of Wall Street, the brigands of the tariff, and the whole shootin' match of grain gamblers, land grabbers, and government sneak thieves." Ignatius Donnelly, the sage of Nininger and storm-center of Minnesota politics for thirty years, became their prophet. He wrote in the Populist platform of 1892 that "the people are demoralized . . . our homes covered with mortgages, labor impoverished, and the land concentrating into the hands of the capitalists. . . . The fruits of the toil of millions are boldly stolen to build up colossal fortunes for a few . . . we breed . . . two great classes of tramps and millionaires."

When Governor Merriam took office, he found thirty-three Farmers' Alliance members in the Minnesota House of Representatives, full of the spirit of revolt and holding the balance of power. In the next election, Merriam won again, but the two candidates of the Democrats and the Farmers' Alliance, together, polled more votes than he. The message was clear. The Republicans, skillfully adapting to the wind blasting hot out of the wheatlands, sought a new "image" and nominated the first of Minnesota's Scandinavian governors, Knute Nelson. Nelson's administration provided a series of measures directed against those same excesses of avarice and abuses of power which had provided the construction funds for many a great mansion.

Knute Nelson was cautious, orthodox, and skilled in timely adjustments to the realities of economic power. He was a reformer, not, like some of the earlier agrarian leaders, a revolutionary. He was at ease in the United States Senate, to which he was later elevated, in the company of the moderate, middle-class men whose careers spanned the period during which Populism modulated into Progressivism. Populism had been passionate—it always had fire in the belly. Progressivism was in earnest, but it kept a cool head and a dry palm. Populism was an upsurge of the unsophisticated; Progressivism was avowed by an impressive assemblage of intellect and education.

The palaces of the nabobs had effectively symbolized the growth of a class possessing much power and relatively unconcerned about democratic values. Progressive architecture, which began to develop in the 1890s, not only symbolized, but was the conscious expression of, a protest against the heedlessness and vulgarity of the plutocracy; it was an affirmation of those democratic values. Many politically sensitive architects who had worked in the stick style and in the free, exuberant wooden styles of the 1880s, and those who hoped to develop a free expression of the new century, were appalled by the classicist emphasis upon a dull decorum and a deadly antiquarianism. These men mixed ethics with esthetics in decrying the cult of the neo-Renaissance as both ugly and immoral. John C. Stevens and Albert W. Cobb asked Americans to recall the social context of the typical Renaissance palace in Italy "at the portals of which swarm specimens of that breed of beggars evolved in the process of its erection." Palaces of this kind, they said, were "inspired by an admiration of tyrants." Louis Sullivan agreed. To him, there was "a certain grim, ghastly humor in . . . a banker sitting in a Roman temple; railroad tracks running into a Roman bath; a rich vulgarian living in a Trianon."

To be affronted implied an alternate set of standards; if it was wrong to create palaces amid a swarm of beggars, or, as Donnelly had said, to divide society into tramps and millionaires, then there must be another image of America in mind. And so there was, in the minds of both the Populists and the Progressives: a commonwealth of independent citizens, neither too rich nor too poor. Their proper habitation, if not a family farm, should be at least a patch of greensward. Orson Fowler had called this a home for all, evoking a concept which had been constant throughout American architectural history and which came surging back in full force during the Progressive era. It has been, also, a primary theme of this book.

The ideal of the independent householder, uncorrupted by cities or large industrial establishments, had been symbolized in the Greek revival temple. The prophet of the domestic Gothic revival, Andrew Jackson Downing, agreed with the ideal, but held that a simple, suburban, creeper-covered cottage was more fit for its symbol than a temple. These concepts were imperiled by the great social changes wrought by the Civil War, but, as Vincent Scully has pointed out, they were later reasserted: "the colonial and Queen Anne revival and the shingle style . . . emerged in reaction against the industrialized world, and its architects attempted to create a new cottage and suburban refuge."

The Populists were, in general, farmers and small-town people who rose up against specific economic abuses from which they were suffering at the hands of rich and powerful city folk; the Progressives included many who feared what cities would do to its own inhabitants as well. Cities had been growing, of course, for a century and more, but in the 1880s and 1890s the old agrarian America went into its long, final agony. It was a time of concentration of power, concentration of industry into trusts, concentration of people into slums, a process which Louis Sullivan called feudalism. Frank Lloyd Wright spoke of New York as a "volcanic center of confused energy bred by money-power, no wise control of enormous mechanical forces, pushing up to crowd and be crowded, to grind against each other with a blind force moved by common greed." The city was, to him, an "incongruous mousetrap of monstrous proportions . . . Moloch . . . Anti-Christ." He espoused Sullivan's "theory of democracy, especially, in its relation to art as the self-expression of free men." Wright joined the ranks of the reformers with his dream of "Usonia" (borrowing the term from Samuel Butler), where production was keyed to the needs of the consumer, where there was universal free education, a popular vote required before going to war, and where "congestion of human life in great ugly centers was reversed."

There were many voices speaking through Wright: William Morris, John Ruskin, Henry George, and Walt Whitman among them, voices heard by many of the architects of the Progressive movement resisting the crushing of individualism in the cogs of industry, committed to the ideal of each free family in a home of its own. Wright called this an inalienable right.

In Minneapolis, Chicago, Syracuse, and elsewhere, circles were established by people influenced by William Morris's Arts and Crafts ideals to make their decoration and their own furniture, thereby to assert individuality, freedom from the machine, and independence of mass culture. Gustav Stickley established a magazine, known as *The Craftsman,* to espouse the cause of small houses of good design for the average family. The maximum cost was to be $4,000. In the Arts and Crafts spirit, Progressive architecture included designing furniture, fixtures, tiles, hangings, paintings, and sculpture to make an integrated whole of each house, with the active participation of the householder himself.

In the fullness of the Progressive ideal, there was to be a renewal of the mutual respect which had ennobled both the patron and the master builder in the Jeffersonian era, when the client was an amateur of architecture and the builder a craftsman. As the editor of the *Western Architect* wrote in March 1913, "A democratic architecture . . . is evolved by a close and constant relation between the architect and his client, the people, which results in a complete understanding as to the latter's needs. . . . Instead of 'handing' a client an 'exquisite little colonial' or a 'magnificent Italian Renaissance' our democratic architect must know his client's habits, the climate in which he lives, the location, possibilities of his site. . . ."

Progressive architecture was a part of a broad social movement grounded—then and now—in the university communities and suburbs such as Oak Park, Illinois. Sullivan, Wright, William G. Purcell, and George G. Elmslie all were affected by the atmosphere of Oak Park, where Wright had his first workrooms and where Purcell's journalist-grandfather, William Cunningham Gray, was the leader of the Progressive intellectuals. Another center of patronage was the University of Wisconsin, where Richard T. Ely was sheltering faculty members against charges of "radical anarchism" and was barely acquitted of the charge by the regents. David Gebhard, Purcell and Elmslie's biographer, has analyzed the composition of the Progressive group and found that "to a considerable extent they were the same men who supported the many social and economic reforms . . . inaugurated by Theodore Roosevelt, Robert M. LaFollette, Woodrow Wilson and others."

To Sullivan, Wright, Purcell, and Elmslie, who produced the great monuments of Progressive architecture in Minnesota, these economic and social questions were of intense interest, and their affirmation of Progressive social ideals was central to their aesthetic philosophy. To Purcell's delight, their dedication was appreciated by their European colleagues. When he made an architectural tour of Scandinavia in 1906, he found that the designers of "fully functional, wholly modern buildings . . . wanted to ask him as a kind of architectural student envoy from the United States of Louis Sullivan, first, 'Tell us about Theodore Roosevelt. Is it true, the stories they tell about his "trust busting" . . . "democracy for the common man"?'" Purcell there had no doubt that an alliance of reactionary architecture and reactionary politics stood in the way. "In 1891 those who were privileged and successful looked right through all the old familiar architecture and saw with horror, a crowd of revolutionary insistences which appeared certain to ruin the comfort of upper middle class prosperity. . . ."

Purcell and his partner George Elmslie articulated in domestic architecture the Progressive ideal. Sullivan and Wright, for different reasons, disqualified themselves for such a mission. Sullivan was never very interested in residential work and recent scholarship has suggested that his most famous houses were largely the work either of Wright or, later, of Elmslie. In Minnesota, he completed no residential commissions and his greatest concept for a house, designed for Carl Bennett (owner of the famous Farmers and Mechanics Bank which Sullivan and Elmslie had built in Owatonna) betrayed a total indifference to its site, its inhabitants, and its budget. It was a superb abstract design but not a house.

Wright, of course, designed scores of houses (his Minnesota work is listed in the appendix to chapter 10) but the defensive arrogance he developed during the long years when his clients were few and the critics were derisive made it difficult in his celebrated and successful old age for him to engage in the kind of dialogue with clients required by the Progressive ideal. In his view, the act of creation came from the great man, and from the client came money and gratitude. "No man," he said, "can build a building for another who does not believe in him . . . who has not chosen him because of his faith. . . . This is the nature of the architect and client as I see it." The hostility of critics and the indifference of the public in his middle years enhanced Wright's feeling that his talent set him so far above those for whom he deigned to execute commissions that he could not be expected to solicit their opinions. He became cynical. The Great Man would give a client a house (probably too good for him) "so his home environment may now face forward and portray his own character by way of his own 'tastes' and preferably his ideas (if he has any). Every man has some—somewhere about him?" The quotation marks about 'tastes' and the question mark as to both taste and ideas are Wright's own, and so also is his view that there was a quantum leap between himself and the rest of mankind.

Though Wright designed ten houses for Minnesota, all but one were built after the Progressive period, and after the timespan covered by this book. That exception was one of his greatest creations, however. Across a knoll on the south shore of Lake Minnetonka, near Minneapolis, more than two hundred and fifty feet long, was his residence for Francis W. Little. Little was a utility executive who had come to Minnesota from Peoria, Illinois (where he had commissioned an earlier Wright house). "Northome" was a grand summer pavilion, inhabited only in part during the winter, centering on a baronial hall lit by windows leaded in geometric shapes. The rectilinear—almost cubist—wood sculpture and furniture which Wright was creating simultaneously for the Imperial Hotel in Tokyo are represented in the Little house, as is a largeness of scale and a breadth of conception more monumental than domestic. It is a house full of sudden changes, explosions of space, surprising angles, a creation from the hand of a master.

Because their work best demonstrates the ideals and the capabilities of Progressive domestic architecture, and because they did nearly all of it in Minnesota, Purcell and Elmslie occupy a central position in this study. (A list of their houses in the state appears as the appendix to chapter 10.) Some of their houses will be scanned in the next few pages, but at the outset it is important to emphasize their ideological and professional background, for they were always conscious of the ideology represented by their work.

George G. Elmslie was born and educated in Scotland, where from childhood he was imbued with the spirit of the anti-industrial Arts and Crafts Movement of Morris and Ruskin. He came to America in 1887, and joined the firm of Joseph L. Silsbee in Chicago. There he met Wright and, two years later, through Wright, he was hired as a draftsman by Louis Sullivan. He remained with Sullivan during the next decade of success, and continued to work as his faithful associate until 1909, long after Sullivan had lost the capacity to execute most of the commissions received by the firm—until, according to David S. Gebhard, in the final years of Sullivan's practice, "the last designs were almost entirely from his [Elmslie's] hands."

William Gray Purcell was brought up in Oak Park, which Wright had found so congenial, largely by his maternal grandparents, Dr. and Mrs. William C. Gray. Dr. Gray was a newspaper editor and columnist, a late disciple of New England transcendentalism. From the idealism of Oak Park (and from the experience of spending his summers living in primitive conditions in northern Wisconsin) Purcell "came to despise the meretricious, to value the goodness of plain 'uneducated people,' and to accept democratic relations with all men as the normal way of life." When he was at college, he encountered the writings of Sullivan. After his graduation, in 1903, he met Elmslie who introduced him to Sullivan. He worked in their office for five months; however, it was not the length of time in which he was actually employed there which counted. There was little work for the firm at the time, but Purcell's commitment to Sullivan's ideas was reinforced and a long friendship with Elmslie was established. Purcell went to the West Coast for four years, and then returned to establish his own firm in Minneapolis in 1907. Elmslie finally left Sullivan and joined him in 1909, though he had contributed some ideas to work done by Purcell in the previous year. The partnership officially dissolved in 1920 when Purcell departed to work, once again, in the Pacific Northwest and Elmslie made his office in Chicago.

Purcell and Elmslie's work can be described in general terms which would be applicable to Wright's early houses or to those of other mem-

W. G. Purcell House,
Minneapolis, 1913

E. S. Hoyt House,
Red Wing,
1913

bers of what came to be called the Prairie School. They employed strips of casement windows, patterns in leaded or colored glass, and emphasized the long lines of the midwestern landscape; they united windows with horizontal strips of wood in dark colors contrasting with the generally light-colored plaster of the upper portions of the facade; and they often employed horizontal board and batten or brick on the lower portions. Deep eaves sheltered the windows like eyebrows. Ornament was of great significance. Terra-cotta appeared on fireplace walls or over doorways, sometimes as elaborately colored and molded as the famous designs for the Owatonna Bank. Elmslie often established a motif which appeared in stained-glass doors, in interior cabinets, in carven woodwork, and recurred in the strip windows, entrance doors, and sawed wooden panels which were frequently set into the termination of supporting members and about the doorways. Purcell's house on Lake Place in Minneapolis and the Hoyt house in Red Wing are particularly distinguished by their wooden ornament and the Powers house in Minneapolis by its extraordinary terra-cotta.

Purcell and Elmslie did not turn their backs on the technology of their time to retreat into Arts and Crafts as a refuge from the twentieth century. Others were preaching a medieval revival but building Elizabethan country houses upon a framework of concrete and steel. Purcell and Elmslie recognized that labor-saving devices were a boon to people of limited means and they, like Orson Fowler, thought machines could be made fit servants for "independent yeomen." As early as 1915, they were using sliding-glass doors, central lighting and heating controls, and a centralized pump to provide vacuum cleaner outlets in each room. Their work outside the residential field indicates that they did not disdain the effort to create beauty out of mundane material: they designed phonograph salesrooms, a commercial garage, street lamps, stationery, magazine covers, and, for one very large but uncompleted residential project, an indoor swimming pool.

The largest residential commission completed by the firm in Minnesota was a house for Minneapolis banker Edward M. Decker, begun in 1913, the same year as Wright's house for Francis Little, and not far distant on the shore of Lake Minnetonka. Decker was a creative and uninhibited figure in the financial community, a scholar of Lincolniana, and a fervent admirer of Theodore Roosevelt. Family recollection is hazy as to his reasons for choosing Purcell and Elmslie, but the firm designed, for Decker, a house full of innovations at a time when most of his colleagues were commissioning Renaissance reproductions. Today, only the garage and service buildings remain on the site. The great house which was a monument to Decker and to his architects has been torn down.

Most of Purcell and Elmslie's houses, however, were small. They attacked the problem of the fifty-foot lot and the small budget as a poet might attack the constrictions imposed by the form of a sonnet. Purcell's own house cost $14,500 complete with its furniture, its frescoes, and its specially designed fixtures and was built on a lot 50 by 120 feet. Setback requirements were answered by pushing the structure to the rear of the lot so that it enjoyed the space and breeze of neighboring backyards, leaving a sunken garden with a 10- by 15-foot pool in front to screen the windows, which were patterned in leaded glass to enhance interior privacy. Their house for T. C. Bachus was built in 1915 for $2,992, including built-in furniture in the living and dining rooms, three bedrooms, a bath, and five large closets. The Bachus house, incidentally, separated the two children's bedrooms with a folding screen. All their houses, large or small, were designed with free-flowing interior space. While large commissions were executed for some wealthy clients, the majority of their residential work was done within budgets below $15,000, and those below $5,000, which were many, were actually built within their stated limits. (This would not have been the case, for example, with Wright's famous $5,000 house designed in 1906 for *The Ladies Home Journal*).

Our story comes to an end with Purcell and Elmslie, who asserted in Minnesota once again the great American tradition of domestic architecture. Though craftsmanship is a universal phenomenon, the impulse requiring men to work proudly in the humblest materials has a special significance in America, where homebuilding has been ennobled by the creed that the house of any man is a worthy theater for the exertion of talent, whatever may be his station in society or his function in the economy. It has never been the size of a house which determined its importance, but the quality of its design, its execution, and the quality of the life within.

There have been many references in this book to the symbolic function of residential architecture. I have throughout assumed that it was as important to ask how a house came to be as to appraise it as an object. Further, I believe that without the exertion of an owner's taste and creative will, a house becomes the product of outsiders, a thing laid up by strangers, however skilled. Therefore, I hope that these pages may encourage those who, on building a house, would shape it themselves, would give it their own character, undeterred by fashion or the smallness of their fortune. Most architects welcome a dialogue with their clients and do not scorn small commissions. Those of whom this cannot be said should not be entrusted with so serious a work as the creation of human habitation.

There is a second object in the writing of this book, an effort to enhance a consciousness of the wonders of this broad and fertile valleyland, of the profusion of human achievement here, of the color and vigor and variety of its history.

Boldness of individuality and sharpness of eye are the virtues to which this book is dedicated.

Appendixes

Appendix to chapter 1:
Some Minnesota Log Buildings

(From Paul Klammer, "Building With Logs," *Gopher Historian* (Fall 1963): 17.)

Beltrami County One-room log school in excellent condition. Located in Saum, Minnesota.

Carver County Scandia Swedish Baptist Church, one mile east of Waconia, built in 1858. Exterior covered with siding, but the logs may be seen inside the building.

Cook County (1) Forest ranger cabin on county fairgrounds, Grand Marais. (2) Holy Rosary Catholic Church, Grand Portage. Of tamarack logs covered with siding. Open during the summer.

Cottonwood County Cabin, built in 1868, now in Island Park, Windom. Originally had sod roof.

Freeborn County Livedalen Cabin of oak logs, built in 1853, now part of historical village on county fairgrounds, Albert Lea.

Itasca County Pioneer forest ranger cabin, on Little Cut Foot Sioux Lake.

Jackson County Cabin built before 1860, now in Ashley Park, Jackson. Former home of pioneer Norwegian settlers.

Kandiyohi County Cabin of Guri Endreson, heroine of Dakota War, northwest of Willmar near Solomon Lake.

Lac Qui Parle County Cabin made of large elm and cottonwood logs, on county fairgrounds, Madison. Open during annual fair.

Marshall County Pioneer cabin south on county fairgrounds in Settler's Square, Warren. Built in 1880.

Murray County Andrew Koch cabin of small logs, built before Dakota War of 1862, in Lake Shetek State Park.

Nicollet County (1) Cabin at Traverse des Sioux state wayside. (2) Restored log powder house in Fort Ridgely State Park.

Olmsted County Cabin built 1862, now on grounds of county historical society, Rochester.

Polk County Ole Bakken cabin near McIntosh on farm. The best example of pioneer log home in the state. Privately owned, but visitors welcomed.

Pope County Pioneer log home which served as first county courthouse. Now on lawn of courthouse, Glenwood. One room, squared logs, roof of hand-split shakes.

Ramsey County Muskego Lutheran Church, a small log chapel on the campus of Luther Theological Seminary, Como Avenue, St. Paul. Built in the 1840s; the logs now covered with siding.

Renville County Lerud Cabin built of logs in 1869 in Morton, and maintained by the Renville County Historical Society.

Traverse County Two-story log house, built in 1864 by Samuel J. Brown, now a museum in Sam Brown Memorial Park, Browns Valley.

Wadena County Pioneer log cabin located in city park, Sebeka.

Washington County Two mentioned in text in Marine-on-St. Croix; one on west side of Highway 97 between Marine and Copas.

Watonwan County Cabin built in 1857, now in Flanders Park, Madelia, and maintained by the county historical society.

■ ■ ■ ■

Appendix to chapter 4:
More Greek Revival Houses

THE GABLE-FRONT FORM

In Clearwater a fine small Grecian house was built between 1858 and 1860 by Nahum Walker, a millwright known as "Deacon Walker," a stern New Englander who was a pillar of the Congregational church built soon after his house (and used as a fort during the Dakota War in 1862).

In Dundas, across from the Episcopal church, Lorenzo Hamblin built a similar house in 1859. Local deeds show that it was bought soon afterward by Edward T. Archibald, of the family which was pioneering new flour-milling techniques on the river nearby. What it looked like before it was unporched is demonstrated by a more recent house said to have been built by a "Colonel Catterson" at 523 Main Street in Sauk Centre.

In Elk River, at 1033 4th Street, is a small two-story house which retains only the Grecian doorway under a lowered roof, but the doorway is a proud achievement in itself. Owatonna had a brick version of the same style at 218 South Oak Street, complete with half-returns and entablature board, now "modernized" with a jutting porch and flanking wing of a later vintage. In 1856, James and Frank Clark built a small Grecian house for Henry Jones at

506 Walnut Street in St. Peter using limestone blocks which have since been covered by cement. Jones was a pharmacist and an early associate of townsite promoter F. A. Donahower, who acquired the house some years later.

In Hastings, there is a house at 418 2nd Street which is unequivocally Grecian only in its doorway, but has about it the pride and the careful proportions which makes the style so welcome an encounter on dusty roads or in old villages. This was the Pringle House, built in 1855 or 1856 by Justice Benjamin Pringle of the United States Supreme Court, as a wedding present for his son George, a promising young attorney. George Pringle died at 29, but his family lived in the house until the 1890s.

One of the craftsmen brought from Kentucky to work on General Israel Garrard's St. Hubert's Lodge at Frontenac was Joseph Weich, who built his own house in the Grecian manner, drawing on examples he found at Lake City, the blooming port ten miles to the south. Lake City still has a dozen such houses which might once have caught his eye, though all are now encrusted by later carpentry.

A Red Wing attorney, Eli Wilder, built a larger Greek revival house at 805 3rd Street, about 1857.

BROADSIDE TYPES—THE ABERRANT THREE-BAY FORM

The three-bay "broadside Grecian" house, a reduced and generally non-symmetrical version of the more stately five-bay style, had some popularity. In Lake City, at Third and Oak Streets, one example of this type remains, of uncertain history, though probably built in the late 1850s. It still retains a front porch whose pillars, cut away into light trellises like those of the Folsom House, show the fanciful work of early homebuilders who were not intimidated by the Grecian mode.

At Second and Eighth Streets in Sauk Rapids, there is another version: William H. Fletcher built his "Sunnyside Farm" during the Civil War years. Pictures of the house in the 1870s show it with a small portico and a formal entry, and an un-Grecian jumble of appendages to the rear. It has survived virtually unchanged. Fletcher was born in Muskingum County, Ohio, in 1842. His family followed the westering trail to the Mississippi, thence up to St. Anthony in 1857, to Little Falls in 1858, and, finally, settled at Sauk Rapids in 1859. Fletcher himself manufactured wagons and harnesses, but his chief interest, apparently, was building hives and apiary materials.

The finest "broadside Grecian" house in the state lies on the west side of the main street in Franconia, one of the original lumber-milling towns of the St. Croix Valley, now a summer colony. It probably was built in the 1860s by the same Munch family that commissioned the fine gable-end house beside the St. Croix a few miles upstream in Taylors Falls.

■ ■ ■ ■

Appendix to chapter 5:
More Gothic Houses

There are many Gothic houses in Minnesota, the most prominent of which have been described in chapter 5. Here is a list of a number of others which are worthy of note.

In Fergus Falls, there are two: the first, built by a Judge Chapman at 309 Oakland, is a variation of the 1880s on the theme of the John Nichols house in Stillwater. The other, at 831 Mt. Faith, was built by Charles J. Wright at about the same time. Wright's daughter, who also lived in the house, believes that it was copied from a southern house he fancied, and was constructed by a bridge contractor.

In Stillwater, at 205 East Walnut, Rose Spencer built a tall house in the early 1870s at the base of a bluff, amid tall trees. It has no tracery, but displays double lancet windows and a buff-yellow color approved by Downing.

In Lake City, there are a number of houses whose only Gothic characteristic is a tall triple window set within an ogival arch, a staple feature of Victorian versions of the Venetian Gothic. The finest of these is at 310 South Oak Street. It may have been built in the late 1870s, but local records are uncertain. In Princeton, at 311 South 8th Street there is an L-shaped red-brick farmhouse, with a two-story section facing the street, bearing a beautiful sawtooth rhythm of carved wood along its eaves, and to the side is a wing with crested dormers and a confectioner's cresting above the porch. It was built by Dr. Ephraim C. Gile about 1875. Gile was a native of Steuben County, New York, where such houses usually wore Greek revival mouldings. The Greek revival had expired by the 1870s and the Gothic revival was still lively.

A more elaborate tossed-salad of styles, but still predominantly Gothic, is the farmhouse built at about the same time by Dennison T. Melandy in Greenwood Prairie, near Plainview, when he arrived from Vermont to start all over again at the age of 56. Like so many others, he had dented too many plows on too many fieldstones, and he went west to find deep, black prairie earth. The principal gable of his house has three lancet windows, and a dormer to the side has tracery and a Gothic pendent, but the doorway and lower windows are Grecian and there are Italianate brackets under the eaves. Variants of this type are to be found all along Highway 247 between Plainview and Highway 63.

In Rushford, George Stevens's son-in-law, G. R. Parker, erected a house about 1870 just a hundred yards away from Stevens's house, but miles apart in spirit. Stevens's had blended quietly into the land. It was built of stone, unobtrusively, but with an intention to last, to establish "order and culture." Parker's balloon-frame house rears up, vaunting wild, elaborate scroll-saw ornament, encrusted with shingles. It wears Tudor hood molds made anxious by cresting, and though it has a bright, lively character of its own, it has none of the literary, romantic character of earlier Gothic houses.

■ ■ ■ ■

Appendix to chapter 6:
The Origin of the Bracket

The appearance of the bracket in American architecture has never been satisfactorily explained. A number of hypotheses have been suggested: (1) The ornithological theory: the bracket grew out of the corbel, a sort of extended rafter, abstracted in stone for decorative purposes in many Renaissance buildings and Gothic buildings before them. The term "corbel" descends from the Latin *corvellus* or "little raven." Therefore, since brackets, at least at the outset of the bracketed style, were normally placed in pairs under the eaves, they may have arisen from an elaborate visual pun by a literate architect. This elaborate unlikelihood might be called the "perching bird" theory. (2) The theory of a classic precedent: J. Frazer Smith, in his *White Columns*, a study of the architecture of the Lower Mississippi Valley, suggests that they may be "the outgrowth of the modillion of the Corinthian Order combined with the triglyph of the Doric. This combination is apparent on Vignola's so-called cantilever cornice at Caprarola. Another ancient form which may serve as precedent for the bracket is the distorted form taken by the triglyph of the fourth order of the Colossum." Vignola was a great Italian Renaissance architect whose masterpiece is often said to be his villa at Caprarola, built for the Farnese family in 1535. His work was well known to Americans traveling in Italy. (3) The "boiling oil" or early Renaissance theory. A Farnese palace older than that at Caprarola, in Rome, would have been far more accessible to impressionable Americans, and it displays eaves supported by brackets considerably more like those which appeared later in America than those of the cantilever cornice. The eye is led from the Farnese Palace to another far more dramatic Roman cornice, that of the first great Renaissance palace of the city, the Palazzo Venezia. Begun in 1455, it has very long stone supports quite like those of the first great Renaissance palace in Siena, the Spanocchi Palace, of 1479, and the first of the famous country houses of the Medici, at Careggi near Florence, enlarged by Michelozzo for Cosimo il Vecchio in 1417. These are all transition buildings, marking the passing of the fortified house, whose eaves were extended to provide a platform for defenders, perforated to afford convenient dumping of boiling oil on the heads of besiegers, and supported by machicolations, stone supports spaced so as to let the oil and rocks fall unimpeded. These later palaces retained the machicolations for their decorative value, but omitted the perforations, and their roofs soon lost their battlements as well. The search for picturesque details may well have been rewarded by these celebrated ancient structures, which presented an element readily applicable to any sort of structure. The machicolations may have been merged in the anonymous architectural composite mind which developed the bracketed style with a fourth possible source: (4) The medieval bracket possibility. The Parson Capon house was merely one of many in New England in the seventeenth century whereon an overhanging second story was not actually supported, but merely provided occasion for showy carven brackets. Brackets were probably used elsewhere, though the Cupola house in Edenton, North Carolina, seems to be the only surviving southern example. In the 1840s, Americans were beginning to look to their own past for precedents, and it is possible that brackets were the first signs of the later colonial revival. (5) The picturesque chalet theory. Scholarly readers seem to prefer the thesis suggested in the text that brackets were taken from picturesque wooden houses like Swiss chalets, which appeared in the pattern books in the 1840s and 1850s, and spread from thence to many picturesque styles, particularly the Italianate. The author himself reserves judgment.

■ ■ ■ ■

Appendix to chapter 10:
The Houses of Frank Lloyd Wright and
Purcell & Elmslie in Minnesota

FRANK LLOYD WRIGHT HOUSES OF IN MINNESOTA

Original Owner	Date	Address
R. W. Lindholm	1955	Cloquet
Donald Lovness	1954	Route 3, Woodpile Lake, Stillwater
Malcolm M. Willey	1934	255 Bedford Street, Minneapolis
Henry J. Neils	1951	2815 Burnham Boulevard, Minneapolis
Dr. A. H. Bulbulian	1951	Skyway Drive, Rochester
Thomas E. Keyes	1951	Skyway Drive, Rochester
S. P. Elam	1951	107 Eastwood Road, Austin
Paul C. Olfelt	1960	St. Louis Park

(There is at least one more of Wright's design, but disavowed by him because he disapproved of its site.)

■ ■ ■ ■

PURCELL AND ELMSLIE HOUSES IN MINNESOTA

(A list compiled, with descriptions, by David S. Gebhard.)

Adair, Dr. John, M.D.—dwelling, 1913
322 East Vine Street, Owatonna
In excellent condition, both exterior and interior.

Bachus, C. T.—dwelling, 1915
212 West 36th Street, Minneapolis
An outstanding example of the firm's small, open-plan houses. This house remains as originally built. Built for less than $3,000.

Baker, W. E.—dwelling, 1910
1805 Fremont Avenue South, Minneapolis
Basic form remains unchanged; exterior has been partially re-covered with shingles, several modifications in interior. This is an interesting example of the firm's early open-plan houses.

Beebe, Dr. Ward, M.D.—dwelling, 1912
2022 Summit Avenue, St. Paul
In original condition, both exterior and interior; present exterior color not
original.

Buxton, C. L.—bungalow, 1912
424 East Main Street, Owatonna
In excellent condition, both interior and exterior; garage not designed by
firm. Two-level plan with bedrooms on ground floor, living area opening to
rear garden.

Carlson, Fritz C.—dwelling, 1917
3612 17th Avenue South, Minneapolis
One of the firm's small, open-plan houses; built by construction foreman on
many and varied Purcell and Elmslie operations.

Decker, Edward W.—dwelling, 1912–13
Route 101 at Holdridge, Lake Minnetonka
House no longer standing, but the garage and service buildings, including
apartment for chauffeur, are still in existence. Original house of concrete and
steel in the form of large cross.

Gallager, J. W. S.—dwelling, 1913
457 Broadway, Winona
In excellent condition; both interior and exterior; planting box by front entrance not original, nor present color of stucco.

Gallaher, H. P.—dwelling, 1909–10
Route 1, Zumbra Heights, Lake Minnetonka
The exterior still preserves its original forceful design. The interior has been
extensively remodeled.

Goetzenberger, Edward—dwelling, 1910
2621 Emerson Avenue South, Minneapolis
A number of later remodelings have somewhat changed the interior and exterior design of this house. Nevertheless it is a good example of the firm's
small, inexpensive, open-plan houses.

Goodnow, M. D.—dwelling, 1913
446 Main Street, Hutchinson
In excellent condition, both interior and exterior.

Gray, Catherine—dwelling, 1907
2409 East Lake of the Isles Boulevard, Minneapolis
Very little of the original house now remains after continuous remodelings
over four decades. Only original section is the street facade, side entrance, and
stair bay. The house is a Purcell-Feick project. Although Elmslie produced its

plan, Purcell did the facades. Thus, it is one of the first Purcell and Elmslie houses.

Hineline, Harold E.—dwelling, 1910
4920 Dupont Avenue South, Minneapolis
In good condition with some interior changes; side and rear screened porches recently enclosed.

Hoyt, E. S.—dwelling, 1913
300 Hill Street, Red Wing
In excellent condition both interior and exterior. This is in excellent state of preservation. Red color of exterior plaster is original and gives an accurate indication of how colored plaster was used by the firm. The covered walk and garage were added in 1915 by the firm, entailing a unique parking and entrance solution for the garage.

Mueller, Paul—studio and office, 1910–11
4845 Bryant Avenue South, Minneapolis
Although a number of changes have been made in this small building, it still retains its original Purcell and Elmslie quality. The basement garage in front was added at a later date. This dwelling originally stood in a grove of tall white pines.

Owre, Dr. Oscar, D.D.—dwelling, 1911–12
2625 Newton Avenue South, Minneapolis
In excellent condition, both interior and exterior. Fence and garage added by the firm in 1918. This is one of the firm's first examples of the open-plan house.

Parker, Charles J.—dwelling, 1912–13
4829 Colfax Avenue South, Minneapolis
In excellent condition, both interior and exterior; upper attic dormers not a part of the original design nor is the present garage.

Powers, E. L.—dwelling, 1910–11
1635 26th Street West, Minneapolis
In excellent condition, both interior and exterior; present exterior plaster not original (originally plaster was a light red brick).

Purcell, William Gray—dwelling, 1913
2328 Lake Place, Minneapolis
The high point of the firm's domestic work. In excellent condition, both interior and exterior. Still contains mural paintings by Charles Livingston Bull and Lawton Gray Parker.

Tillotson, E. C.—dwelling, 1912
2316 Oliver Avenue South, Minneapolis
In excellent condition on exterior with the exception of the light plaster color;

some alterations on interior. An example of the firm's larger open-plan houses. Plan and design especially related to the narrow, north-facing lot with close, built-in houses on either side. Idea being to secure all possible sun from the front and rear garden.

Wakefield, Lyman E.—dwelling, 1911
4700 Fremont Avenue South, Minneapolis
In excellent condition; both interior and exterior. Garage not designed by firm.

Wiethoff, Charles—dwelling, 1917
4609 Humboldt Avenue South, Minneapolis
Some interior alterations, exterior in good condition. A good example of a late Purcell and Elmslie open-plan house.

Wolf, Maurice I.—dwelling, 1912–13
4109 Dupont Avenue South, Minneapolis
The firm did not supervise construction and some changes were made in the original design. Later alterations have been made to both the interior and exterior. Garage not designed by firm.

Notes

Note to chapter 1: The Sources of Pioneer Architecture

1. A local history pamphlet—Guide to Galena.

Notes to chapter 3: The Houses the Germans Built

1. No one can write conscientiously about this field without relying heavily upon the research of Bishop James P. Shannon, represented in his book *Catholic Colonization on the Western Frontier,* New Haven, 1957, and of Father Colman J. Barry, former president of St. John's University in Collegeville which appeared in his work on *The Catholic Church and German Americans,* Milwaukee, 1953. Neither could be held responsible for any of the sometimes unorthodox suggestions advanced in this chapter, but they have supplied the basic materials from which all of us who follow must mold our own conclusions. There is probably no more controversial area of American religious history than that which surrounds the conflict of Archbishop John Ireland and Peter Paul Cahensly, and that conflict lies in the center of this story. It illuminates German-American architecture, and can be better understood after examining that architecture. Therefore, the method of this book requires us to examine it with considerable care. Father Colman Barry's book, in particular, makes that examination possible for a layman.

2. Faust himself, the dark angel of German liberalism, "becomes the settler, the frontiersman on a vast ocean of savagery, he becomes the American, transforming a wild continent into the habitable abode of rational men. Often we have said, much oftener have we thought, that this Second Part of *Faust* in many portions becomes an American book, or rather the *Mythus* of America. . . ." (Carl J. Friedrich, *The Forty-Eighters,* edited by A. E. Zucker, NY, 1950, 12). For Carl Schurz, the intellectual leader of the Forty-Eighters, America was the seat of a new race of men. Speaking at Faneuil Hall in Boston, he spoke of Americans as "led together by the irresistible attraction of free and broad principles . . . in the colony of free humanity, whose mother-country is the world, they establish the Republic of equal rights, where the title of manhood is the title to citizenship. My friends, if I had a thousand tongues and a voice strong as the thunder of heaven, they would not be sufficient to impress upon your minds forcibly enough greatness of this idea. . . ." As to German classicism: "Periclean Athens and Republican Rome were seen

as universal teachers of a creed that included all nations" (*The Forty-Eighters*, 19). Thomas Jefferson's Virginia State Capitol in Richmond was paralleled, in Germany, by such vast projects as Friedrich Gilly's monument to Frederick the Great, and the Walhalla, built at Regensburg by Leo Von Klenze, a new Parthenon, on a new Acropolis. It is not strange that New Ulm, founded in 1854 by a group of Forty-Eighters, looked very much like Taylors Falls. They were both Greek revival, white-frame towns. New Ulm was built by men who sought to accord, as much as possible, to patterns of an America they admired, and who already shared a body of ideas with those Americans who had embraced the Greek revival.

3. See Plate XXXVII of Morris's *Select Architecture*, which appears in T. T. Waterman, *Mansions of Virginia, 1706–1776* (1946), 379; and Plate XVIII in Talbot Hamlin, *The Greek Revivals* (1944).

4. New Ulm was never so Jacobin as some communities in Wisconsin. Twenty-three freethinker societies were established in that state, where children were baptized "in the name of the United States of America," where the liberty pole and the cap of freedom, symbols brought into Germany by the armies of the French Revolution, could be seen well into the twentieth century. The desire to embrace American ways, including American architecture and language, was part of a determination to leave Old Germany behind. Frederick Holmes reports of one of the citadels of these '48ers, Thiensville, that "for eighty years Thiensville resisted Christianizing influences. They had their dead buried under memorials to their name only." They were married without benefit of clergy, in what was called in the neighborhood that "God-forsaken Village," where a collection for a church met with an offer of twice as much not to build one. It was not until 1919 that a Catholic church was erected in Thiensville, not until 1929 that it had its first Protestant church (Holmes, *Old World Wisconsin*, Eau Claire, 1944).

5. Fearing that Cahenslyite views might prevail in Rome, Ireland cabled his friend Monsignor O'Connell that "great disturbance, danger of schism and persecution unless Rome denounce Cahensly, and denounce once for all, and for time being name no German Bishops" (Barry, *The Catholic Church*, 142). A year later he was called to Rome to defend his "Americanizing" policy, especially his permitting the towns of Faribault and Stillwater to take over two parochial schools against the vehement objections of the Jesuits and Archbishop Corrigan of New York. On April 21 a committee of five cardinals approved Ireland's actions, and Cahensly wrote that "Msgr. Ireland has won so much influence in Rome and so charmed the Holy Father and the Cardinals, that it would be hard to shake that influence" (Barry, 199).

6. On January 14, 1885, the *New Ulm Review* recorded that one building projected for the year by Ruemke and Schapekahm was a building for August Schell, and, a year later, that the cost was $6,000.

Herman G. Schapekahm was born in Germany in 1855, and went to New Ulm at sixteen where he learned a carpenter's trade. In 1878 he went to St. Louis to study architectural drawing and building. Returning to New Ulm in 1880 he established himself as an architect and contractor. Many of the largest structures in New Ulm were built under his direction and supervision.

Notes to chapter 5: The Gothic Revival

1. Geoffrey Scott, *The Architecture of Humanism* (New York: Doubleday Anchor Ed., undated, 62).

2. John Vanbrugh, the stage designer, dramatist, and architect who probably initiated the Gothic revival in England with his own castle-like house in 1717, had said: "The contemplation on ancient ruins moves lively and pleasing reflections . . . on the persons who have inhabited them [and] on the remarkable things which have been transacted in them" (Morrison, 573).

3. Beckford ordered his architect to fashion "an ornamental building . . . partly in ruins and yet contain some weatherproof apartments," and, before he was done, had enclosed within eight miles of twelve-foot walls a tower as high as a twenty-seven-story building, around which spread a great castellated mansion of which the wings, running to the north and south, were four hundred feet in length. (Beside this, the great American Gothic House, "Staunton Hill," in Virginia, was a cottage. Its walls were only a mile and three-quarters by a mile and a half, and it had only thirteen rooms in the main block, to Fonthill's fifty.)

4. One of Mr. Downing's followers invoked a sort of nostalgic colonialism, asserting that "we of this Saxon race feel somehow always a home-whispering voice at the heart when we gaze upon some crumbling beauty of Gothic Art in our nation's birth place across the ocean different and more dear than the emotions that fill our souls in Greece or Italy" (Quoted in Maass, 61). For many, the home-whispering voice was shouted down by practical objections: Said the *New York Mirror* on October 17, 1846: "It was quite pardonable in Horace Walpole and Sir Walter Scott to build gingerbread houses with rusty old armour, lances, drinking horns and mouldy tapestry, and they were surrounded by the memorials of the times they were idly trying to revive. But there can be nothing more grotesque, more absurd, or more affected, than for a quiet gentleman, who has made his fortune in the peaceful occupation of selling calicos, and who knows no more of the middle ages than they know of him to erect for his family residence a gimcrack of a Gothic castle . . . as though he anticipated an attack upon his roost from some Front de Boeuf in the neighborhood."

5. Downing went to some pains to disclaim any effort to prettify houses with details "at variance with propriety, comfort or sound workmanship," but there was difficulty in deciding what propriety permitted and when sound workmanship became whimsical decoration. James Russell Lowell satirized "the Rural Cot of Mr. Knott . . . the greenest of antiques

> (whose) architect worked for weeks
> Inventing all his private peaks
> Upon the roof etc. . . .

Downing quoted Lowell's lines with approval as a cautionary tale against what he did not have in mind, but the lesson was lost.

6. In his doctorate thesis on "Minneapolis Architecture and Architects, 1848–1908" (1951, available in the University of Minn. library), Donald Torbert suggests that it is based on two Downing patterns, "a Gatehouse for Blithewood on the Hudson," designed by Alexander J. Davis and pictured in

Rural Residences of 1837, and " A Cottage in the English or Rural Gothic Style," shown in the second edition of *Cottage Residences* of 1844. Another Davis design, a cottage for William H. Drake in Hartford, Connecticut, seems a possible contender.

7. Op cit., 47. Drip-caps, incidentally, are also called hood molds and were originally employed to prevent rain from coursing down stone surfaces onto the glass or parchment windows. They generally took two forms in Minnesota: the "basket-handle" type, flattened on the top, and the "horse-collar" type, rounded or arched.

8. Sibley was returning to an area of the state where he had already suffered one disappointment: an abortive town promotion he, Alexander Ramsey, William G. Le Duc, and Henry M. Rice had organized on "Minnesota Point," a sandpit in Duluth's harbor.

9. The Minneapolis suburb of Morningside was an early picturesque development, laid out by landscape architect Jonathan T. Grimes according to Downing's ideas. Grimes's house, at 4200 W. Forty-Fourth Street, is of mixed Gothic and Italian design, and was built about 1869.

Notes to chapter 6: The Italianate Styles

1. The early eighteenth-century palaces designed by Sir John Vanbrugh in England possessed such towers. A man of the theater, he may have borrowed the concept, quite literally, from Italian stage scenery. The evidence is inconclusive.

2. At Eighth and Vermillion, in Hastings, is the Byron Howes House, which may have been very similar (it was built about the same time) but was considerably altered in the 1880s.

3. The mansion built by wholesale grocer F. A. Theopold at 29 First Street sw in Faribault carried the trend further. The center gable now has a large, framed circular window, and the roof, rising up toward a mansard, has acquired dormers, and there is an out-thrust center section.

4. The persistence of older, simpler forms of decoration in communities far from the urban cockpit of competing fashions is illustrated in the severe horizontal supports under the eaves of an Italianate house of the intermediate, gable-roofed variety built in Redwood Falls by Henry D. Chollar, in 1878. Chollar came from the second staging area of New England westering, upstate New York, and had accumulated some capital as a traveling salesman. He began his house soon after he arrived in Redwood Falls to establish a lumber business. Its grave but impressive bulk, at Fourth and Minnesota, a block from the main street, established his respectability. He became mayor of the town and died in 1887 after falling from the Redwood River Bridge, where he had been watching a threshing machine work its way across the rickety structure. Dr. S. F. Ceplecha later transformed the interior into a clinic, but its graceful circular staircase and fine paneling remain intact. Its corbels have elongated to earn the name of consoles, but they had not yet yielded to the fashion, long since established elsewhere, to dip and curve and become true brackets.

5. William Channing Whitney, one of the most versatile of the fashionable architects working in Minneapolis in the early years of the twentieth century,

created the finest of these monuments to scholarship in the Elbert L. Carpenter house on Clifton Avenue in Minneapolis, in 1906. It is certainly a more beautiful structure than the naive bracketed houses a generation older, but it is an architect's house, not an owner's house. It tells us that Mr. Carpenter had the taste to select a good architect and, perhaps, to make suggestions as to the style he preferred, but the directing influence has ceased to be that of the owner and had become that of the architect.

Note to chapter 7: Architecture at Mid-century

1. Norrish and his neighbor, Dr. William Thorne, had both come from Devonshire to the boomtown of Hastings. Both built houses of stone overlooking the river. Thorne's bracketed cube has suffered from later additions; Norrish's octagon was later sold to H. B. Clafin and divided into five apartments.

Another house on the same scale, but with a slightly higher mansard was built by banker John H. Ray at 217 Lincoln in Mankato. It is chiefly noteworthy for the leaded-glass fanlight over the door. The Blue Earth County Historical Society in Mankato inhabits a fine mansard mansion built in 1868, but considerably remodeled in the 1880s. In Hastings, the mansion at 612 Vermillion Street, on which Wilson J. Van Dyke lavished $25,000, a great sum in 1868, was accounted "one of the finest residences in the state." It has declined since into an apartment house carrying a slatternly wing to the side.

Notes to chapter 9: The Architecture of Propriety

1. The Panic of 1857 smote Minnesota hard, but its effect was brief. Architecturally, it occurred at a time when classicism was still vigorous, and the Greek revival, its final flowering, was in full bloom. Therefore, no "classicizing" or sobering effect upon architecture could be observed: the result was white upon white.

2. The quotation continues:

> Occasionally, however, there looms up in the field of the ordinary and practical some example of lavish monied expenditure which at once assures an intelligent observer that culture and refinement have combined with wealth in its production. . . . To convey anything like an adequate idea of the character and convenience of this model and modern home—which equals the most pretentious in any of our American cities and surpasses the general average of the finest residences in cities like Cleveland, Detroit, Buffalo, Milwaukee and others of that class— would require a minute and technical description of every apartment. . . . The ball room is fifty feet square and in some important features is probably unsurpassed by that in any private home in the country. . . . Relatively considered, the average man and trained architect and specialist would probably consider Mr. Harrington's stables even a more complete utilitarian and scientific triumph than is the residence. It is undoubtedly the most perfect building for its purposes that has yet been constructed either in this country or in Europe. . . . So perfect is the heating, ventilating and flushing, which is that of the recently perfected American Sanitary Stall system, that not a trace of antimonial

odors are possible anywhere in the building, not even in the stalls. Indeed, there are comparatively few residences in which the problems in sanitation have been so perfectly solved. . . . The carriage floors each side of the runway affords opportunity for pleasing decoration, which is utilized by the foreman in charge by a light covering of snow-white sand upon which he has stenciled conventional designs in brilliant colors. For the week of the Fourth of July the designs will consist of "Old Glory" and other evidences of patriotic citizenship.

[The Harrington house has become the clubhouse of a Masonic order.]

3. Vincent Scully has noted how houses of this sort comported with the social background outlined in the previous chapter, which America in the late nineteenth century had in common with Italy in the late sixteenth: "The association of colonial architecture with 'good breeding' is typical of both an antiquarian and academic point of view since the phrase, with all its connotations, expresses the psychological drives leading to both positions. . . . Much of the impetus leading toward the establishment of academies in the sixteenth century was apparently a desire for security, and the *American Architect's* statement [enjoining a strict adherence to the Renaissance tradition even though the result be monotonous and uninteresting] . . . reveals a distrust of the ever-changing present which feeds at similar sources."

4. These photographs, in a monograph on Cram's work in the St. Paul Public Library, solemnly repeat, on page after page, the address "Winona, Illinois" (*Cram and Ferguson,* New York, 1929).

Glossary

Architrave The lowest division of the entablature.

Balustrade A row of short pillars of circular section, surmounted by rail or coping.

Barbican An extension of a fortified place.

Bargeboards Decorated boards along the sloping edges of a gable roof.

Belvedere The upper story of a structure, designed to provide a fine view, often in the form of a cupola.

Broadside A convenient term to describe that type of gable-roofed Greek revival house which confronts the street with its door and turns its gables to the sides.

Captain's walk A flat deck on a roof enclosed with balustrades.

Center gable A term to describe that type of Gothic revival house which presents to the street a gable in the center of the facade.

Cornice A horizontal molding projecting from the line formed by the roof meeting the wall; the uppermost part of an entablature.

Cupola A rounded vault or dome forming the roof of a building or part of a building.

Dentils A row of small blocks along an entablature.

Dormer window A window cut into the roof to provide light for attic rooms.

Entablature That part of a classic architectural order which rests horizontally upon the columns and consists of the architrave, frieze, and cornice.

Facade The face or front of a building.

Frieze A band of painted or sculptured decoration.

Gable front A convenient term to describe that type of gable-roofed Greek revival house which is turned so the gable faces the street and the door is situated in the front facing the street.

Hip roof A roof which rises by equally inclined planes from all four sides of a building.

Hood mold The heavy molding over a window.

Hooked gable Defined in the text: a convenient term to describe a pedimented gable upon which the horizontal element linking the feet of the cornice has been indicated only, the center portion having been removed.

Lintel A horizontal supporting beam over an opening.

Loggia A gallery or arcade open to the air on at least one side, often a succession of arches.

Mansard roof A form of roof with two slopes, the lower slope approaching the vertical and the upper slope nearly flat.

Oriel window A bay window, especially on an upper story, having several sides.

Parget Ornamental or fine plasterwork bearing designs in low relief.

Pavilion A building dependent upon a larger or principal building, as a summer house; more especially a dependent residential building or a projecting element on the front or side of a building.

Pedimented gable A gable upon which the foot of the cornice is connected with the opposite foot with a horizontal string course or board.

Pendant A hanging ornament.

Pilaster A flat square column attached to a wall and projecting from it, simulating a pillar.

Porte-cochère A porch at the door of a house which shelters persons entering and leaving vehicles.

Quoins Blocks of stone laid either flush with the wall at the corners of a building or projecting from it.

Rustication Grooving of walls made of wooden planks to simulate stone masonry.

Sidelight A vertical row of windows on either side of a doorway.

Weatherboards Horizontal wood siding.

A Selected, Annotated Bibliography

The best way to approach Minnesota history for the first time is with the humane and gently humorous Theodore C. Blegen as a guide. His one volume *Minnesota History*, published in 1963, is convenient, comprehensive, and incorporates a lifetime of study. It also includes a lengthy bibliographical section covering sources for the study of all major aspects of the growth of the state, and there is no need to duplicate his effort. The earlier great work was William Watts Folwell's four-volume *History of Minnesota* (1921–30) for Folwell was a participant as well as a chronicler. Return I. Holcomb and his associates produced a good anthological history in 1908 which has some excellent biographical material. And of late the Minnesota AIA has produced *100 Places + 1: An Unofficial Architectural Survey of Favorite Minnesota Sites:* http://www.aia-mn.org/101_places.cfm

Now, to pick up the bibliography where I left it forty-odd years ago, and add a few thoughts.

In 2005 the first good book of the French colonial architecture appeared, *French America: French Architecture From Colonization To The Birth Of A Nation,* by Ron Katz, with photography by Arielle De La Tour D'Auvergne, whose mother, the indomitable Princesse Marisol de la Tour D'Auvergne, got the job done, charming a lot of people, including me, to write pieces of the book, in my case the introduction as well. Minnesotans have the good fortune to have the benefit of Grace Lee Nute's specialized studies in the fur trade and good amateur works like Hamilton N. Ross's study of *La Pointe* (1960). My *Orders from France* was intended to fill some of the void with regard to the neoclassical period.

Hugh Morrison's *Early American Architecture* (1952) is the great work in that field, more comprehensive than Fiske Kimball's *Domestic Architecture of the American Colonies* (1922) and Harold D. Eberlein's *Architecture in Colonial America* (1927). Rexford Newcomb examines a more restricted territory in his *Architecture in the Old Northwest Territory* (1950). A number of shorter and more popular surveys have appeared, the best of which is *Identifying American Architecture: A Pictorial Guide to Styles and Terms : 1600-1945* by John J. G. Blumenson. Others include *American House Styles: A Concise Guide* by John Milnes Baker; *American Houses : A Field Guide to the Architecture of the Home* by Gerald L. Foste, and *What Style Is It? A Guide to Ameri-*

can Architecture by John C. Poppeliers. The best of state architectural studies is Thomas T. Waterman's *The Early Architecture of North Carolina* (1941). Waterman's *Mansions of Virginia 1706-1776* (1946) is difficult to obtain but well worth the effort, as is Richard W. E. Perrin's *Wisconsin's Pioneer Architecture*, a pamphlet which deserves the opulent treatment given by the Indiana Historical Society, and the Lilly Endowment to Wilber D. Peat's *Indiana Houses of the Nineteenth Century* (1962). Another local study is Thomas E. Tallmadge's pleasantly opinionated *Architecture of Old Chicago*. The best kind of committee work produced *Historic St. Paul Buildings* with text by H. F. Koeper (1964), to which I have attempted some additions in this volume. While Mills Lane was alive he saw to it that the Southern states got good books of photographs of their antebellum architecture, with elegant, accurate texts.

Specific periods of architectural history have gathered treatments of their own, though the profession of architectural history has not in recent years encouraged grand syntheses in intelligible prose, produced great writers interested in attempting to cover the whole story, except for one. My *Greek Revival America* benefited from a subsidy from the Polaroid Corporation to pay excellent photographers, and won some awards; it was intended to make more accessible, visual, and contextual the work of previous scholars such as Talbot Hamlin, in his *The Greek Revival of 1944*, and to suggest some of the social and psychological context of the Greek Revivial—quotation marks probably best provided, because it wasn't very Greek.

Hamlin's work has been reissued in paperback, and so has Vincent Scully's *The Shingle Style*. Lewis Mumford takes a broad swath, including architecture, in his *Sticks and Stones* (1924) and *The Brown Decades* (1931), both fortunately reissued in paperback, as does John Gloag in his *Victorian Taste* (1962). Kenneth Clark's august volume on *The Gothic Revival* (1928) is limited to Britain but its language is beautiful, and the same can be said of Geoffrey Scott's *The Architecture of Humanism*, which Mr. Clark acknowledged as the work which led him into the field, and which has now also been reissued in paperback. The British have a long tradition of writing architectural criticism in a style which is itself an art form. There is not yet an elegant, inviting, and capacious book on the American Gothic revival, though there are some competent textbooks for college courses.

If the British generalists are writing belle-lettres, some of the Americans whose books give delight as well as information are too often dismissed as "mere" journalists, presumably because much of their work first appeared in magazines of general circulation, without footnotes. Among the best of these are Russell Lynes, *The Tastemakers* (1949); John Maass, *The Gingerbread Age* (1957); and Wayne Andrews, *Architecture, Ambition and Americans,* reissued in 1964. Oliver Larkin's *Art and Life in America* (1960) is a well-written survey of a large field. And speaking of Larkins, David Larkin has produced a series of splendid illustrated books on American architecture, including several with entries from Minnesota.

There are many monographs on individual architects, of which the following were particularly useful in this study. R. H. Newton's *Town and Davis* (1942); studies of Louis Sullivan by Hugh Morrison (1935), by Albert Bush-

Brown (1960), and more journalistically, by Willard Connelly (1960). Crombie Taylor's magnificent collection of Sullivan's own selection of photographs of his work shows how Sullivan wanted his buildings to be seen, and was recently published by the University of Virginia Press. The Frank Lloyd Wright bibliography is huge—take your pick. It is shameful that Andrew Jackson Downing and Orson Squire Fowler are still in the limbo of the out-of-print. Though I did my best for parts of the story in *Architecture, Men, Women, and Money*, and *Rediscovering America*, and both Wayne Andrews and Leonard Eaton bit off other pieces, there still is no answer to William Gray Purcell's cry for a comprehensive study of the work of the Progressives or the Prairie School and their clients. Michael Conforti and his colleagues did a fine job of presenting the social and artistic world in which the Progressives thrived in their *Art and Life on the Upper Mississippi (1890–1915)* (1994).

In Minnesota history, some reference to individual works should be made, despite the fact that Dean Blegen has covered the bibliographical field, to serve the interests of readers who are particularly interested in the relationship of architectural and social history. C. W. G. Hyde and William Stoddard's *History of the Great Northwest* (1901) gives the sort of information about the Minnesota-Dakota borderland not available elsewhere. William H. C. Folsom did the same for the St. Croix region in *Fifty Years in the Northwest* (1888). He has been seconded by James T. Dunn's *The St. Croix* (1965), a good popular work by the expert in the field. The Rev. Edward D. Neill presided over a history of the *Minnesota Valley* (1882) and of the *Upper Mississippi Valley* which are really anthologies of anonymous contributions. Wilson P. Shortridge used Henry Hastings Sibley as the central figure in his thesis on *The Passing of a Typical Frontier* (1919), but Rhoda R. Gilman recently published a wonderful biography on Sibley, *Henry Hastings Sibley: Divided Heart* (2004).

James J. Hill deserves much better than Joseph G. Pyle's dutiful official biography, *The Life of James J. Hill* (1917) and Stuart Holbrook's short and informal volume of 1955. It's a pity that the only scholar-statesman who was interested in doing better by Hill, Bishop James P. Shannon, never got around to it—but he did so much other good in his extraordinary life that one less accomplishment can be forgiven him. The files of *Minnesota History* include a wealth of articles on many phases of the state's development and a comprehensive Web index is now available to the layperson. Tribute should be accorded to June L. Holmquist and Jean A. Brookin's *Minnesota's Major Historic Sites* (1963). It is indispensible to residents of the state who have any curiosity about its history. For those interested in specific aspects of economic development, the definitive works are Agnes M. Larson's *The White Pine Industry in Minnesota* (1949) and Merrill E. Jarchow's agricultural history, *The Earth Brought Forth* (1949), and Jeff Forrester's engaging and feisty *The Forest for the Trees* (2004).

Since Frederick Jackson Turner read his famous paper to the historians assembled for the Chicago Columbian Exposition of 1893, the literature of the frontier has outgrown section after section of the stacks. I have found the following books particularly useful, and I'm sure I've missed a dozen more: Turner's own essays collected in a paperback, *The Frontier in American His-*

tory (1962); another collection by his disciple Ray Allen Billington, *The Western Movement in the United States,* paperback (1959); Walter Prescott Webb's great speculation *The Great Frontier* (1952); Henry Nash Smith's *Virgin Land* (1950), and several of David Lavender's evocations of specific men and places, the latest of which is his chronicle of Ramsey Crooks and the fur trade, *A Fist In The Wilderness* (1963).

Cited in the text and footnotes as readable and useful, and so much so that their qualities should be reaffirmed here, are *The Forty-Eighters,* edited by A. E. Zuker (1950); *Catholic Colonization on the Western Frontier,* James P. Shannon (1957); *The Catholic Church and German Americans,* Colman J. Berry (1953).

Finally, as becomes a great state historical society—in my view the nation's best—the Minnesota Historical Society has provided: *Building Community, Keeping the Faith: German Catholic Vernacular Architecture in a Rural Minnesota Parish,* Fred W Peterson (1998); *Cap Wigington: An Architectural Legacy in Ice and Stone,* David Vassar Taylor and Paul Clifford Larson (2001); *Cass Gilbert: The Early Years,* Geoffrey Blodgett (2001); *Germans in Minnesota* (People of Minnesota series), Kathleen Neils Conzen (2003); *Lost Twin Cities,* Larry Millett (1992); *Mill City: A Visual History of Minneapolis Mill District,* edited by Shannon M. Pennefeather (2003); *The National Register of Historic Places in Minnesota,* compiled by Mary Ann Nord (2003); *Minnesota Treasures: Stories behind the State's Historic Places,* Denis P. Gardner (2004).

Listing of Houses

Note: Page numbers in *italic* indicate illustrations.

Winslow, C. A.	Government Rd., Taylors Falls	68, *69*
Clay County		
Comstock, Solomon	506 Eighth St. S., Moorhead	147–48
Dakota County		
du Puis, Hypolite	1357 Sibley Memorial Hwy., Mendota	35
Faribault, Jean Baptiste	1357 Sibley Memorial Hwy., Mendota	28, *29*
Freeman, Reuben	9091 Inver Grove Trail, lnver Grove Heights	45–46, *46*
Sibley, Henry Hastings	1357 Sibley Memorial Hwy., Mendota	23–25, *25*
Dodge County		
Doig, Andrew	Wasioja	41, *42*, 43
Douglas County		
Johnson, J. B.	north side of Hwy. 52, Osakis	134
Fillmore County		
Stevens, George	Rushford	83–84, *85*, 150
Goodhue County		
Garrard, Israel	Frontenac	6–8, *7*, 127
Hoyt, E. S.	300 Hill St., Red Wing	114, 197, *197*, 208
Lawther, James L.	Third and Hill Sts., Red Wing	113, 131–32, *132*, 134
Rich, John H.	1015 Fourth St., Red Wing	170
Sheldon, Theodore B.	805 Fourth St., Red Wing	137–38
Sprague, Philander	Third and Hill Sts., Red Wing	*113*, 113–14
Westervelt, Evert	Frontenac	78, *79*
Hennepin County		
Akeley, H. C.	2300 Park Ave., Minneapolis	185
Armstrong, John A.	242 S. Fifth St., Minneapolis	119–20, *121*
Atwater, Isaac	1607 S. Fifth St., Minneapolis	97
Bachus, C. T.	212 W. 36th St., Minneapolis	198–99
Cutter, B. O.	Tenth Ave. and Fourth St., Minneapolis	97–99, *98*
Decker, Edward W.	Route 101 at Holdridge, Lake Minnetonka	xi, 198
Florida-Stork House	on the Crow River, Rockford	19
Gale, Edward	2115 Stevens Ave., Minneapolis	178, *179*
Godfrey, Ard	50 University Ave. NE, Minneapolis	75, *75*
Harrington, Charles M.	2540 Park Ave., Minneapolis	168
Little, Francis	Deephaven, razed in 1972	xi, 194
Pond, Gideon H.	401 E. 104th St., Bloomington	35–36
Powers, E. L	1635 26th St. W., Minneapolis	197
Purcell, William Gray	2328 Lake Place, Minneapolis	xi, *196*, 197, 198
Semple, Frank B.	Blaisdell and Franklin Aves., Minneapolis	179
Smith, C. Alden	1403 Harmon Pl., Minneapolis	185
Snyder, John P.	2118 Blaisdell Ave., Minneapolis	178
Stevens, John H.	Minnehaha Park, Minneapolis	75–76
Turnblad, Swan J.	2600 Park Ave., Minneapolis	159–61, *160*, 162
Van Dusen, George W.	1900 LaSalle, Minneapolis	157, *158*
unknown	2500 Portland Ave., Minneapolis	155

Houston County

Cameron, Daniel J.	429 S. Seventh St., La Crescent	116

Kandiyohi County

Frost, Edward S.	321 W. Seventh St., Willmar	119

Le Sueur County

Snow, George D.	129 S. Second St., Le Sueur	*74*, 74–75
Taylor, George W.	Second and Bridge Sts., Le Sueur	*155*, 155–56

Nicollet County

Cox, Eugene St. Julien	213 Broadway, St. Peter	95
Cox, Eugene St. Julien	Washington St., St. Peter	95, *96*, 111
Moll, Henry	Washington St., St. Peter	156

Olmsted County

Mattison, Truman	County Rds. O and 7, Eyota	132, *133*

Otter Tail County

Austin, Jacob	Guttenburg Heights, Fergus Falls	152
Clement, Charles C.	604 Burlington St., Fergus Falls	161–62, *162*
Page, Henry G.	219 Whitford St., Fergus Falls	*115*

Ramsey County

Apitz, Doris	320 Smith Ave., St. Paul	46
Burbank, James C.	432 Summit Ave., St. Paul	106–8, *107*, 109, 116
Cutler, E. H.	360 Summit Ave., St. Paul	150
Davidson, Watson P.	344 Summit Ave., St. Paul	177
Dean, William B.	514 Grand Ave., St. Paul	170
Gibbs, Herman	2097 Larpenteur Ave., St. Paul	43
Gilbert, Cass	One Heather Pl., St. Paul	xii–xiii, 147
Hill, James J.	240 Summit Ave., St. Paul	183–85, *184*
Hill, Louis W.	206 Summit Ave., St. Paul	170, *171*
Irvine, Horace	1006 Summit Ave., St. Paul	181
Kellogg, Frank B.	633 Fairmount Ave., St. Paul	185, *186*
Kittson, Norman	Summit Ave., St. Paul	xii, 116
Luckert, George D.	480 Iglehart, St. Paul	46
Noyes, Charles P.	Virginia Ave., St. Paul	173, *174*
Oakes, Charles H.	Eighth St. in Lowertown, St. Paul	8
Ramsey, Alexander	265 S. Exchange St., St. Paul	37–39, *38*, 136
Ramsey, Justus C.	252 W. Seventh St., St. Paul	*40*, 40–41
Scott, Thomas B.	340 Summit Ave., St. Paul	177
Shipman, Henry & Herman Greve	445 Summit Ave., St. Paul	144–45, *145*, 146
Spangenberg, Frederick	375 Mount Curve Ave., St. Paul	47
Thompson, Horace E.	Summit Ave. and Avon, St. Paul	177

Rice County

Buck, Cassius M.	124 sw First Ave., Faribault	170, *172*
Erb house	628 nw 3rd Ave., Faribault	67

Index

Cowles, John and Sage, xiii
Craggencroft Classical Institute for
    Young Ladies, 102
Cram, Goodhue and Ferguson, 179, 180
Cram, Ralph Adams, 179, 180, 182,
    187–88
Crane Library, 183
Crow Wing, 44
cupolas, 21, 103, 105, 106, 111, 114,
    115–16, 119, 120, 131, 178, 205
Curtis, Philip Johnson, xiii
Curtiss-Wedge, Franklin, 83, 89

D

Dakota County Historical Society, 95
Dakota Indians, 36
Dakota War of 1862, 23, 27, 30, 33, 50,
    72, 82, 95, 140
Dakotah House hotel, 51
Davidson, Commodore, 178
Davidson, Watson P., 177–78
Davis, Alexander J., 213n6
Davis, Cushman K., 55
Davis, Jefferson, 15
Dayton family , xiii
Dean, William B., 169–70
Decker, Edward M., 198
Deere, John, 124
Delaware Valley, 14
dentils, 34, 68
depression of 1870s, 140
Dickinson, William, 90, 91
Doane, George W., 105
Dodge County, 41
Doig, Andrew, 40–43
Doig, James/John, 40
Donahower, F. A., 156, 203
Donnelly, Ignatius, 136, 189, 191
dormers, 35, 59, 77, 106, 111, 112, 127,
    152, 156, 204, 214n3
Dousman, Hercules L., 8, 26, 108–9
Downie, Mary, xii
Downing, Andrew Jackson, 86–89,
    91–93, 100, 102, 104, 111, 112, 114,
    191, 204, 213nn5–6
Drake, William H., 213–14n6
Dressler, Marie, 6
du Puis, Hypolite, 35, 72
Dubuque, Iowa, 108, 142
Duluth, 100–102, 136, 147, 148, 176, 187
Duluth Savings Bank, 100

Dunnell, Mark Hill, 117–19
Dutch influence, 14
Duveen, Lord, 165

E

École des Beaux-Arts, 166, 172, 187
Elizabethan mode, 106, 179, 180, 198
Ellis, Harvey, xii, xiv, 146, 156, 157, 182
Ellringer family, 47
Elmslie, George, xi, xii, 192, 193, 194–99
Ely, Richard T., 193
Emerson, Ralph Waldo, 126
Emmett, Lafayette, 29
Encampment Forest, xiii
England, 87, 105, 213n2, 214n1
entablature, 67, 68, 74, 78, 202
Erie Canal, 16

F

facade, 8, 28, 34, 35, 73, 74, 75, 86, 89,
    106, 117, 166, 180, 187, 197
Fairmount Park, 142
false gables, 106, 119, 156, 187
Faribault, 150
Faribault, Alexander, 72–73, 93
Faribault, Jean Baptiste, 27–28, 36, 72
Faribault (city), 40
Farmer, Silas, 16
Farmers and Mechanics Bank,
    Owatonna, 193, 197
Farmers' Bank, 156
Farther and Gay castle (Joseph R.
    Brown), 30
Faust, 211n2
Fawcett and Pearson, 149
Federal style, 19, 75, 121, 174–75
Fergus, James, 114
Fergus Falls, 161
Ferguson, Frank W., 179
fieldstone houses, 45
Fillmore County, 66, 83
First Minnesota Volunteer Infantry
    Regiment, 81–82
First National Bank, 114
First National Bank of Minneapolis, 99
First Presbyterian Church, Stillwater, 92
Fisk, Jim, 82
Fitch, James Marsden, 64, 89
Flandrau, Charles E, 97
Fletcher, Jonathan E., 32–35, 36, 37
Fletcher, William H., 203

Kees and Colburn, architects, 178
Kees and Fisk, Minneapolis, 148
Kelker, Miss — (mother of A. Ramsey), 37
Kellogg, Frank B., 185–86
Kellogg, Oliver, 15
Kennedy, Ernest, 178
Kennedy, John S., 91
Kenosha, Wisconsin, 109
Kent, William, 126
Kieffer family, 47–48
Kimball, Fiske, 10
kinetic approach to architecture, 170, 172
Kittson, Norman H., 108, 148
Klammer, Paul M., 11, 12
Klenze, Leo von, 212n2
Knight, Richard Payne, 104
Knights of the Forest, 35
Know-Nothingism, 52, 53
Konen, Frank, 59
Krichmayer, John, 184

L
La Crescent, 116
La Farge, Grant, 6
Lac qui Parle, 25–26, 36
LaFarge, John, 6
LaFollett, Robert M., 193
Laird-Norton Company, 152
Lake Calhoun, 36
Lake City, 138, 203
Lake Pepin, 6
Lake Vermilion, 100
Lakeland, 127, 131
Lamberton, Henry W., 110
Lamberton, Mrs. Henry W., 110, 155
Langworthy house, 131–32
Lanesboro, 155
Lanz, Gustave, 60
Lanz, Michael, 60
Lazor, Charles, xiv
Le Duc, Mrs. Mary, 93
Le Duc, William G., 90, 93–94, 114, 167, 214n8
Le Sueur, 74–75
Lease, Mary Elizabeth, 189
Leavenworth, Henry, 28
LeFever, Minard, 51
Lewis and Clark expeditions, 3
limestone buildings, 24, 46–48, 129

Lincoln, Abraham, 42, 125
Linden Place, Minneapolis, 147
lintels, 57
Little Crow, 27
log buildings, 10–12, 32, 36, 37, 43, 83, 201–2
Log Cabin Tradition, 11
loggia, 187
Long, Clyde W., 134
Long, F. B. and L. L., 179
Long Branch, 136
Long Prairie, 34
Lorrain, Claude, 104
Louis Napoleon. *See* Napoleon III
Louisiana State Capitol, 88
Louvre, 135
Lowell, James Russell, 213n5
Lowery, W. D., 116
Lowry Hill, Minneapolis, 189
Ludwig, king of Bavaria, 54
lumber in buildings. *See* wood in buildings
lumber industry, 30, 71, 75, 76, 78, 100, 104, 111, 120, 132, 138, 141–42, 151, 152, 153, 154, 161, 164, 178, 187, 203, 214n4
Lundie, Edwin, xiii, 184–85

M
Maass, John, 89
Macfarlane, Angus Roderick, 100
Madeline Island, xiii
Maher, George, xi
Maine, 143
Maison Carré, 64
Majerus family, 47
Manhattan, 14
Mankato, 215n2
mansard roof, xii, 39, 59, 106, 111, 112, 114, 123, 135–36, 137, 138, 143, 214n3, 215n1
Mansion House (Alexander Ramsey), 37–39, 136
Mantorville, 41
manufacturing, 81
Marine Lumber Company, 78
Marine-on-St. Croix, 12, 16, 30, 32
Marnach family, 47–48
Marshall, William R., 29
Martineau, Harriet, 65
Maryland, 32, 43

Progressive Era, xi, xii, xiv, 189–99
Prussian Court Gardner's house (Karl Friedrich von Schinkel), 105
Purcell, William Gray, xi, xii, xiii, xiv, 192, 193, 194–99

Q
Quebec, 4
Queen Anne style, 143, 191
quoins, 58, 59, 61, 101

R
Rahilly, Patrick Henry, 116
railroads, 141
Ramsey, Alexander, 29, 37–40, 81, 93, 214n8
Ramsey, Justus C., 40
Ramsey County, 65
Rapson, Ralph, xiii
rationalism, 63–64
Ravoux, Augustin, 72
Red River, 108, 148
Red River valley, 141
Red Wing, 134, 137
Reed and Stem, architects, 177
Renaissance, 79, 89, 99, 106, 127, 143, 157, 166, 169, 170, 174, 175, 180, 187, 198, 205, 216n3. *See also* American Renaissance; Italian Renaissance; neo-Renaissance
Renville, Joseph, 25–26
Republican Party, 53
revivalism, 125
Rhode Island, 143
Rice, Henry M., 34, 73, 108, 214n8
Richards, John house, 124, 133–34
Richardson, Henry Hobson, xii, 111, 144–45, 157, 163, 181–83, 184, 185, 187, 188
Robert, Louis, 109
Roch, John, 59
Rochester, 43, 147
Rock Island, Illinois, 142
Rockefeller, John D., 164
Rockford, 20
Roi, Francis cottage, 5
Roman revival style. *See* Greek revival style
Roosevelt, James A., 91
Roosevelt, Theodore, 154, 193
Root, John H., 172

Root, John W., 20
Ruemke and Schapekahm, architects, 212n6
Rum River valley, 120
Rushford, 83
Ruskin, John, 84, 192, 195
rustication, 21

S
St. Anthony, 65, 120
St. Clair, 33–34
St. Cloud, 44, 59, 91
St. Croix River, 142
St. Croix Valley, 16, 17–18, 36, 76–78, 111, 120, 140
St. Hubert's Lodge (Israel Garrard), 6–8
St. John's Abbey, 44–45
St. Julien Cox, Eugene, 90, 95–96
St. Louis (city), 4, 5, 8, 51
St. Louis River, 100
St. Paul, xii–xii, 5, 8, 21, 37, 40, 43, 44, 46–47, 65, 93, 108, 115, 120, 141, 142, 157, 173, 177, 186
St. Paul and Pacific Railroad, 141
St. Paul Central Library, 177
St. Paul Fire and Marine Insurance Company, 109
St. Peter, 95–96, 127
Ste. Geneviéve, Missouri, 4, 5
Salmela, David, xiv
San Gimignano, Italy, 115
Sanborn, John B., 81
Saracen architecture, 154–55
Sauk Rapids, 44
Sauk River valley, 45
Sault Ste. Marie, Michigan, 4
Saunders, E. N., 120
Scandinavian influence, 12
Schapekahm, Herman G., 60, 212n6
Schell, August, 60–62, 212n6
Schell's brewery, 61–62
Schmidt, Martin, 51
Schurz, Carl, 53, 211n2
Schuylkill River, 142
Scotch-Irish influence, 10
Scott, Geoffrey, 86
Scott, Walter, 87, 102
Scott County, 59–60
Scully, Vincent, 146, 151, 177, 182, 191, 216n3
Seabury Divinity School, 73

Turnblad, Swan J., 159
Turner, Frederick Jackson, 65
Twain, Mark, 87–88, 123

U
United States Capitol, 126, 167
United States Steel Company, 178, 180
University of Minnesota, 157, 170, 175
University of Virginia, 64, 66
University of Wisconsin, 193
Upjohn, Richard, 125–26
urbanization, 100

V
Valbricht, William, 60
Valley Creek, 71–72
Van Rensselaer, Steven, 91
Vanbrugh, John, 213n2, 214n1
verandahs, 6, 51, 67, 81, 106, 111, 119, 120, 131, 146
Victorian houses, 89, 143, 204
Villa style, 51, 103, 111, 152
Villard, Henry (Ferdinand Heinrich Gustav Hilgard), 176, 177
villas, 104, 105, 106, 109, 111, 112, 114, 117, 143, 172, 205
Virginia, 43
Virginia Avenue, St. Paul, 147
Virginia State Capitol, 64, 125, 212n2
Virning, Christ, 59
von Schinkel, Karl Friedrich, 105

W
Wabasha, Chief, 109
Wabasha Street bridge, 93
Walbridge, Mrs. Walter, 111
Walk-on-the-Water (steamer), 16
Walker family , xiii
Walker, Orange house, 78
Walker Tavern, 72
Walpole, Horace, 87
War Eagle, steamer, 109
War of 1812, 28, 64
Ware, Norman, 125
Washburn, Cadwallander C., 141
Washburn A Mill, 140, 141
Washington County, 127
Wasioja, 41–43
Watkins, Paul, 180, 181

Watt, William, 145
Watts Sherman house (Henry H. Richardson), 144
weatherboards, 77, 135
Webster, Mortimer, 21
Weehouses, xiv
Weich, Joseph, 203
Wells, James "Bully," 26, 78
Wells, Joseph Morrill, 177
West Point, 180
West St. Paul, 93
Weyerhaeuser, Frederick, 152
Whipple, Henry B, 73
Whistler, James McNeill, 145
White, Stanford, 166, 177. *See also* McKim, Mead, and White
Whiteman, Reuben and Alonzo, 164
Whitewater Recreation Area, 47–48
Whitewater Valley, 47–48
Whitford, Joe, 114
Whitman, Walt, 192
Whitney, William Channing, 166, 181, 187, 214n5
Williamsburg, Virginia, 77
Wilson, Woodrow, 193
Windom, William, 153
Winnebago Indians, 32–35
Winona, xi, 47, 70–71, 108, 109, 119, 129, 142, 152
Winona County Historical Society, 91
Winton, Mr. and Mrs. Michael, xiii
Wisconsin, 16, 64, 66, 124, 126, 133, 212n4
wood in buildings, 5, 11, 13, 14, 16, 19–20, 24, 101, 141, 144, 146, 147, 148, 152, 153, 163
Wright, Frank Lloyd, xi, xiii, 89, 149, 150, 166, 168, 169, 174, 182, 191–94

Y
Yaeger, Frank, 59
Yankees. *See* New England style
Yellow Medicine County, 35
Youmans Brothers and Hodgins, 153
Yungbauer, William, 184

Z
Zelles Von Blon family, xiii